IMAGES
of America

PIG 'N WHISTLE

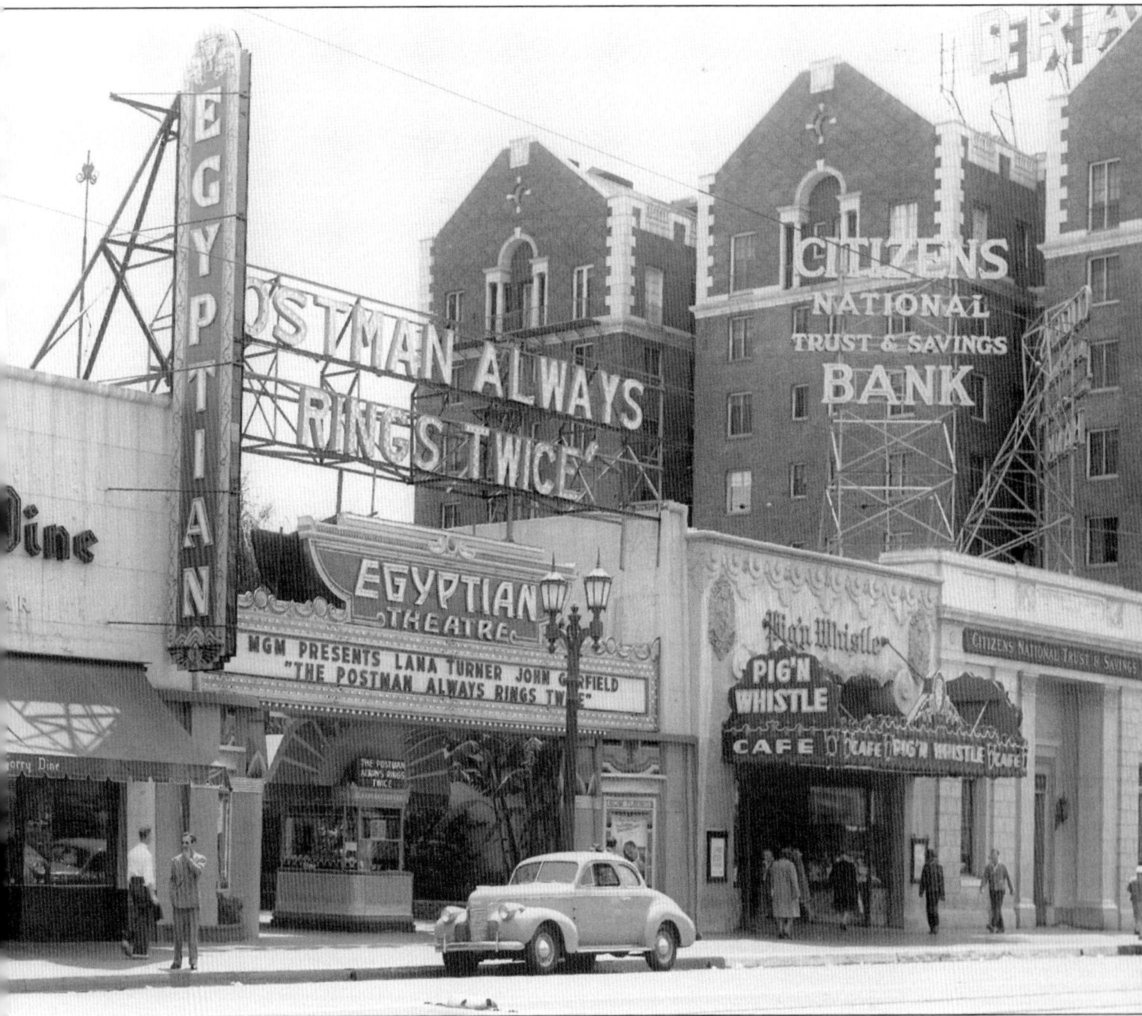

On the Cover: The Pig 'N Whistle at 6714 Hollywood Boulevard opened in 1927 and is adjacent to Grauman's Egyptian Theatre in Hollywood. Seen here in 1946, the marquee advertises *The Postman Always Rings Twice,* starring John Garfield and Lana Turner. The Georgian Colonial–style Christie Hotel at 6724 Hollywood Boulevard opened in 1920 and can be seen next door. (Courtesy Bison Archives.)

IMAGES of America

PIG 'N WHISTLE

Veronica Gelakoska

ARCADIA PUBLISHING

ISBN 978-0-7385-8141-5

Published by Arcadia Publishing
Charleston, South Carolina

Printed in the United States of America

Library of Congress Control Number: 2010929734

For all general information, please contact Arcadia Publishing:
Telephone 843-853-2070
Fax 843-853-0044
E-mail sales@arcadiapublishing.com
For customer service and orders:
Toll-Free 1-888-313-2665

Visit us on the Internet at www.arcadiapublishing.com

This book would not be possible without
Chris Nichols, Marc Wanamaker, and Chris Ralko.
It is dedicated to the memory of Robert Nudelman.

Contents

ACKNOWLEDGMENTS

Many people have helped me follow the Pig's trail. I would like to thank Chris Nichols, Marc Wanamaker and Bison Archives, Sidney "Eddie" Hoedemaker, Jerry Roberts, Teresa Simmons, Kristal Conklin, Katie Kellett, Ashley Boquist McDonald, Tiffany Frary, Arcadia Publishing, Chris Breed, Alain Hajjar, Sunset Entertainment Group, Chris Ralko, Bernadette and Walter Ralko, Ken and Jenice Rosen, Gary Leonard, John Karwin and Fullerton Museum Center, Richard Kaplan, Thomas Carey, Jeff Thomas and the San Francisco Public Library, Wally Shidler, Carla Rickerson and Washington State University, Eric Lynxwiler, Charlene Nichols, Christina Rice, Terri Garst and Los Angeles Public Library, Los Angeles Conservancy, Antoinette Watson, Kathleen Kennedy Knies and Museum of History and Industry, Dorothy Lazard and Oakland Public Library, David Parry, Bob Kerstein and Scripophily.net, Hollywood Heritage Museum, Vincent Chavez, Jack Rivera, Alexandria Hotel, Adam Goldberg and his film *Scotch and Milk*, John Glick, and Rebecca Crawford. Except where noted, all images are from the author's collection.

INTRODUCTION

The Pig 'N Whistle Corporation had its beginnings in the aftermath of San Francisco's great earthquake and fire of 1906. After the fires, the mass exodus from the city included John H. Gage, proprietor of the Hotel America on Market Street, which burned to the ground. Gage decided to move his family to Los Angeles. A native of Boston, Massachusetts, Gage opened a new business—a candy shop and soda fountain named Pig 'N Whistle—next door to Los Angeles's third city hall. Pig 'N Whistle was advertised in the telephone book as a "High Class Candy and Luncheon Place."

It quickly grew successful on Broadway, which by then had become a hot spot for new retail buildings. In 1906 Hamburger's department store opened on the corner of Eighth Street and Broadway, and by 1910, an advertising postcard boasted that Hamburger's was the "Largest Department Store in the West." The Bullocks and Broadway department stores soon followed. Gage decided to return to San Francisco, where he opened a second restaurant next door to the newly rebuilt White House department store, which was destroyed in 1906. By 1911, the White House, an Albert Pissis Beaux-Arts masterpiece, was an inspiration to the people of San Francisco, and it became a leading shopping destination in the Bay Area.

Several more Pig 'N Whistle stores followed: one each in Oakland, Berkeley, Pasadena, and Seattle and several in Los Angeles. By 1920, the Pig 'N Whistle brand name had become synonymous with excellence. To sit at a Pig 'N Whistle soda fountain or to dine at a beautiful mosaic tile table depicting dancing pigs was to be surrounded by the finest in architecture and decor. The finest food was served, and there were hundreds of fountain creations on the ever-changing menus over the years. In some locations, a pipe organ or piano was installed, and patrons were entertained by popular musical numbers of the day.

All of the candy, ice cream, French pastries, and bread were produced in house, and a baking plant and candy factory were added in Los Angeles to keep up with demand. Menus were printed daily, and the Pig 'N Whistle name brand was embossed on various souvenirs such as matchbooks, bookmarks, and postcards. Special pig-shaped porcelain figures were made by the German company Schafer and Vater, and much of the china was made in England. Every piece of tableware had the Pig 'N Whistle logo stamped on it.

By the 1920s, Los Angeles was growing fast. Oil had been discovered in 1892, and by 1923, Los Angeles was producing one quarter of the world's petroleum. Broadway became the home for many opulent theaters and vaudeville houses, and Pig 'N Whistle catered to the ever-growing theater crowd, advertising in all the trade papers and play programs. Much of the chain's success can be credited to Sidney Hoedemaker, a Dutch immigrant who got his start at a hamburger stand, then as a food checker at San Francisco's Fairmont Hotel in 1914. By the early 1920s, he was running a successful line of cafeterias, Leighton Cafeterias, in Los Angeles. Gage wanted Hoedemaker to do for Pig 'N Whistle what he had done for Leighton—expand the chain and dominate the market. Hoedemaker helped Southern California become jokingly referred to as

"Southern Cafeteria" by restaurant insiders. Under Hoedemaker's vice presidency, Pig 'N Whistles operated near every major department store, fine hotel, and popular theater. In 1929, Hollywood had three Pig 'N Whistles, all within several blocks of each other at Grauman's Egyptian Theatre, the Hollywood Plaza Hotel, and next door to the El Capitan Theatre.

A second restaurant concept was added in 1928; Melody Lane was a fine dining extension of the Pig 'N Whistle that included opulent architecture and pipe organ music. After the stock market crash of 1929, many businesses failed, but under Hoedemaker's keen and thrifty eye, the Pig 'N Whistle continued to do well, opening more stores near movie theaters. Americans were still buying movie tickets, and Pig 'N Whistle made the outing more special with one of their many inspired, signature fountain creations, such as the Broadway Melody Sundae or the Show Boat Freeze.

On March 22, 1933, the 18th Amendment, which established Prohibition in 1919, was repealed. Pig 'N Whistle had not served alcohol to this point, but Hoedemaker used this new development as a way to increase patronage. In June 1933, a Pig 'N Whistle advertisement for the 6714 Hollywood Boulevard café announced, "Of Course! Beer served right!" By the end of 1933, a Pig 'N Whistle patron on Wilshire Boulevard could order a manhattan or martini cocktail and also receive a bottle of California Burgundy or Sauterne wine—all for 50¢.

When John Gage passed away in 1938, Sidney Hoedemaker became president of the chain. He added outlets, but kept the focus on Melody Lane for the next 10 years. Three of Melody Lane's popular locations throughout Los Angeles and Beverly Hills were designed by famed architect Wayne McAllister. By the close of the decade, Hoedemaker resigned as president of the Pig 'N Whistle Corporation and decided to open his own chain of restaurants bearing an abbreviated form of his name—Hody's.

By the 1950s, the eating habits of America had changed. Gone were the ornate parlors and soda fountains of the past. The automobile became the main mode of transportation, and automation was a buzzword in food service: It was the dawn of fast food. Frozen food could be delivered to restaurants faster and cheaper than fresh food, and patrons could order, pay, eat, and even watch a movie from the convenience of their automobiles. The downtown areas declined, and the suburbs exploded. Without Hoedemaker at the helm, Pig 'N Whistle struggled through the 1950s and 1960s with less than 10 stores left in operation. Sidney Hoedemaker passed away in 1969 and so did Hody's. Six months later, on April 15, 1970, the Pig 'N Whistle Corporation was finally terminated by the government due to nonpayment of taxes.

After years of several different incarnations, including Vallera's Café Di Lusso owned by Joe Vallera who also owned the famed Italian Kitchen in Los Angeles, the space that housed the last remaining Hollywood Pig 'N Whistle had fallen on hard times. But in 2001, restaurateur Chris Breed of Roxbury fame decided to resurrect the faded shop, which at the time was a Numero Uno Pizza. The Kodak Theatre had just opened nearby at the intersection of Hollywood Boulevard and Highland Avenue and would be the new home of the Academy Awards ceremony. The event had not been hosted in Hollywood for more than 70 years. Chris Breed and Alain Hajjar contributed to the return of Hollywood's Golden Age, and the Pig 'N Whistle is now once again a living part of that legend.

One

From the Ashes

On April 18, 1906, the city of San Francisco was rocked by a 7.9 magnitude earthquake. What was not destroyed by the quake soon burned. The ruptured gas lines were responsible for a massive fire that lasted four days. When it was over, the city lost close to 90 percent of its buildings. The official death toll was set at 350, but today historians estimate that the true number was well over 3,000. The exact number was kept from the public at the time to prevent widespread panic or discourage investors from rebuilding.

This single event caused a shift in the development of California. Two-thirds of the population of San Francisco was left homeless. Many of those displaced moved directly to Southern California. Los Angeles at this time was experiencing a boom. The Southern Pacific Railroad and the discovery of oil opened doors to many seeking a better life. John H. Gage and his wife of three years, Isadora "Dora" Violet Gray, made a comfortable life for themselves in San Francisco. Gage owned the Hotel America on Market Street, and having come from a wealthy Boston family, it was not hard for Gage to pick up the pieces and start anew. He and his wife made the journey south, and within two years, he was back in business with an elegant soda fountain on Broadway—the Pig 'N Whistle.

The Pig 'N Whistle served city hall officials next door as well as the nearby department stores that were establishing themselves in the area—Hamburger's (later renamed The May Company), The Broadway, and Bullocks. The Mason Opera House and the Morosco, Cameo, Arcade, and Palace were popular theaters in the neighborhood. In 1911, Gage traveled back to San Francisco and opened a second Pig 'N Whistle on Post Street, next door to the famous White House department store on Sutter Street and Grant Avenue. Its popularity led the way for more Pig 'N Whistles in the Bay Area. By 1919, there were seven shops in four different cities on the West Coast.

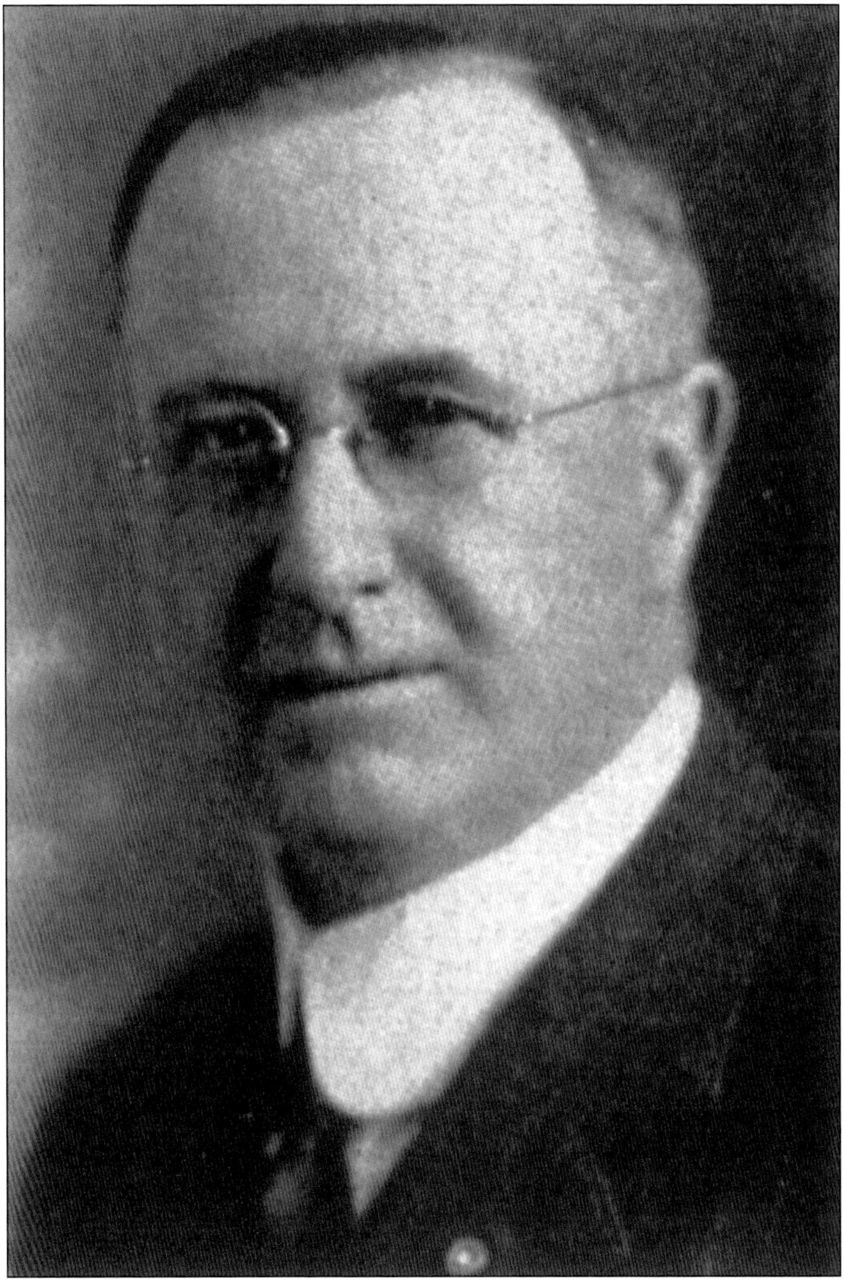

John H. Gage, founder of the Pig 'N Whistle Corporation, is pictured here around 1928. By the time of the great stock market crash of 1929, Gage and partner Sidney Hoedemaker had opened nearly 25 Pig 'N Whistle and Melody Lane restaurants on the West Coast. In 1929, *Who's Who in California* listed him as a member of the Southern California Athletic and Country Club, the Jonathan Club, and former president of the Rotary Club. He was also a member of the Annandale Golf Club in Pasadena, a very exclusive membership that included Henry E. Huntington, who was the owner of the Pacific Electric Railway, and George Patton Sr., father of the famous American general. Gage lived with his family in the fashionable Los Angeles neighborhood of Echo Park at 851 North LaFayette Park Place until his death in 1938.

The Emporium at 835 Market Street is pictured after the 1906 disaster. The Emporium (formerly known as the Parrott building) was a popular department store in the Bay Area from 1896 until 1995. The building was designed by famed Beaux-Arts architect Albert Pissis, who also designed the James Flood Building located across the street. Both buildings survived the earthquake; the Emporium, however, was destroyed by the ensuing fire.

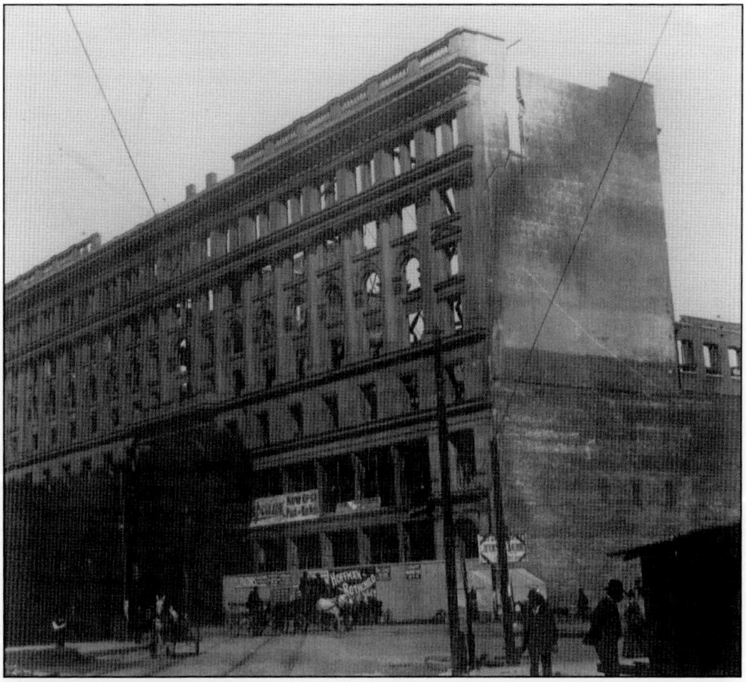

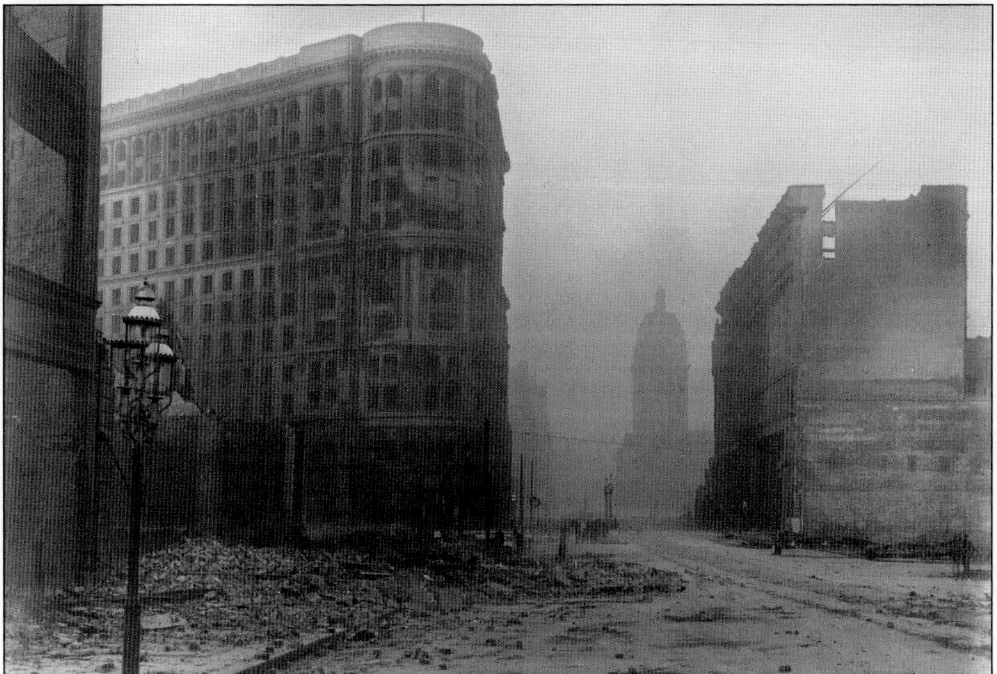

The James Flood Building, at 870 Market Street, and the Emporium, at Powell and Market Streets, are still standing after the earthquake and fire of 1906. Designed by architect Albert Pissis, it was the tallest building in San Francisco in 1904. It survived the quake and fire but had to be renovated; it was restored and reopened in 1907. The Pig 'N Whistle would be located on this corner in seven years. (Courtesy San Francisco Public Library.)

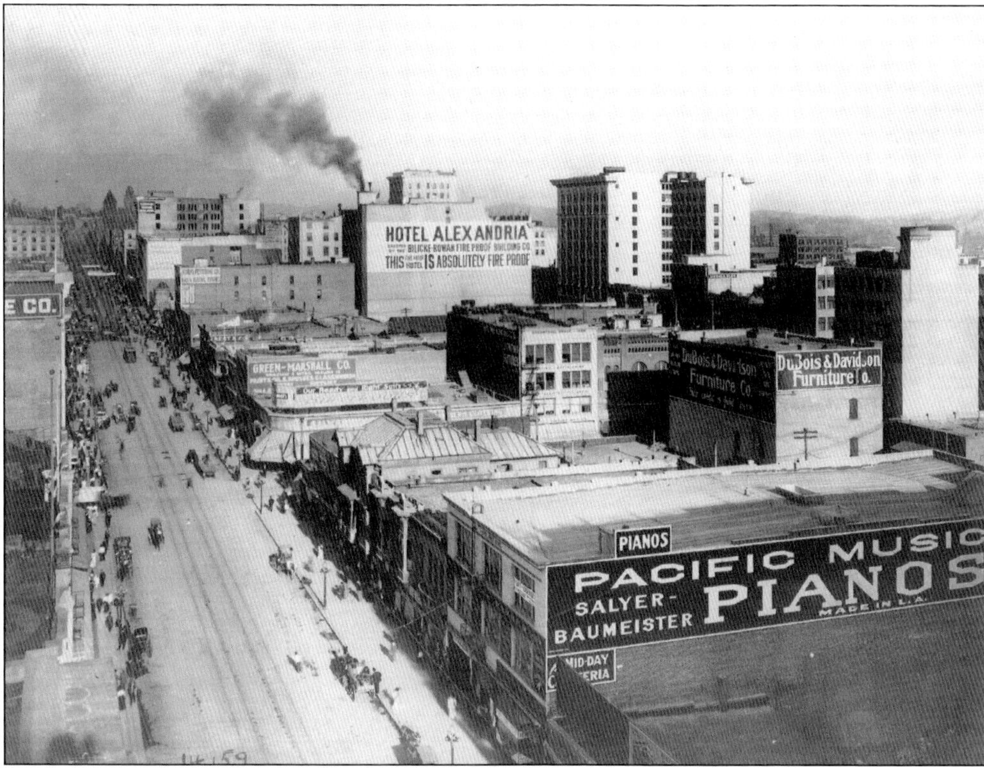

This 1907 view of downtown Los Angeles, looking north up Broadway from Seventh Street, is the Los Angeles that John Gage relocated to after the disaster. Until 1887, Broadway was known as Fort Street. The construction of a newer city hall in 1888 brought many businesses to the area, and the name was changed to Broadway. (Courtesy Security Pacific National Bank Collection/ Los Angeles Public Library.)

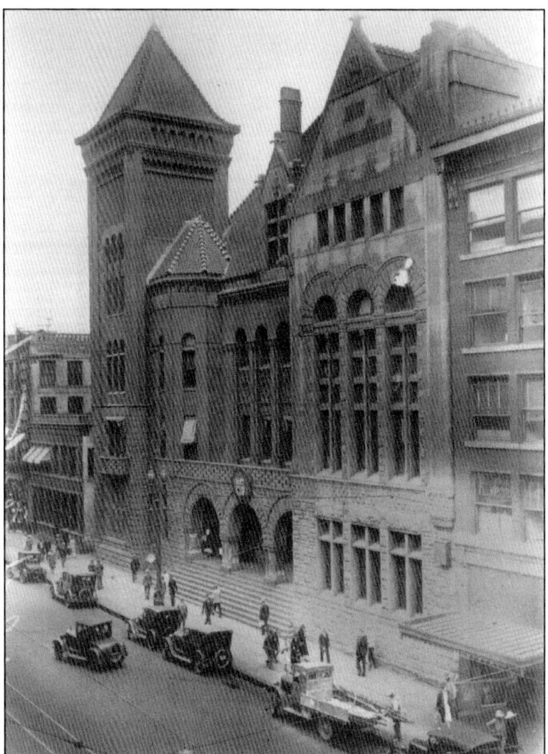

Los Angeles's third city hall was built in 1888 and designed in the Romanesque style by the Caukin and Hass architectural firm. Located at 226 South Broadway, it would also be a neighbor of the future Million Dollar Theatre built by Sid Grauman. The Pig 'N Whistle blade signage can be seen on the far left of the photograph at 224 South Broadway. (Courtesy Security Pacific National Bank Collection/Los Angeles Public Library.)

A Pacific Electric trolley car bound for Angeleno Heights passes the Hall of Records on Broadway and First Street. The Los Angeles Times Building, City Hall, and the Pig 'N Whistle were all located farther south, toward Second Street. When the Los Angeles Times Building was bombed in 1910, an unexploded bomb was also found in the Hall of Records Building.

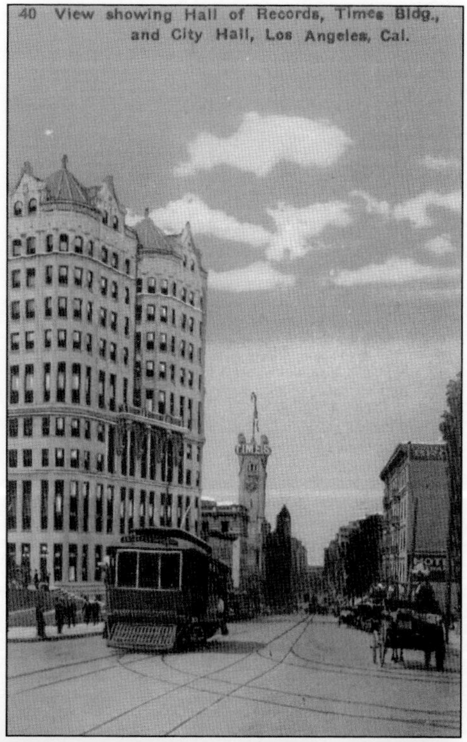

On October 1, 1910, the Los Angeles Times Building, which was one block north of the Pig 'N Whistle, was bombed by union member James McNamara, as Harrison Gray Otis, owner of the *Times*, had strong antiunion feelings. McNamara planted a suitcase full of dynamite behind the building's "Ink Alley." The ink barrels ignited, as did the natural gas lines underneath Broadway. (Courtesy Security Pacific National Bank Collection/Los Angeles Public Library.)

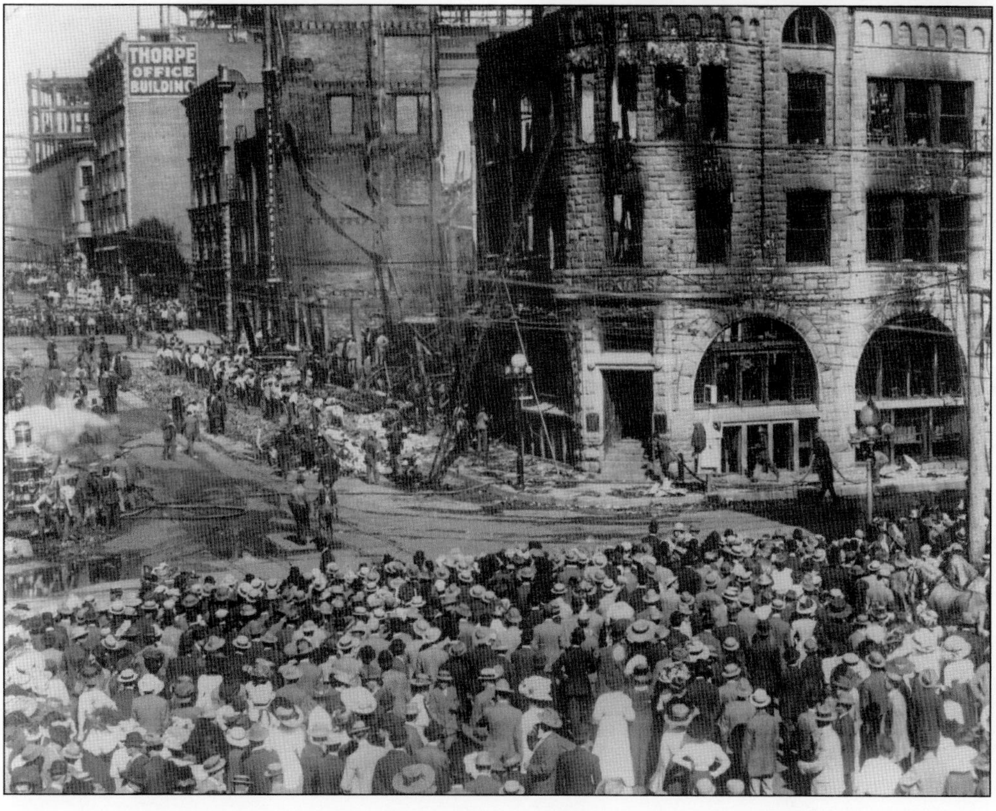

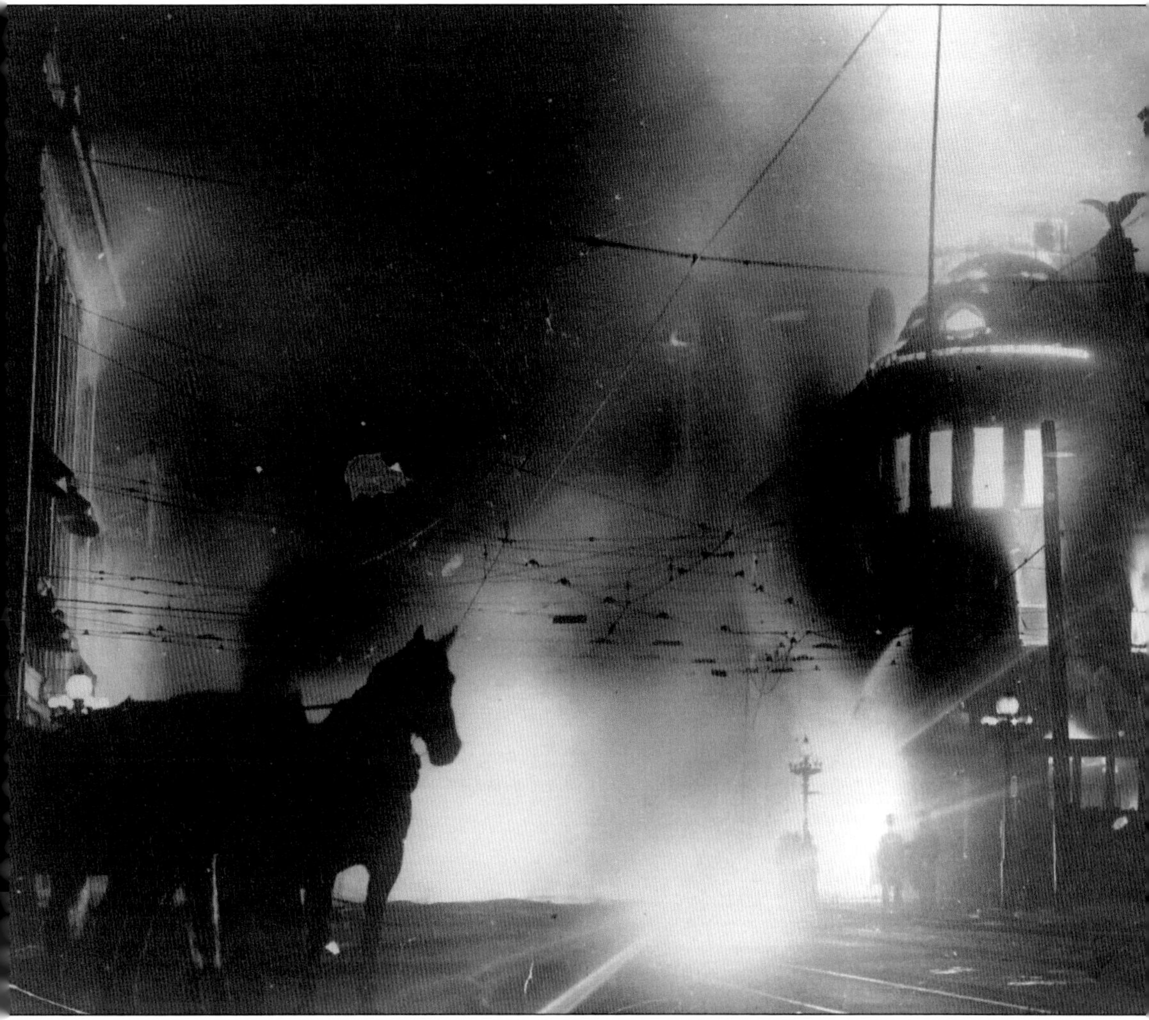

"You were wrong, and I was right. The whole damn world believes in dynamite!" These were the words uttered by James B. McNamara as he was led from the courtroom upon conviction. Pictured here is a scene of the early morning chaos of October 1, 1910, that might easily be mistaken for something out of San Francisco four years earlier. Twenty-one people died in the bombing, and both McNamara and his brother John were found guilty and sentenced to prison. After the initial bombing, unexploded bombs were also found in the Hall of Records Building next door and in the Alexandria Hotel, which at the time had a Pig 'N Whistle restaurant poised to open. The *Los Angeles Times* deemed this the "Crime of the Century." (Courtesy Security Pacific National Bank Collection/Los Angeles Public Library.)

A fashionable woman representing the upper-class leisure world of the *Belle Epoque*, or "Beautiful Era," is featured on this classic Gilded Age menu from 1911. Her box of chocolates cost 50¢ a pound. Ye Pig'n Whistle asks, "Why Not Buy the Best?" Pig 'N Whistle candy appealed to the wealthy upper classes.

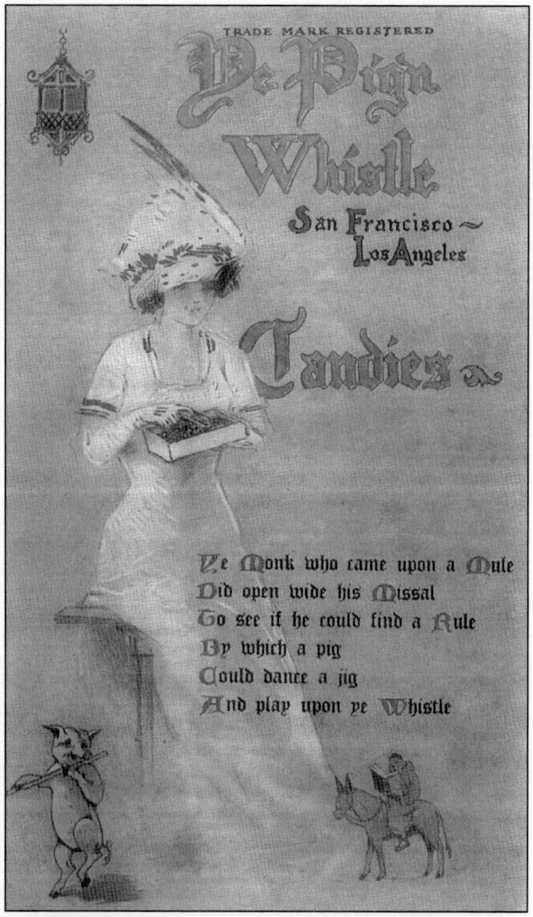

This candy box is inscribed inside: "From Bob Fleming 1916." If a special suitor bought a lady a box of chocolates, "A box where sweets, compacted lie," she may well keep it forever. Candy boxes were treasured items of a remembered beau or a romantic event, sometimes kept to store love letters or similar souvenirs. This paper box has an Art Nouveau influence. (Courtesy Chris Breed.)

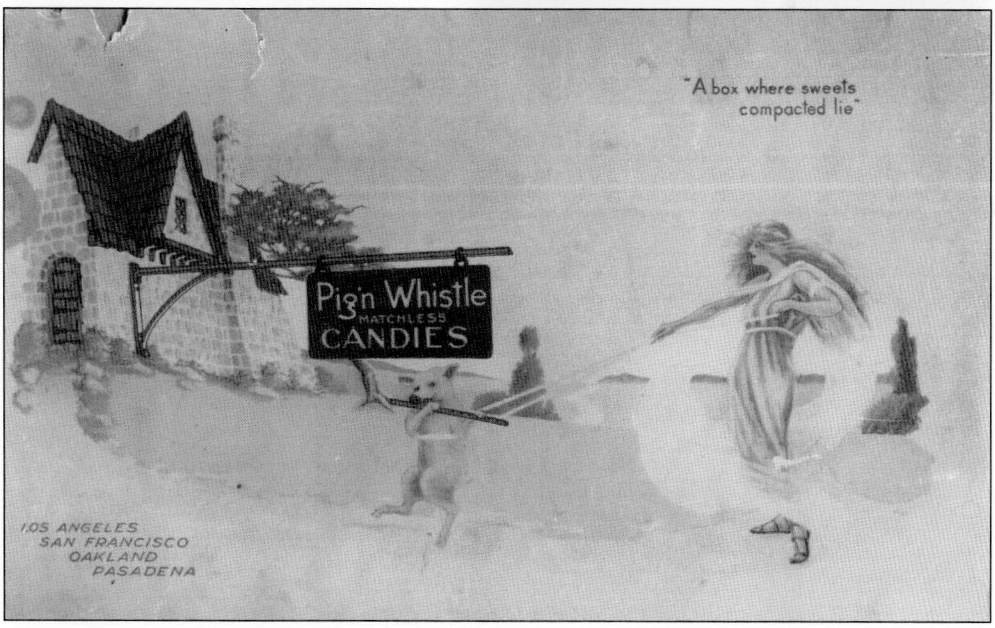

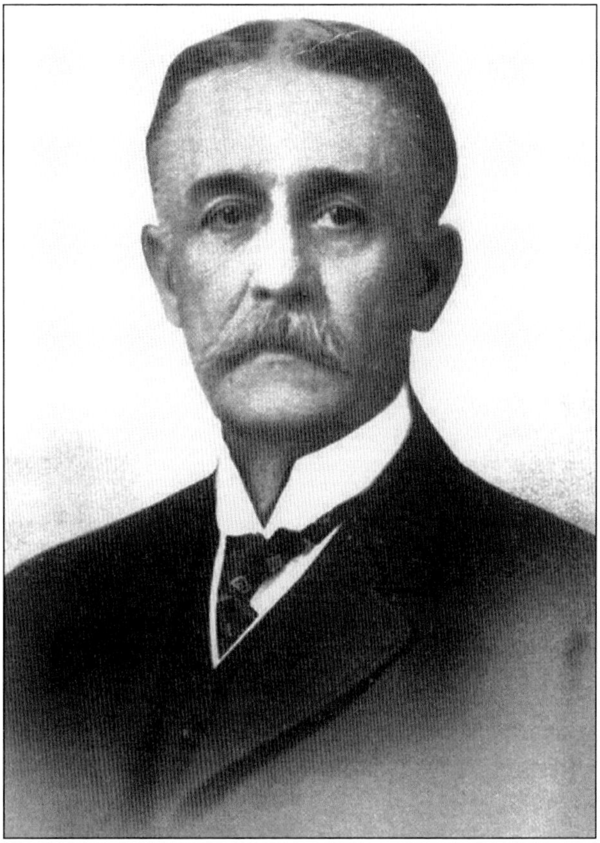

Albert Pissis was born in Guaymas, Sonora, Mexico, in 1852 and moved to the United States when he was six. Trained in the Ecole des Beaux-Arts in Paris, he returned to San Francisco to create some of its most inspired buildings, both before and after the earthquake of 1906. Pig 'N Whistle was located in or around many of his classic Beaux-Arts designs. (Courtesy David Parry.)

The White House department store was the first dry goods house in San Francisco. Founded in 1854 by Raphael Weill, it moved several times throughout its history. Here is the second location, which opened in 1870, at Kearny and Post Streets. It burned down in the 1906 disaster, and Pissis designed its third and final location at Sutter and Grant Streets. (Courtesy San Francisco Public Library.)

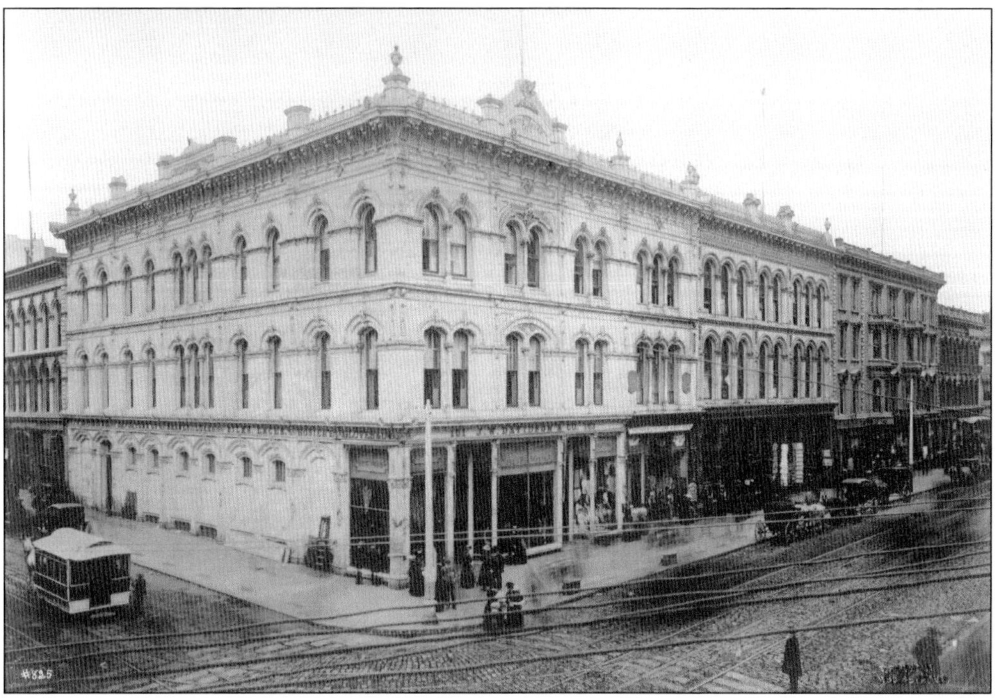

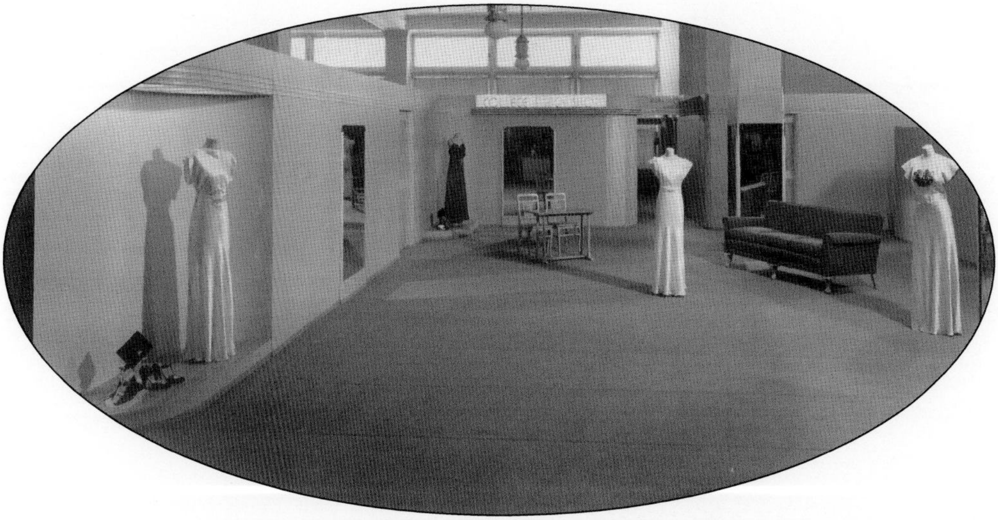

The White House department store had all the latest fashions imported straight from Paris. Pictured here is one of the elegant ladies' salons offering the newest styles from 1938. The White House remained a fixture in San Francisco until it closed on January 1, 1965. (Courtesy San Francisco Public Library.)

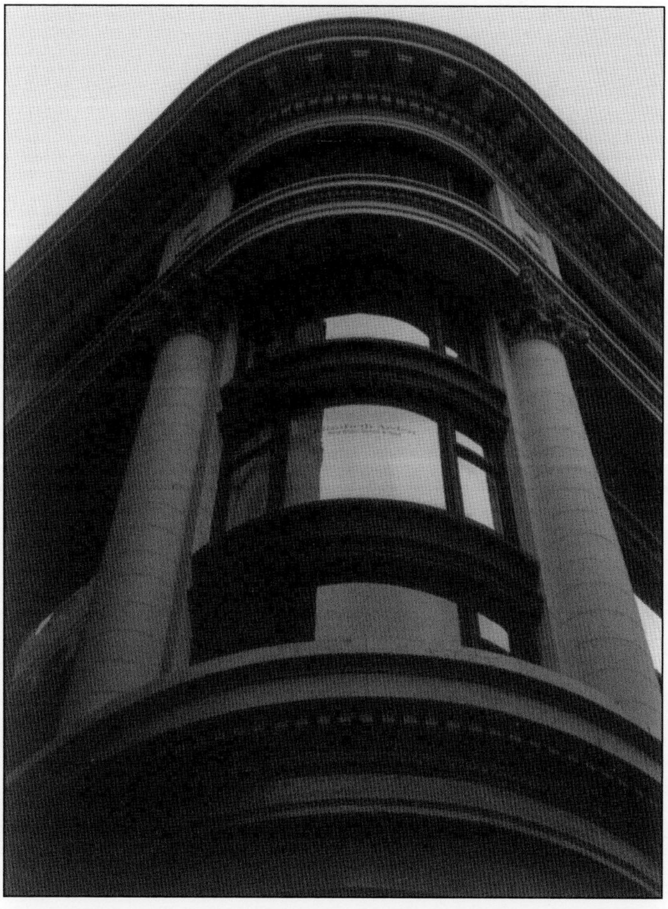

Albert Pissis's Beaux-Arts masterpiece opened on the corner of Sutter and Grant Streets on March 13, 1909. In less than two years, Pig 'N Whistle would open next door at 130 Post Street. John Gage was very proud of this location, which served San Francisco the longest of all his shops. The building still stands today.

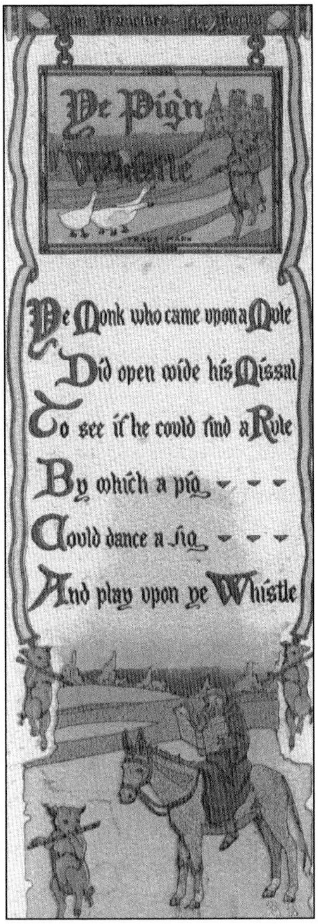

This gold leaf bookmark was printed in San Francisco in 1911 and features a poem about a monk and a pig. Ye Pig'n Whistle was an Old English variation on the name that was sometimes used in advertising. The origin of the name is traced back to English taverns where the Anglo-Saxon "Piggen" (Pig in the diminutive) was a vessel for milk or ale, and the "Wassail" ("Was heal") meant "Be in Health."

A scene from Café Bristol in 1910 Los Angeles gives an idea of the class of people the Pig 'N Whistle appealed to. These were the days of upswept bird's nest hair, large hats, and pearl dog collar necklaces. Dining habits were changing. Heavy 10-course meals that included fish for breakfast gave way to lighter fare. The clubhouse sandwich and the chicken pot pie first made their appearance on menus around 1910.

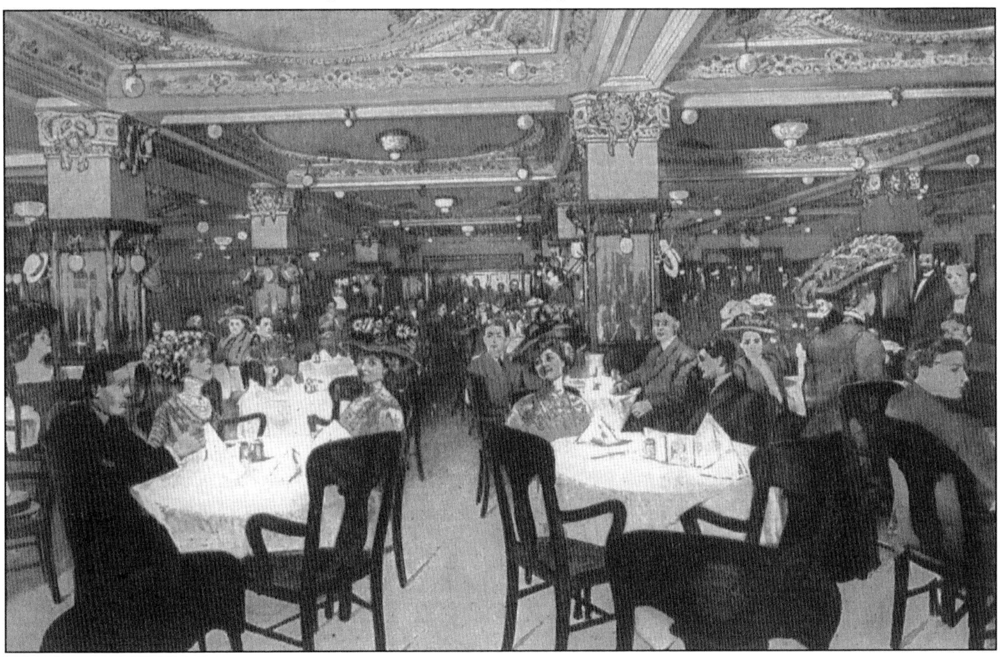

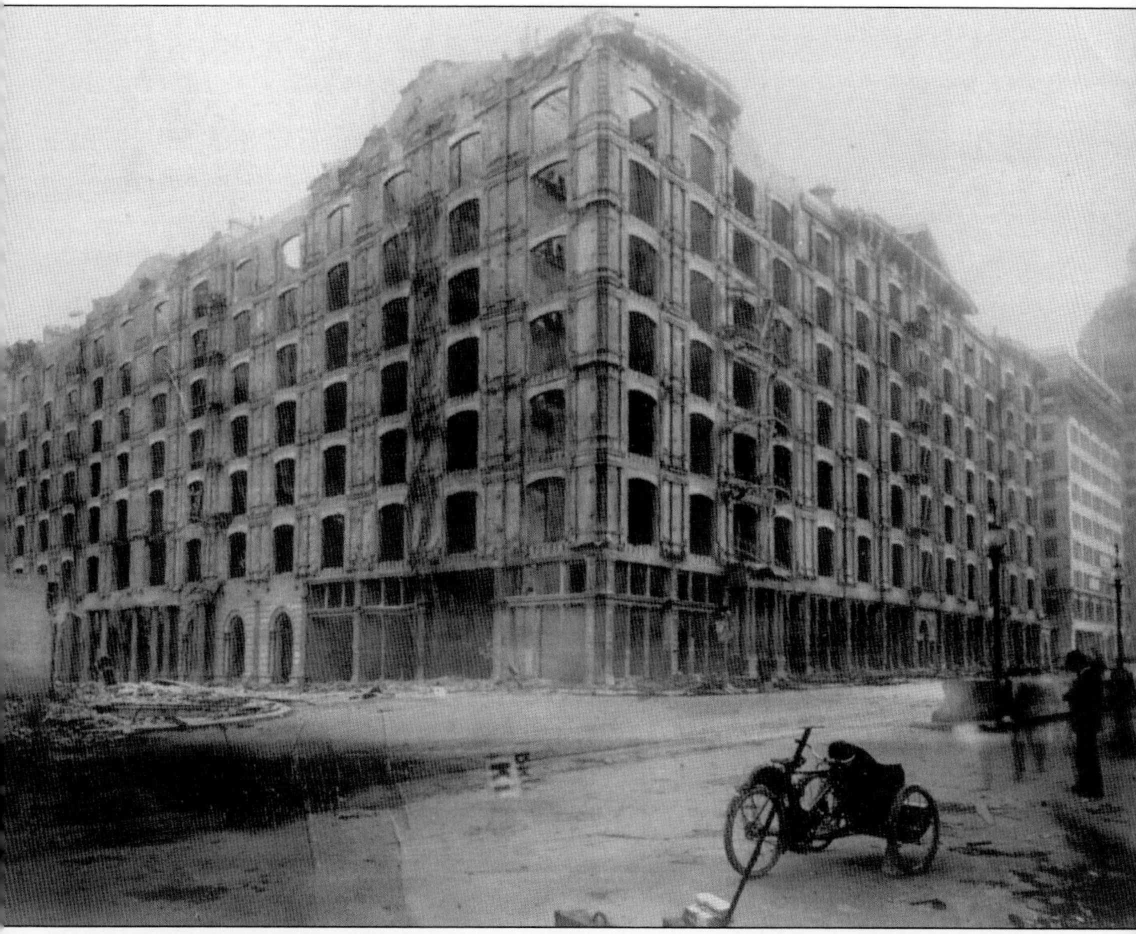

This is the burned-out ruin of San Francisco's Palace Hotel, the grandest and largest hotel in the western United States as of 1906. Built in 1875 to the plan of architect John P. Gaynor, it was located on Market and New Montgomery Streets. Destroyed by the great disaster of 1906 and rebuilt in 1909, it still stands today, though it is now thought of as the New Palace. The Old Palace had a magnificent entranceway for horses and carriages to arrive within the hotel. This grand court was surrounded by a mezzanine on every floor; guests could stand at a rail and gaze down at those arriving in horse-drawn splendor. The night the earthquake struck in 1906, the great tenor Enrico Caruso was a guest; he had just given a performance at the Mission Opera House and was roused from his bed before the ensuing fire engulfed the building. Ten years later, future Pig 'N Whistle president Sidney Hoedemaker would be assistant manager of the hotel. (Courtesy San Francisco Public Library.)

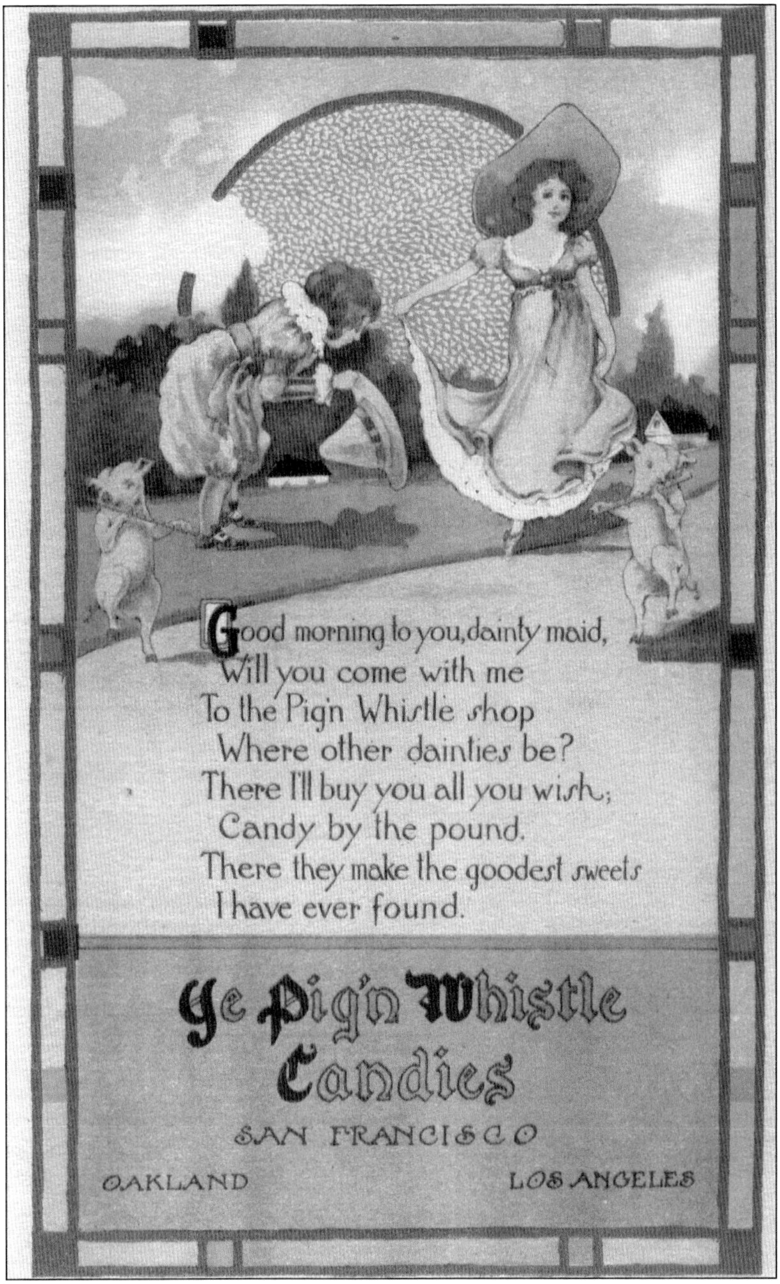

This beautiful gold leaf menu was printed in 1915 to coincide with the Panama Pacific International Exposition that San Francisco was hosting. President Taft awarded the honor to the city, which beat out New Orleans. The Panama Pacific International Exposition was a celebration of the completion of the Panama Canal and also a commemoration of the 400-year anniversary of the discovery of the Pacific Ocean by North American explorers. This event did much to reinvigorate the spirit of San Francisco as well as celebrate the rebuilding of the city since the great disaster of 1906. Albert Pissis was one of five people on the architectural advisory committee, and the exhibit palaces bear his Beaux-Arts influence. This menu features 31 "Fancy Sundaes," with names like the Peter Pan, Chop Suey, Tally Ho, the Tango, and the Wigwam.

Two

Up and Down the Coast

By 1915, the Pig 'N Whistle Corporation had established itself as a name that was very well known on the West Coast. The first two shops had grown with their respective cities, and the demand for clean and respectable places to eat was high. The early years of the 20th century marked the era of the elegant soda fountain. Pig 'N Whistle offered hundreds of different sundaes over the years named for fads and popular crazes. The Tango Sundae was served in 1915 as well as the Automobile Sundae, a whimsical creation inspired by the Ford Model T complete with cookie wafers for tires. The years preceding and following 1920 were characterized by a building boom with nationwide prosperity. California—Los Angeles, in particular—was experiencing a boom within a boom, and Los Angeles had more motor vehicles per capita than any other American city.

The motion picture industry attracted tourists, and thousands of hopeful actors flooded the city in search of fame and fortune. In Los Angeles, the Alexandria Hotel was the most exclusive place to stay. Pig 'N Whistle opened a shop there in 1911. Locations were also added in the cities of Oakland, Pasadena, Berkeley, and all the way up the coast to Seattle. In 1927, John Gage asked famed restaurateur and impresario Sidney Hoedemaker to join the corporation. Hoedemaker had organized the feeding of the navy back in San Francisco during World War I and had also worked at both the Fairmont and the Palace Hotels.

Hoedemaker's war experience taught him about cost and efficiency and how to feed many people, in a small space, in a short amount of time. He took this know-how to Los Angeles in 1921 and ran a line of popular cafeterias. The Leighton Cafeterias and dairy lunches expanded to 20 units in six years. This feat was referred to as the "Hoedemaker touch" by popular restaurant trade magazine *Keeler's Pacific Hotel and Restaurant Review.* With Hoedemaker as vice president and general manager of the corporation, Pig 'N Whistle expanded to even more locations, serving downtown Los Angeles and San Francisco.

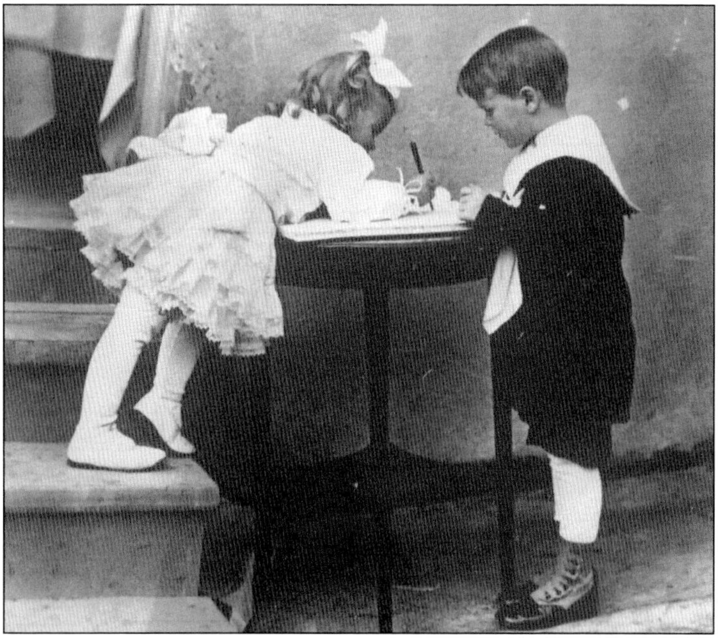

Nancy Bilicke and Albert Bilicke Jr. sign the Alexandria Hotel's guest register on opening day, February 12, 1906. The children's father, millionaire and owner of the Alexandria Hotel (which had a Pig 'N Whistle) was Albert Clay Bilicke. Tragically, Albert and his wife, Gladys, were on board the *Lusitania* in 1915 when a German torpedo struck it. Both made it to a lifeboat, but it capsized and Albert drowned, while his wife survived.

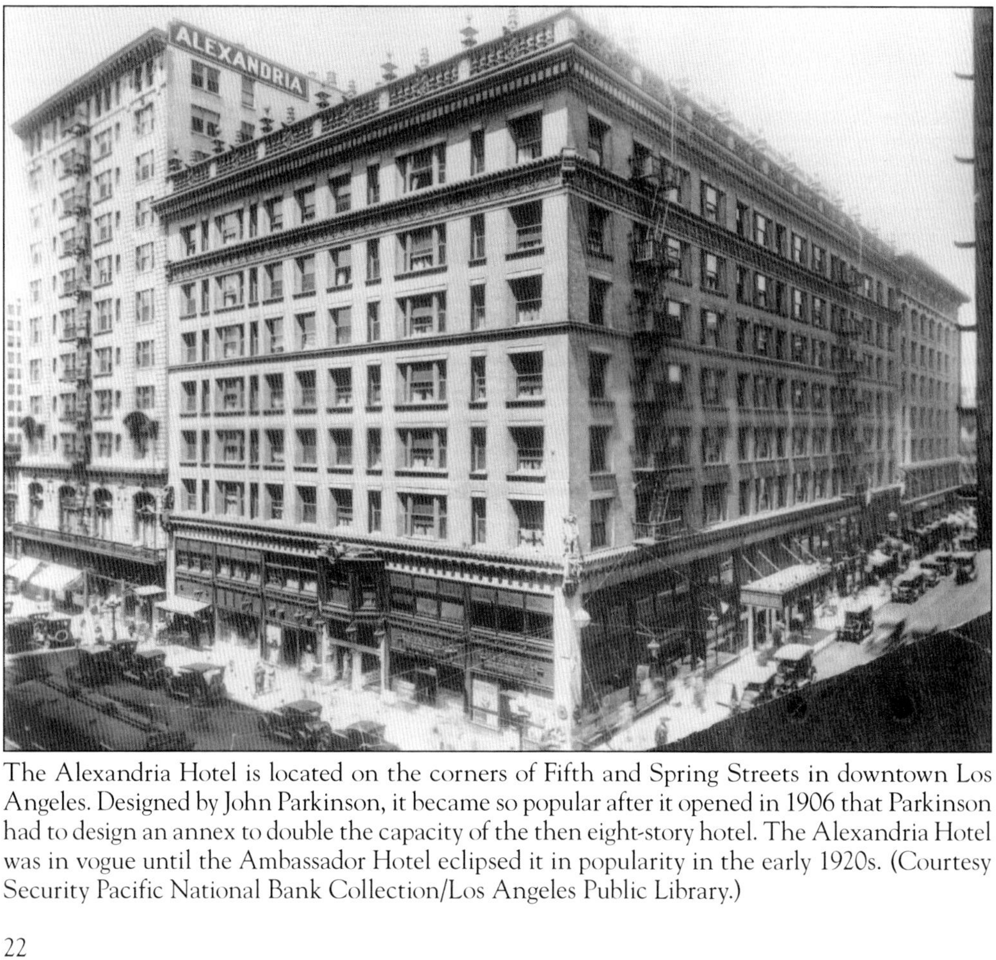

The Alexandria Hotel is located on the corners of Fifth and Spring Streets in downtown Los Angeles. Designed by John Parkinson, it became so popular after it opened in 1906 that Parkinson had to design an annex to double the capacity of the then eight-story hotel. The Alexandria Hotel was in vogue until the Ambassador Hotel eclipsed it in popularity in the early 1920s. (Courtesy Security Pacific National Bank Collection/Los Angeles Public Library.)

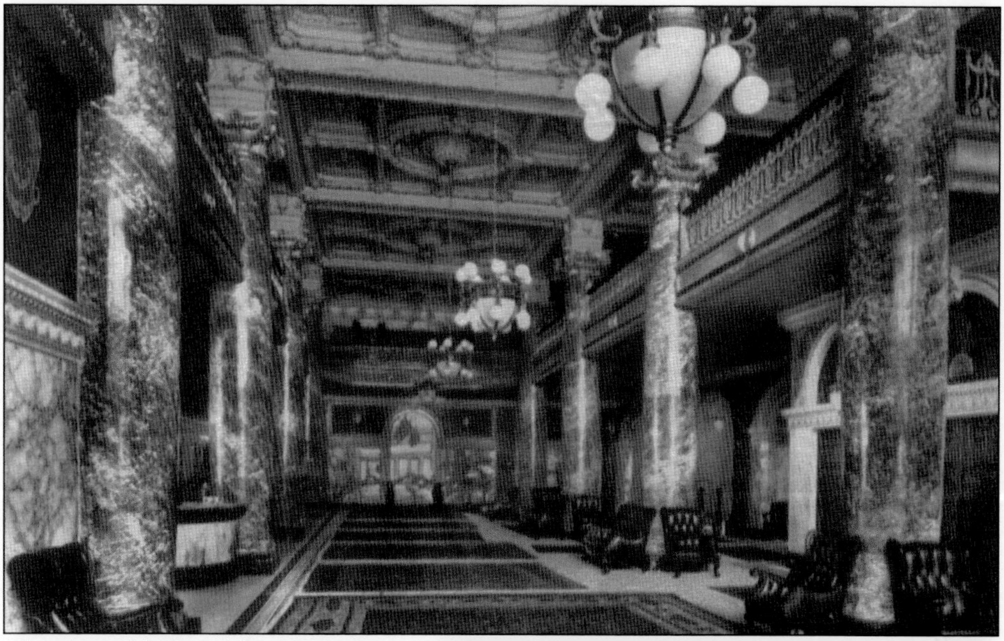

The original lobby of the Alexandria Hotel, with its famed "million-dollar carpet" (so named for the amount of business that was done on it by the moguls of the day), is seen here around 1911. Legend has it that Charlie Chaplin, who had a suite there, would do his pantomime on this carpet to the delight of onlookers overhead on the golden mezzanine.

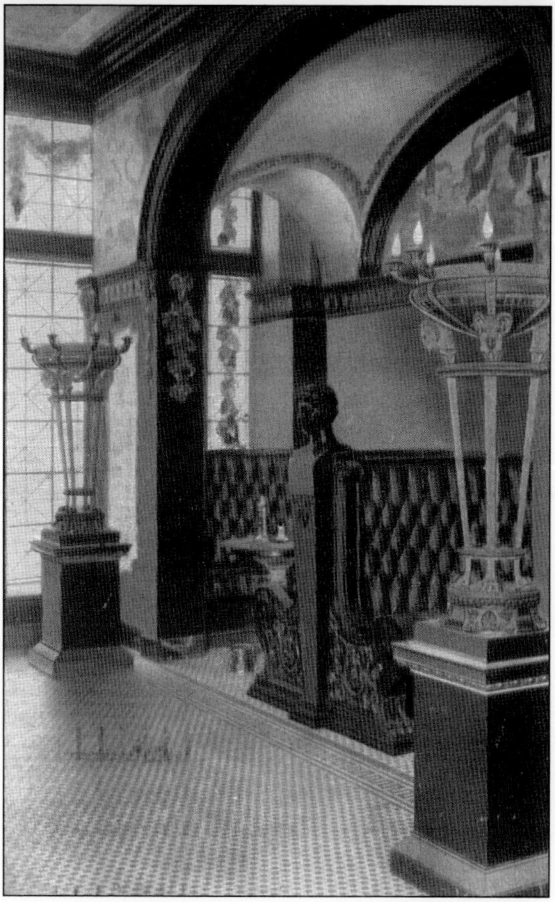

A postcard mailed from the Alexandria Hotel in 1912 shows the Gentleman's Grill. There were golden spittoons underneath the tables, and it was here that men could speak freely, without the worry of offending a lady. Ladies had their own separate lounge in another part of the hotel. Rudolph Valentino, D. W. Griffith, Winston Churchill, and three American presidents were all famous guests here.

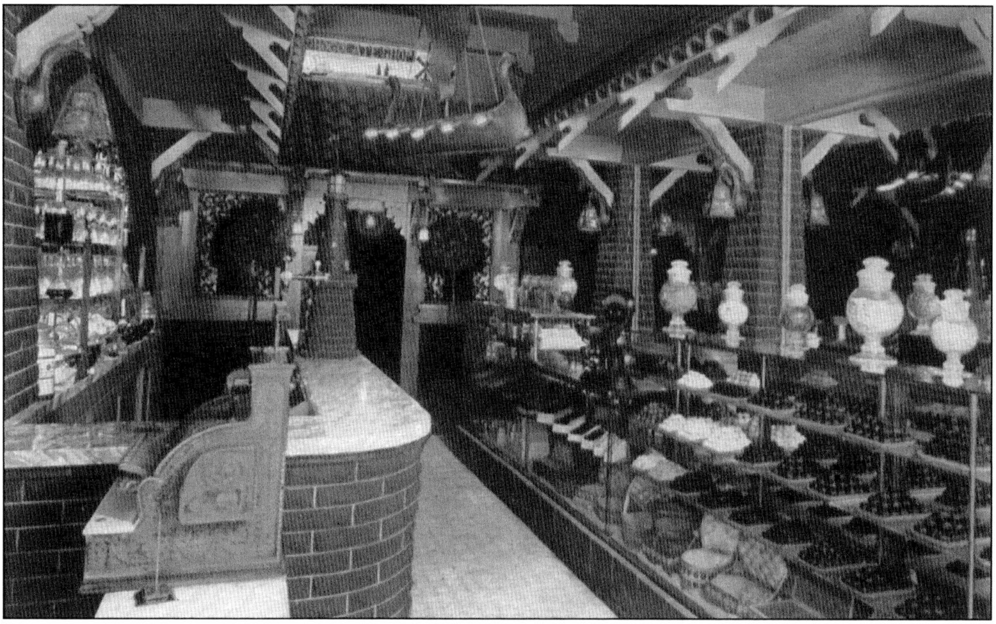

The Pig 'N Whistle at the Alexandria Hotel was most likely a confectionary store only, as the space at 212 West Fifth Street was small, and the Alexandria already had a massive kitchen and a formal dining room in Palm Court. This postcard from 1912 shows the confectionary store at 207 West Fifth Street, across the street from and in direct competition with the Pig 'N Whistle.

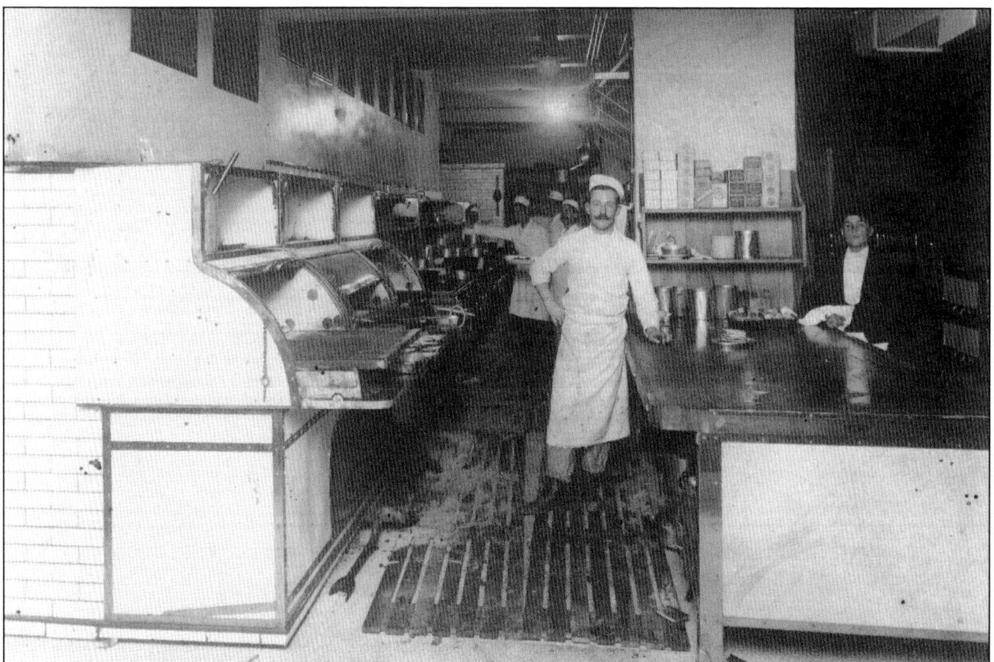

Four line cooks and a busboy are seen here in the Alexandria Hotel's kitchen around 1910. The kitchen closed in the 1970s, and after many years of neglect, it was reopened by the winner of television talent show *Top Chef* as The Gorbals restaurant. (Courtesy Security Pacific National Bank Collection/Los Angeles Public Library.)

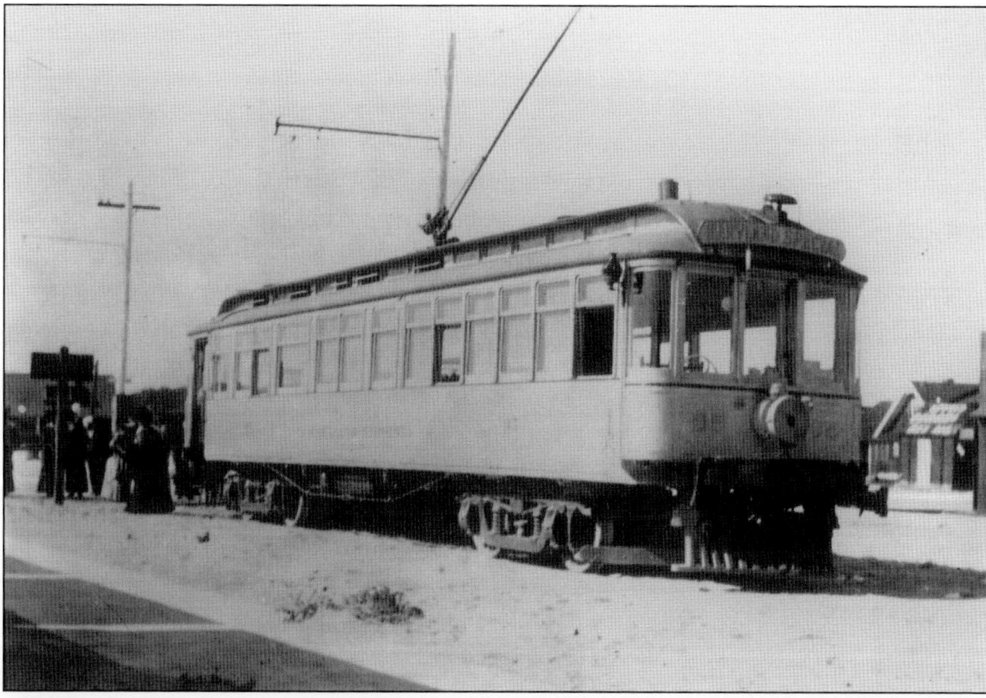

The *Maryland Special* was a streetcar in the Pacific Electric fleet, owned by railroad baron Henry Huntington. This car traveled exclusively between the Virginia Hotel in Long Beach and the Hotel Maryland in Pasadena. Hotel Maryland was served by the Pig 'N Whistle beginning in 1914. (Courtesy Security Pacific National Bank Collection/Los Angeles Public Library.)

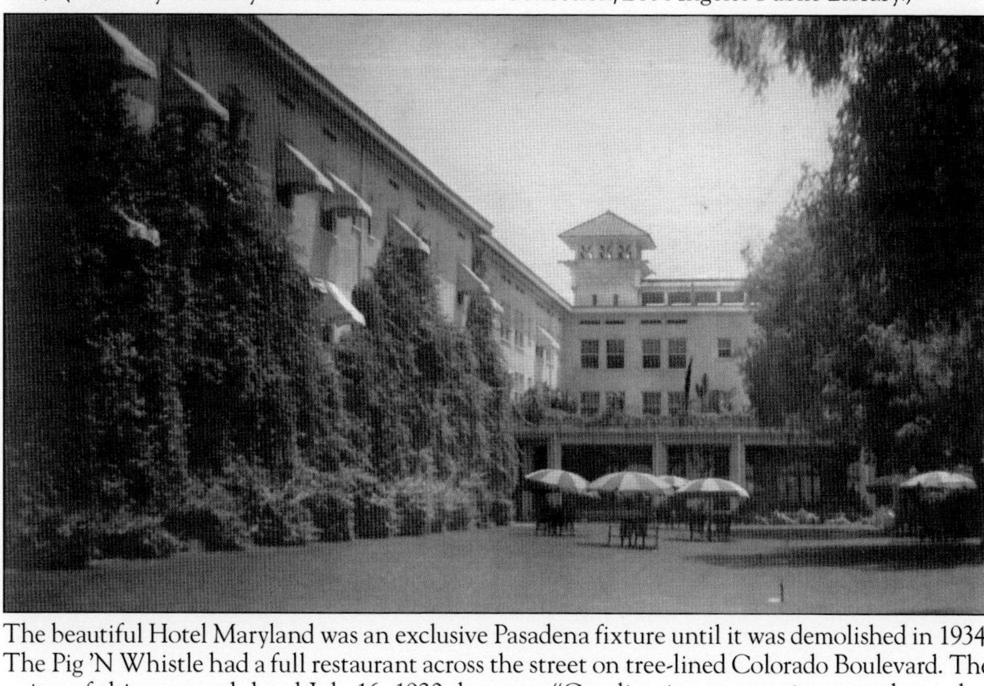

The beautiful Hotel Maryland was an exclusive Pasadena fixture until it was demolished in 1934. The Pig 'N Whistle had a full restaurant across the street on tree-lined Colorado Boulevard. The writer of this postcard dated July 16, 1920, laments, "Gasoline is so scarce just now, here, that people with autos have had to cut down on their riding. What is the world coming to?"

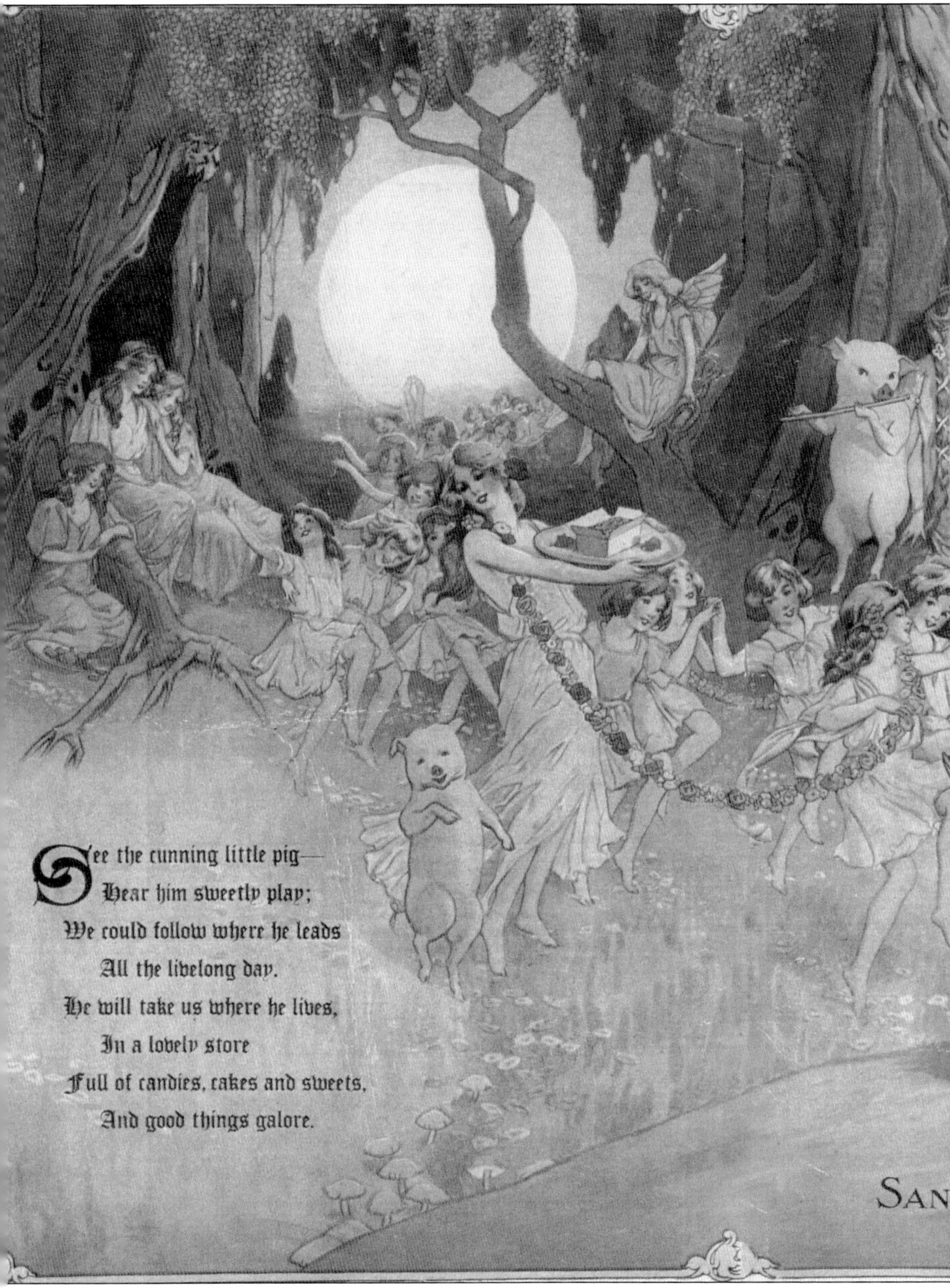
See the cunning little pig—
Hear him sweetly play;
We could follow where he leads
All the livelong day.
He will take us where he lives,
In a lovely store
Full of candies, cakes and sweets,
And good things galore.
SAN

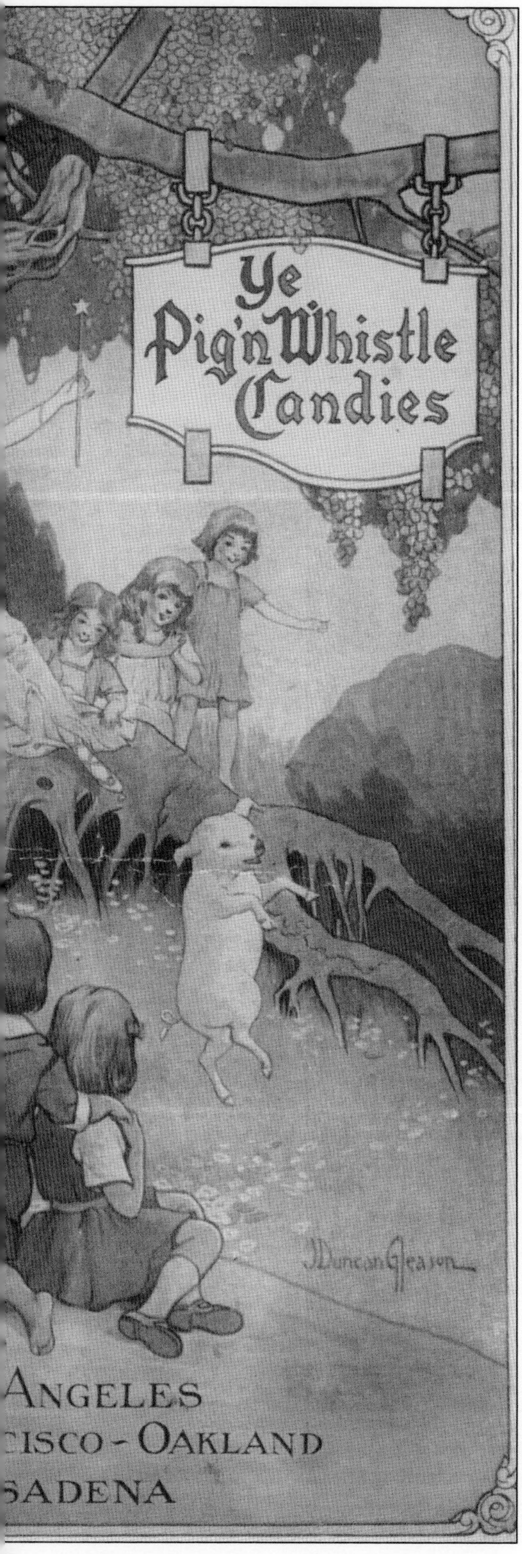

A menu from 1919 depicts children, fairies, and beautiful maidens frolicking with dancing pigs in a wooded setting. It was designed by J. Duncan Gleason, a prominent Los Angeles artist who illustrated many New York magazines, including the *Ladies' Home Journal*. He returned to Los Angeles in 1932, settled in Los Feliz Hills near Hollywood, and worked for MGM and Warner Bros. as a studio artist. By the close of the decade, when this menu was printed, there were "Seven Aristocratic Shops in California." Their locations in Los Angeles were 224 and 712 South Broadway and also 212 West Fifth Street in the Alexandria Hotel. San Francisco had 130 Post Street and 33 Powell Street; in Oakland it was at 511 Fourteenth Street, and in Pasadena it was on 412 East Colorado Boulevard. By 1919 there was also one at 1009 Second Avenue in Seattle.

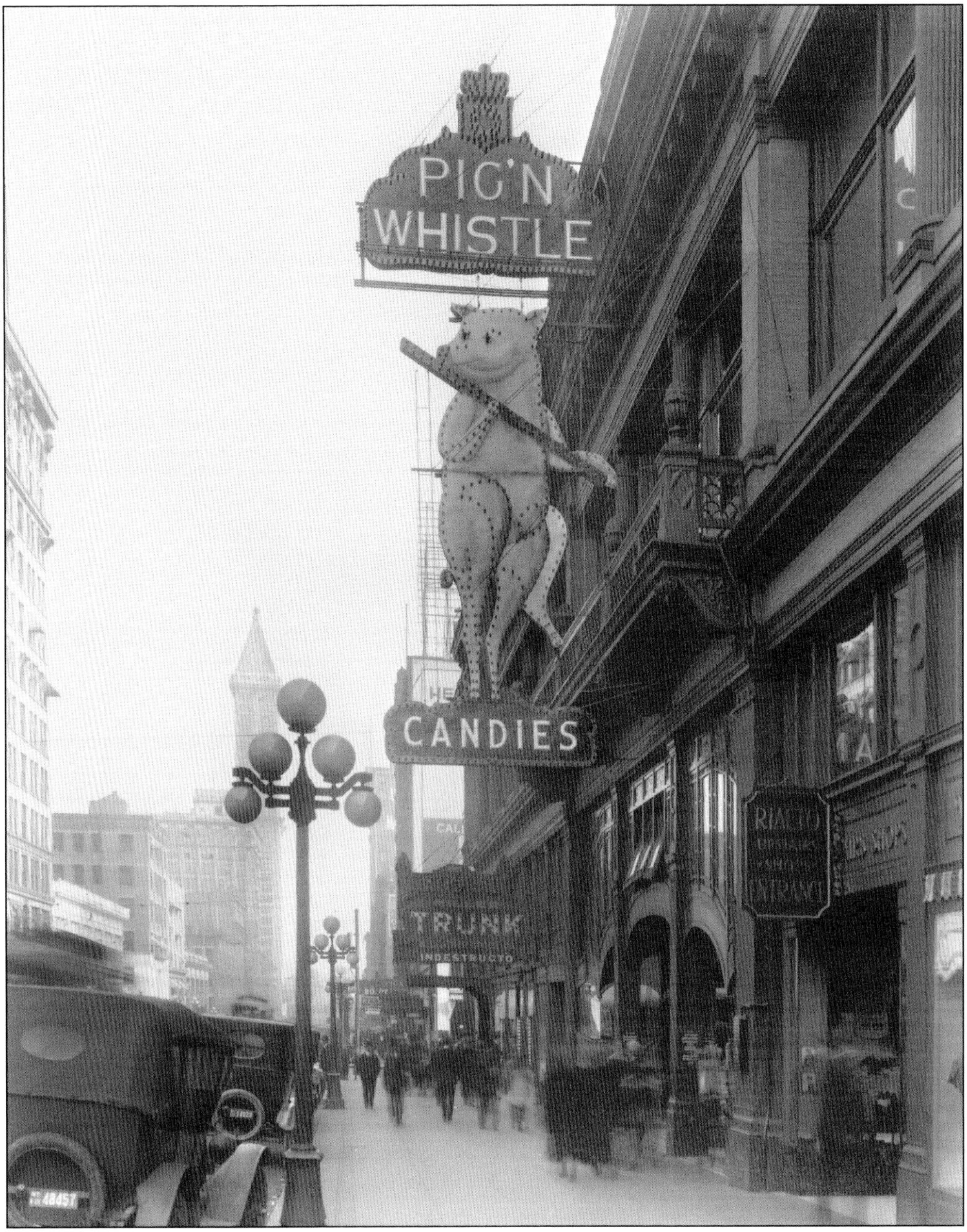

The Pig 'N Whistle made its way up to Seattle in 1919. This huge electric sign—the largest in the chain—is seen here at 1009 Second Avenue; it gives the illusion of a dancing pig. The shop was located in the two-story Rialto Building, which for a short time housed the Seattle Public Library. Visitors could "Dance to a Syncopated Band" in 1923 for a charge of 50¢. Across the street was the Palace Hip at Spring Street. The Palace Hip was the most popular vaudeville theater in Seattle, and the Pig 'N Whistle was the after-theater hangout for the vaudeville crowd. Seattle's only Pig 'N Whistle remained open until 1939. (Courtesy PEMCO Webster and Stevens Collection, Museum of History and Industry.)

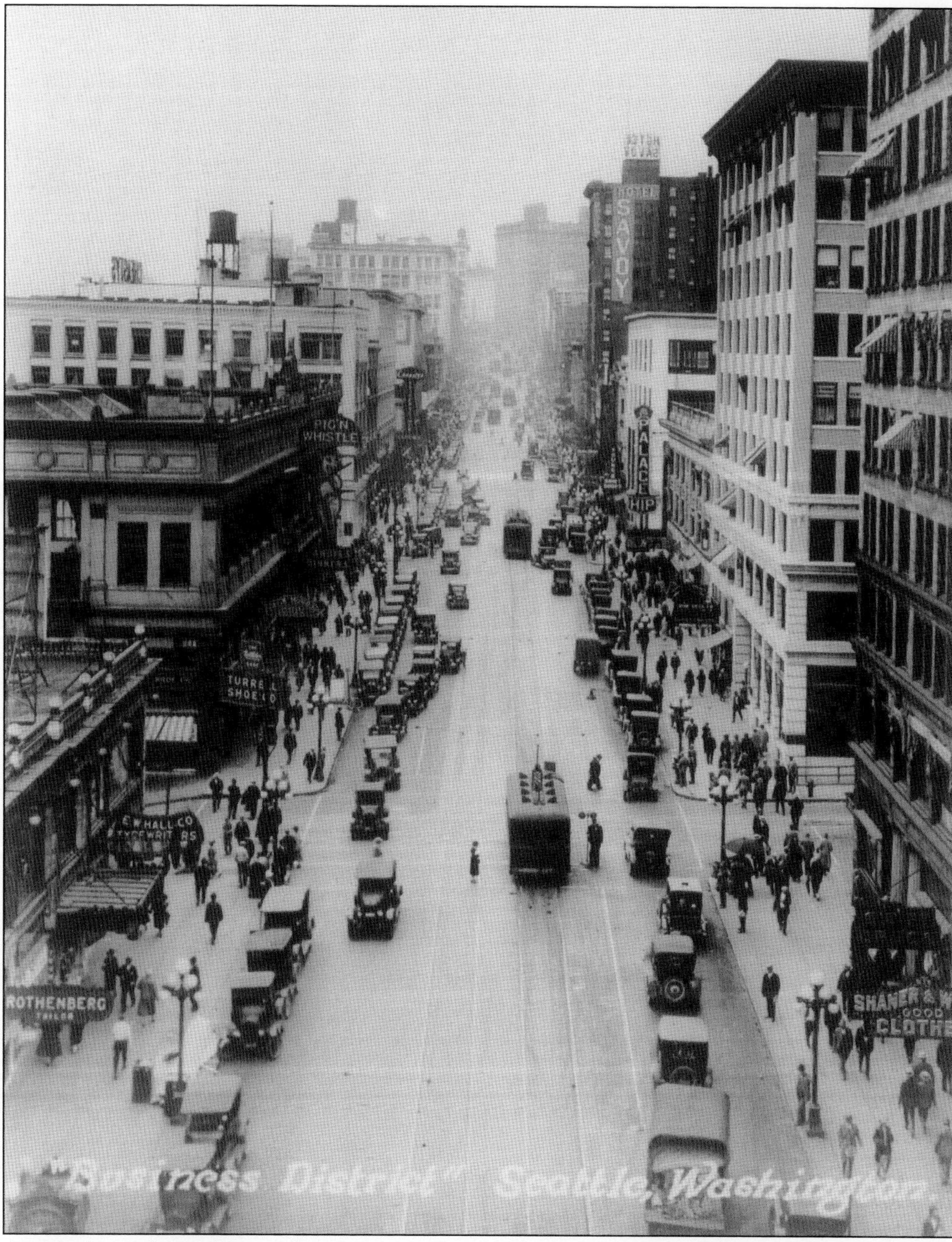

A snapshot taken of Second Avenue in Seattle's business district shows the Pig 'N Whistle signage on the left. This photograph was taken around 1920, shortly after the store moved into the Rialto Building. The Rialto Building was constructed of fire-resistant brick masonry in 1893 and housed many retail shops until it was demolished in 1948. Other businesses that can be seen at street level are the Turrell Shoe Company and Trick-Murray stationery shop. In the foreground at left are Rothenberg Tailor and E. W. Hall Company Typewriters. Also on this block are the Star Drug Company and Swift Drugs. Several Seattle Municipal Street Railway cars can be seen in the distance. The Pig 'N Whistle enjoyed 20 years in Seattle. The Rialto Building lasted 10 years beyond that and was demolished in March 1948.

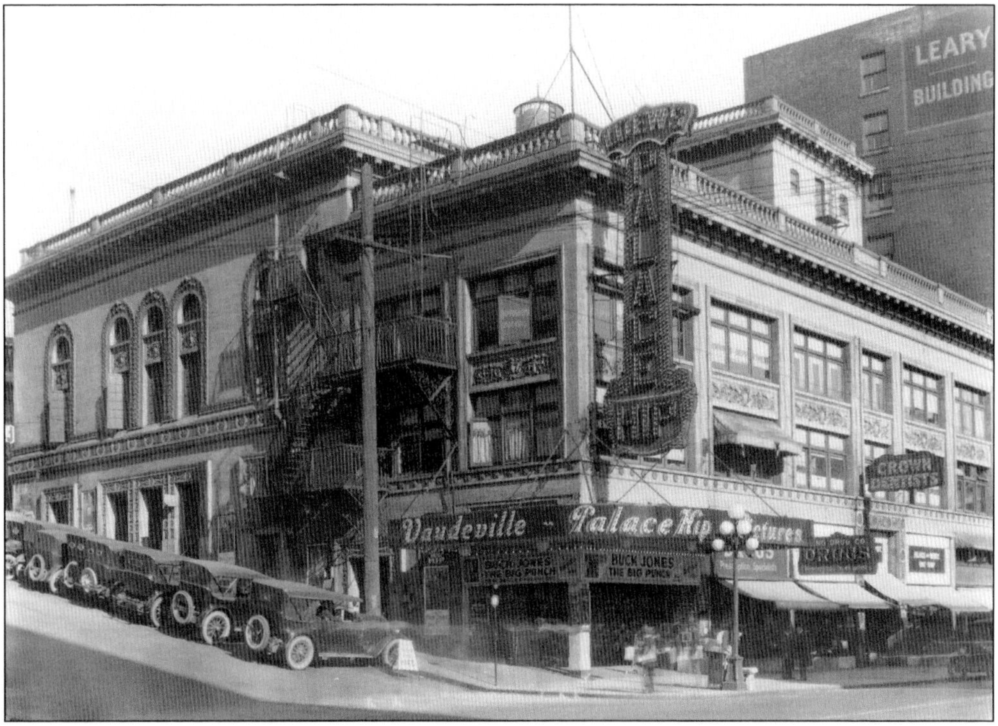

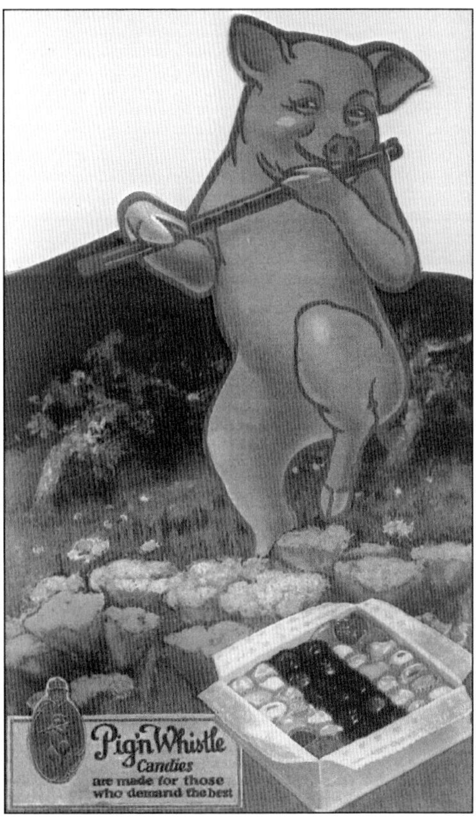

Loew's Palace Hip, or Hippodrome, was a popular vaudeville theater across the street from the Pig 'N Whistle on Second and Spring Streets in Seattle. Seen here in 1921, the marquee is advertising Buck Jones in *The Big Punch*. The Hip had all the big vaudeville acts of the day. It was demolished in 1981. (Courtesy PEMCO Webster and Stevens Collection, Museum of History and Industry.)

The pig on this menu is dancing in a field of California poppies. This evening fountain menu from 1920s Seattle would have served the Palace Theatre crowd across the street. On the menu is the University of Washington Sundae, which had mixed fruit over vanilla ice cream, coconut, whipped cream, nuts, and Nabisco wafers.

Three

Downtown Los Angeles

Downtown Los Angeles in the 1920s and 1930s was bustling with activity, and this period can be considered its golden age. Real estate boomed, and the Pacific Electric Railway, one of the most advanced systems in the United States at the time, had miles of track connecting Los Angeles to cities in Orange County and even in San Bernardino. The California climate was ideal, and the popular notion was that residents could reach out their doorways and pick an orange at any time. Hollywood was the dream factory, and would-be actors flooded the city looking to be discovered. By the time of the Great Depression, America desperately needed these manufactured dreams. The Pig 'N Whistle had several downtown locations in the 1920s, three of them on Broadway.

The many major department stores included Bullocks, Hamburger's (The May Company), Barker Brothers, and The Broadway. Sidney Hoedemaker was keenly aware that women shoppers often brought their youngsters along. He realized that they influenced their mothers' spending habits and made sure that they would want to come back to the Pig 'N Whistle. Special menus were created just for children, as well as whimsical dishes with nursery rhyme characters and dancing pigs. Downtown Los Angeles's beautiful movie palaces included the Orpheum, Palace, Grauman's Million Dollar, Rialto, Pantages, Loew's State, and Tower theaters. Pig 'N Whistle served many patrons before and after a show. Downtown had two of the finest hotels in the Alexandria and the Biltmore, and both had Pig 'N Whistle candy shops.

San Francisco was completely rebuilt by 1915, and eventually there were four Pig 'N Whistles in the city, serving the shopping district, Powell Street, and Market Street's "Movie Row," which included the Paramount (Granada), Orpheum, and Fox theaters. The Pig 'N Whistle was so popular in San Francisco that it was included at the Golden Gate International Exposition in 1939.

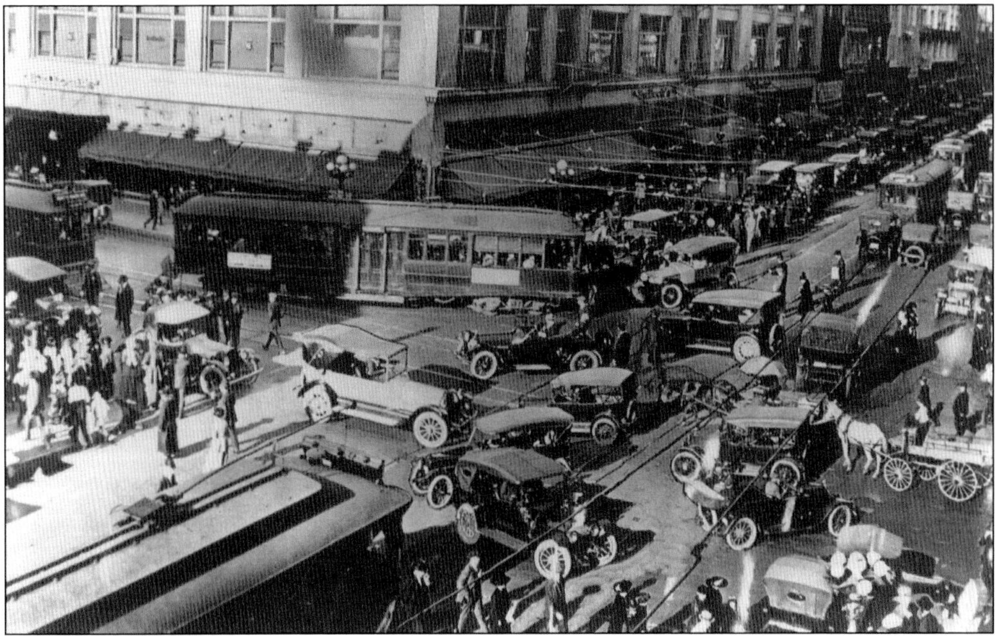

This photograph taken around 1920 underscores the claim that Seventh Street and Broadway was the busiest intersection in all of Los Angeles. In the 1926 travel guide *Greater California*, Broadway is described as "the most traveled thoroughfare in Christendom." Automobiles, streetcars, horse-drawn vehicles, and pedestrians are all tangled up together in a chaotic mess. (Courtesy Security Pacific National Bank Collection/Los Angeles Public Library.)

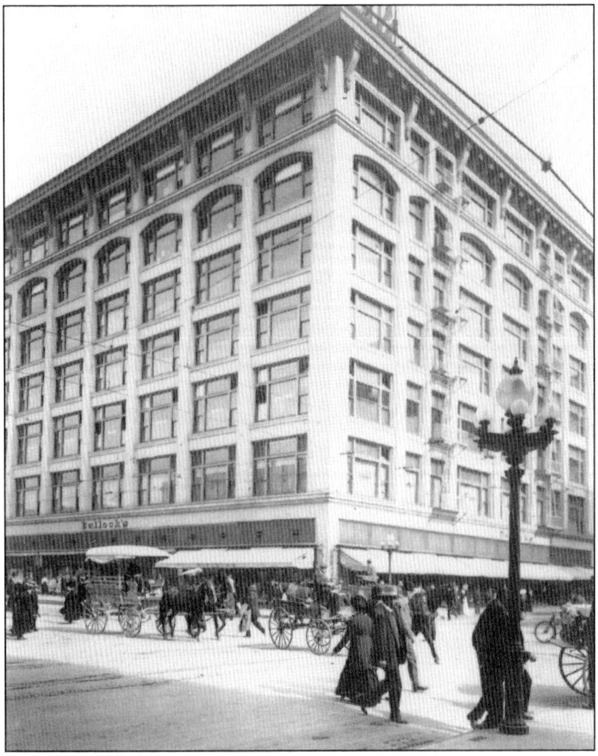

Bullock's department store was founded in 1907 by John G. Bullock It is pictured here in 1910 on the corner of Seventh Street and Broadway. Bullocks specialized in high-end merchandise; it was a popular store, with many locations in California, Arizona, and Nevada, until it went out of business in 1996. (Courtesy Security Pacific National Bank Collection/ Los Angeles Public Library.)

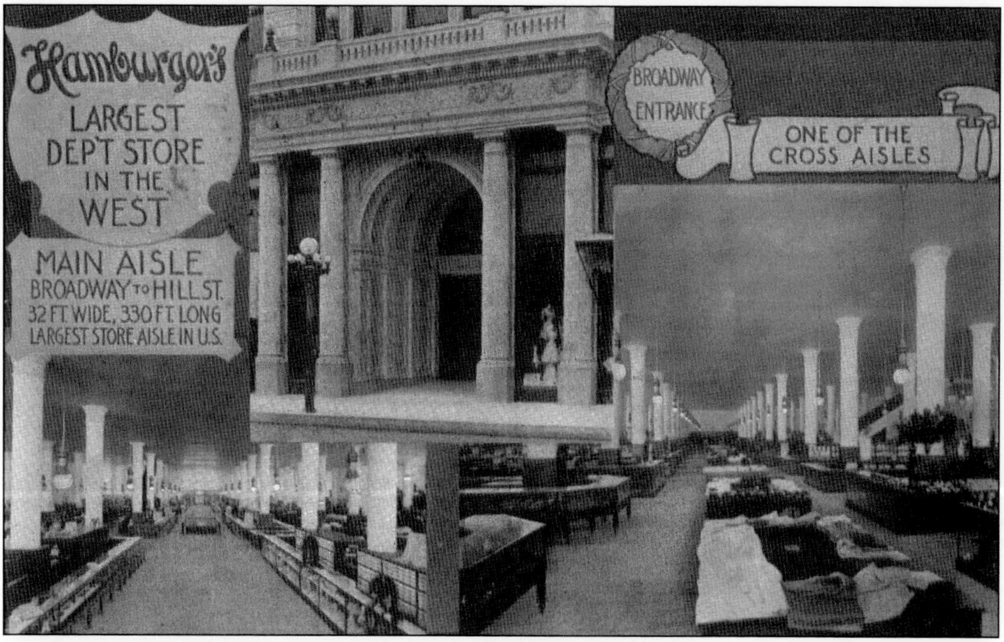

Hamburger's People's Store was founded by Asher Hamburger in 1881 in Los Angeles. Originally it sat on the corner of Spring and Hill Streets, but later moved to Eighth Street and Broadway and became "Hamburger's." By 1923, it was bought out by The May Company. Hamburger's was the largest department store in the west, according to this 1910 postcard.

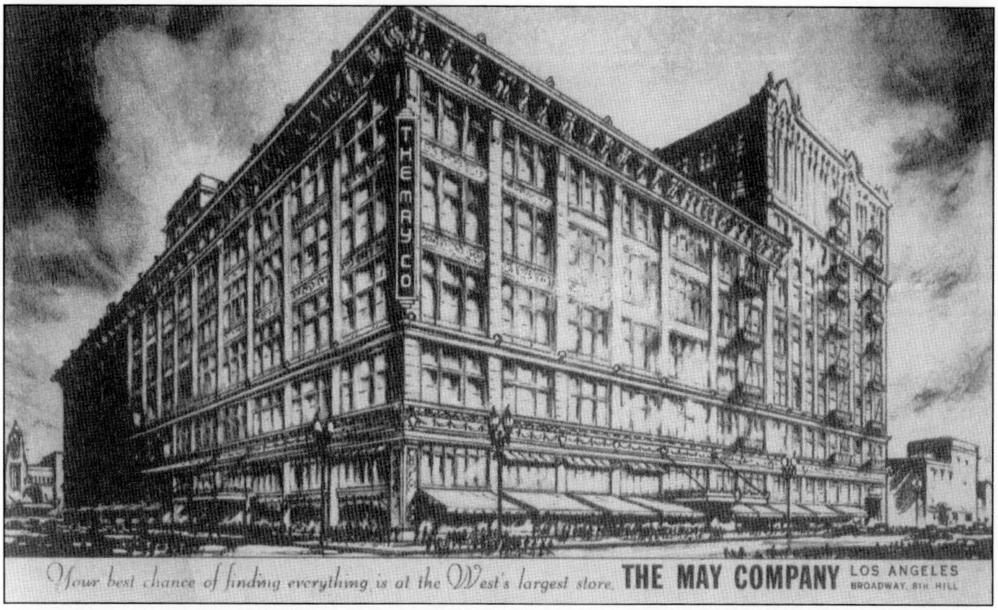

The May Company, founded by David May, took over Hamburger's department store in 1923. This postcard image from the late 1920s depicts the store on the corners of Broadway and Eighth and Hill Streets with the following caption: "Your best chance of finding everything is at the West's largest store." The May Company dissolved in 2005.

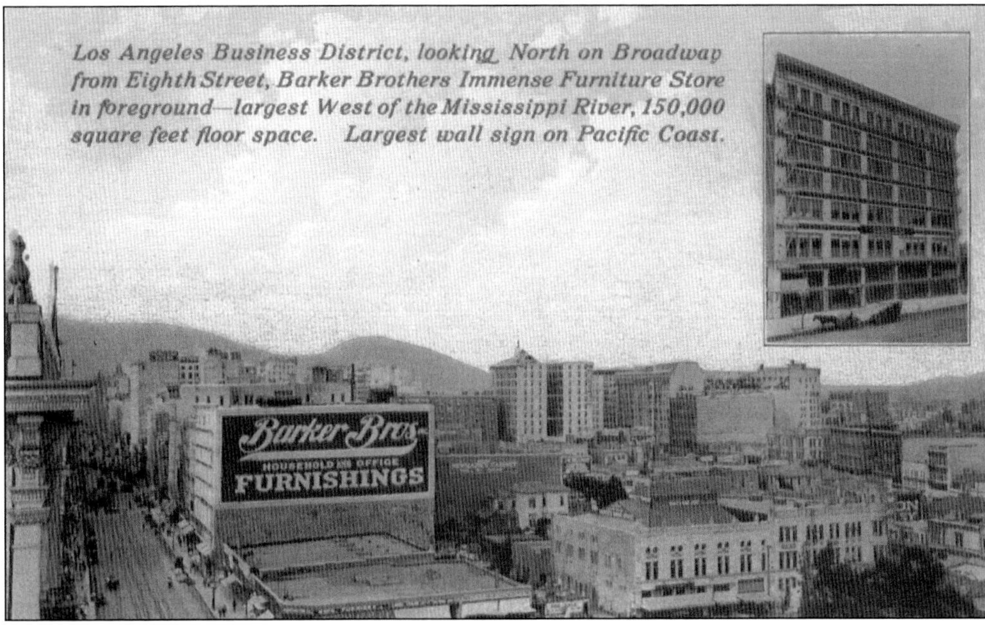

Another major store in the heart of downtown Los Angeles was Barker Brothers furniture store. This postcard noted that Barker Brothers was the largest store west of the Mississippi River. The same corner near Eighth Street and Broadway was also home to Hamburger's. In 10 years Barker Brothers would also have a location near the Hollywood Pig 'N Whistle at 6714 Hollywood Boulevard.

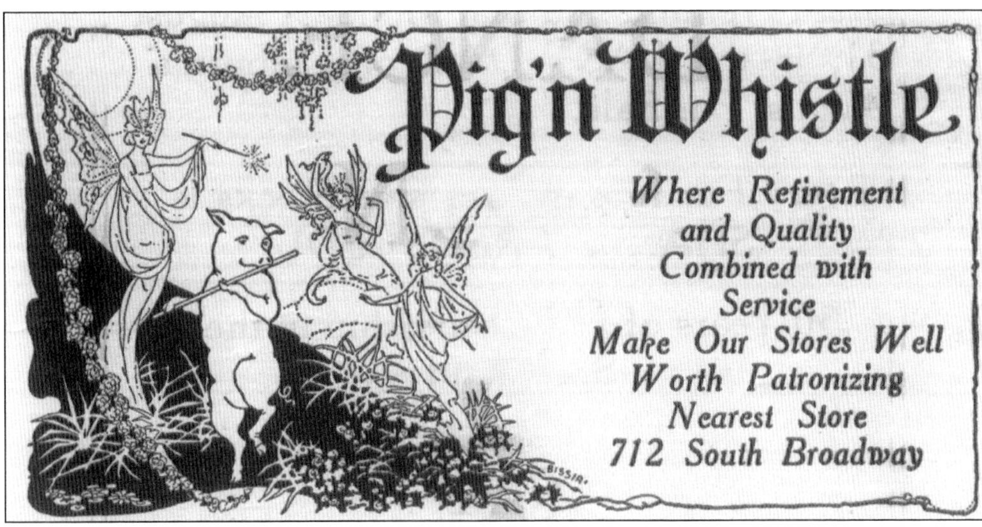

This Pig 'N Whistle advertisement from 1925 was created at Bissiri Studio by Adriano and Augusto Bissiri. Adriano was a title artist for motion pictures, and his brother Augusto is credited as the inventor of television. In 1906, Augusto transmitted a photograph image from one room to another, and in 1917, he successfully transmitted an image from London to New York. He patented his apparatus in Los Angeles in 1928.

Hovsep Pushman, or Pushminian, was an Armenian American artist known for his beautiful paintings of women. The 712 Broadway Pig 'N Whistle had a fine art gallery, and Pushman's painting *Narcissa* was prominently displayed. This menu from 1926 commemorates the reopening of the Shrine Auditorium, which had been destroyed by fire five years before. A special Shriner's Sundae could be ordered for 40¢.

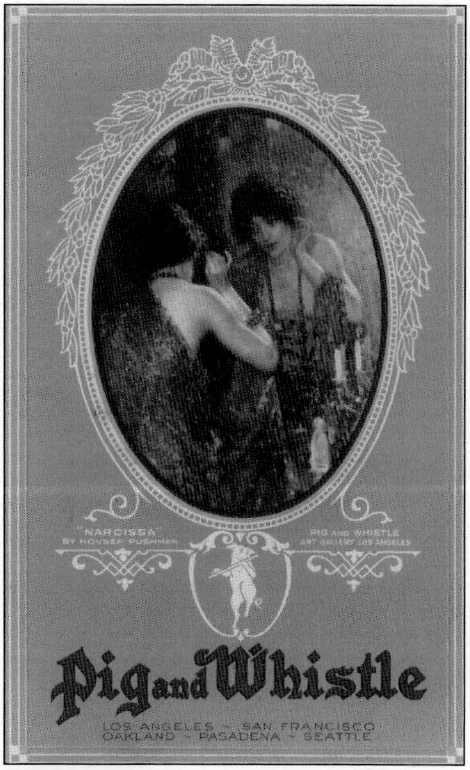

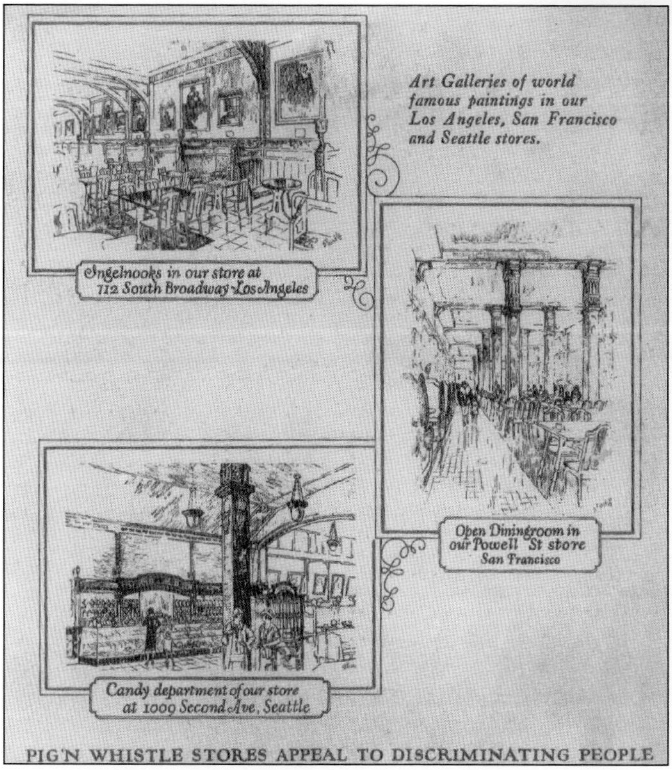

An illustrated menu from 1925 shows the interior of three shops that had "Art Galleries of world famous paintings": Los Angeles, main store at 712 South Broadway; San Francisco, Powell Street; and Seattle, 1009 Second Avenue. The bottom reads, "Pig 'N Whistle stores appeal to discriminating people." The Powell Street store had an open dining room where patrons could see the cable cars turning around outside.

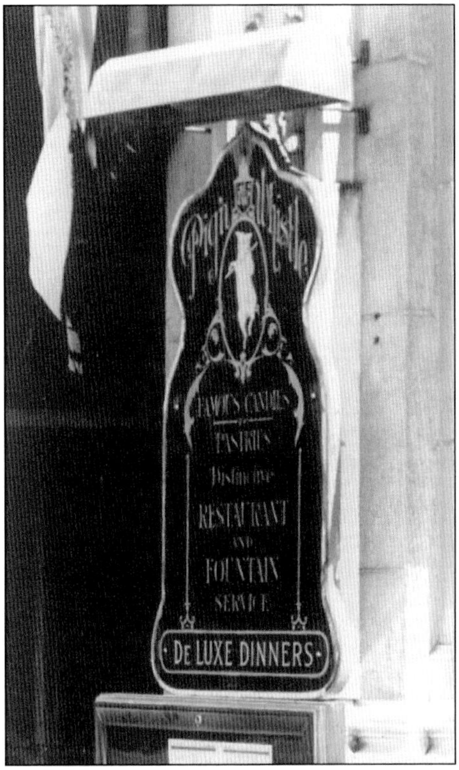

A detail of the storefront electric signage and menu board at 712 South Broadway reads, "Famous Candies Pastries; Distinctive Restaurant and Fountain Service. De Luxe Dinners." This location became the headquarters, or main store, of the restaurant chain. (Courtesy Bison Archives.)

In this interior shot of the 712 South Broadway store, the fine art paintings can be seen on the wall. To the left, the candy counter had beautiful candy boxes and a countertop scale for weighing out custom orders. On the right was the soda fountain. A copy of the *Los Angeles Times* can be seen draped over the back of the waiting bench. (Courtesy Bison Archives.)

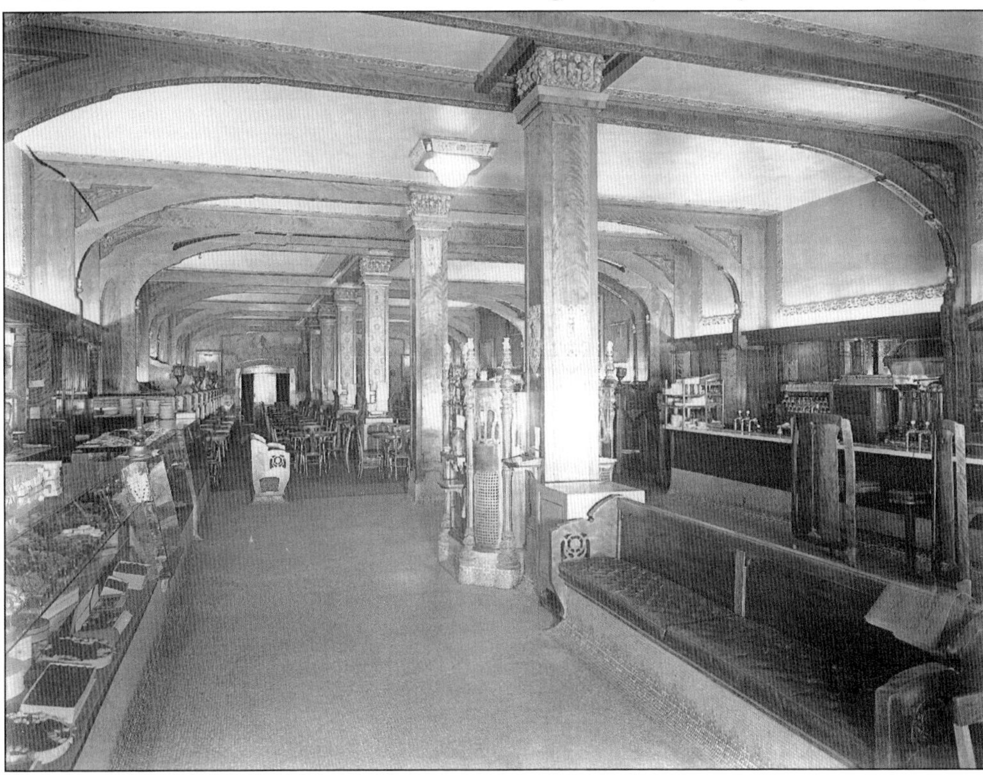

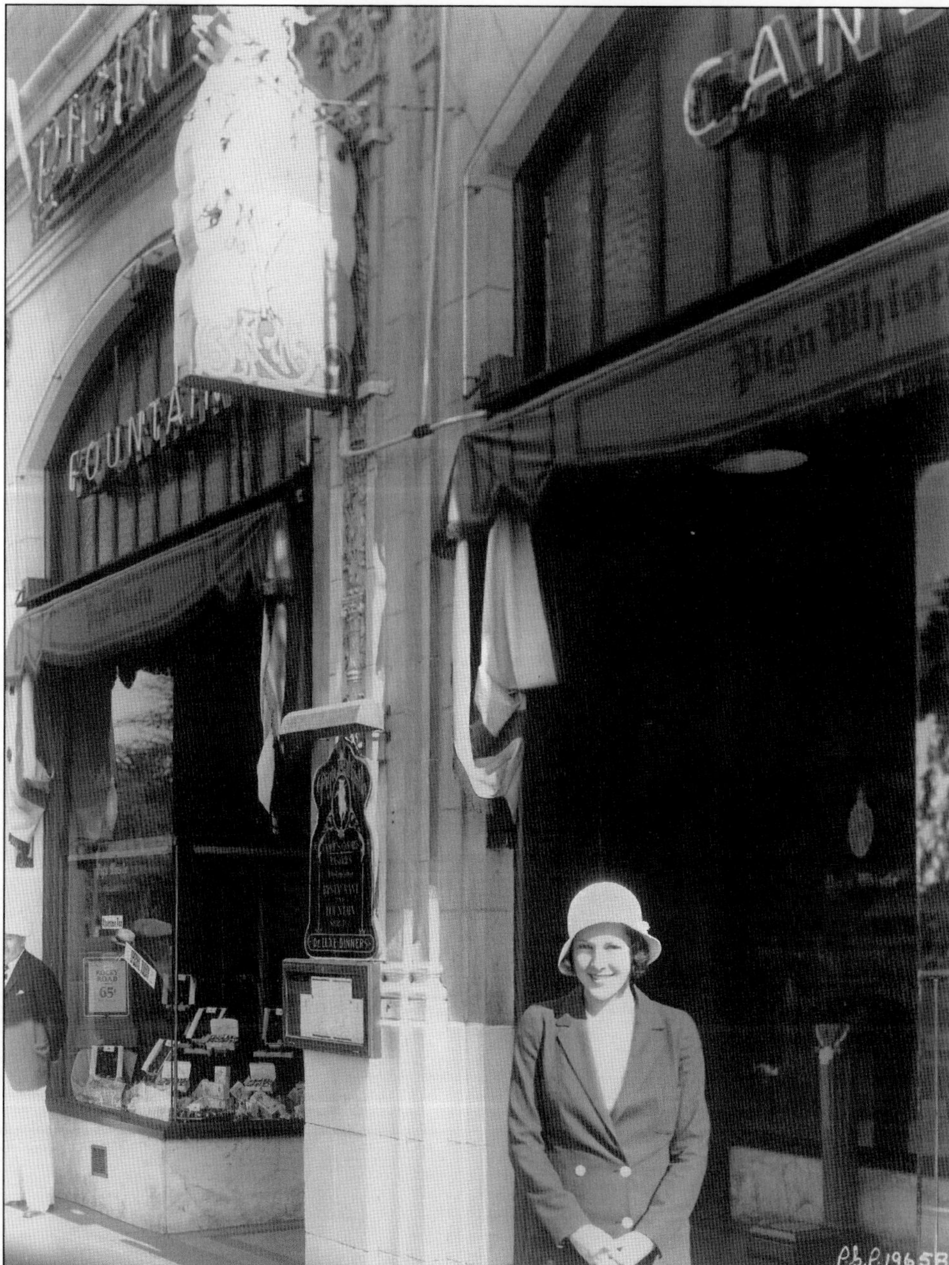

Actress Frances Dee poses outside the Pig 'N Whistle at 712 South Broadway. Frances was considered one of the most beautiful actresses in Hollywood and enjoyed a varied array of roles throughout the 1930s and 1940s. She was a supporting actress in films such as *Little Women*, *Of Human Bondgae*, and *Becky Sharp*. Before she gave up acting in the 1950s, Dee appeared in the 1943 cult classic horror film *I Walked With a Zombie*. David O. Selznick almost cast Dee in the role of Melanie Wilkes in *Gone With the Wind*, but thought her beauty would overshadow that of Vivien Leigh. It is fitting that one of Hollywood's most beautiful actresses should pose in front of one of Los Angeles's most beautiful shops. The special of the day advertised in the window was Rocky Road candy for 65¢ a pound. (Courtesy Bison Archives.)

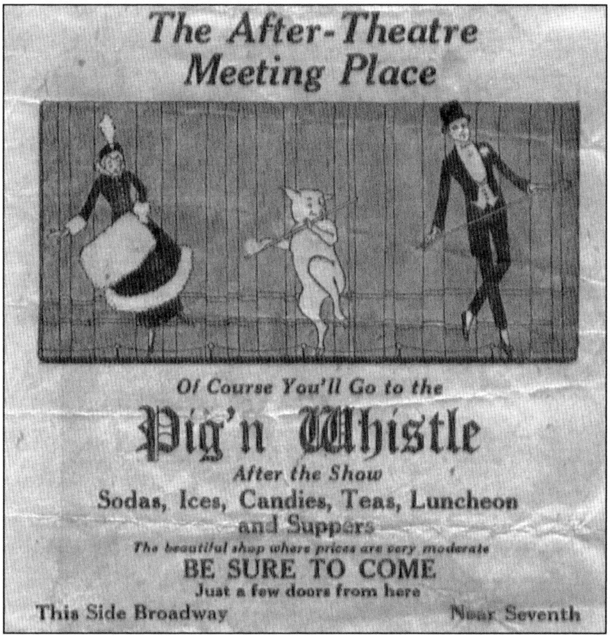

An advertisement from February 1918 comes from a Morosco Theatre program. Producer Oliver Morosco opened the theater in 1913 at 744 Broadway, a few steps down from the Pig 'N Whistle at 712 Broadway. This advertisement accompanied a listing for David Belasco's play *Seven Chances*. It was made into a silent film starring Buster Keaton later in 1925.

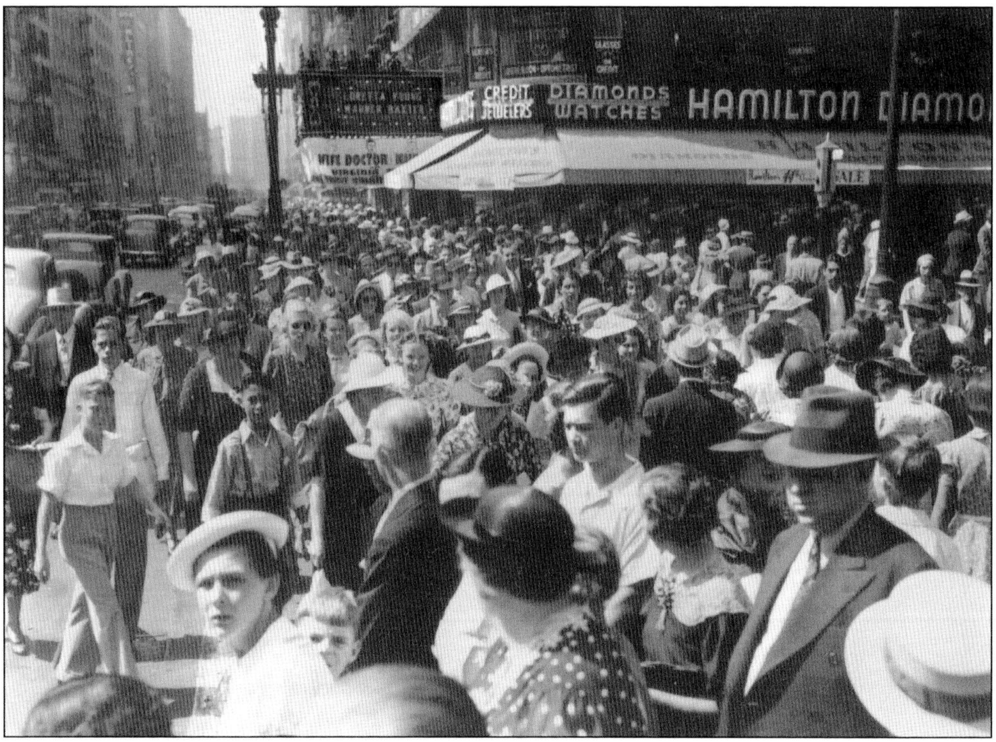

By the time this picture was taken in 1937, downtown Los Angeles was at the height of its popularity. Broadway at Seventh Street was still crowded morning to night. All of the city's retail and entertainment was centered within a 1-mile radius. This would drastically change by the middle of the century. (Courtesy Security Pacific National Bank Collection/Los Angeles Public Library.)

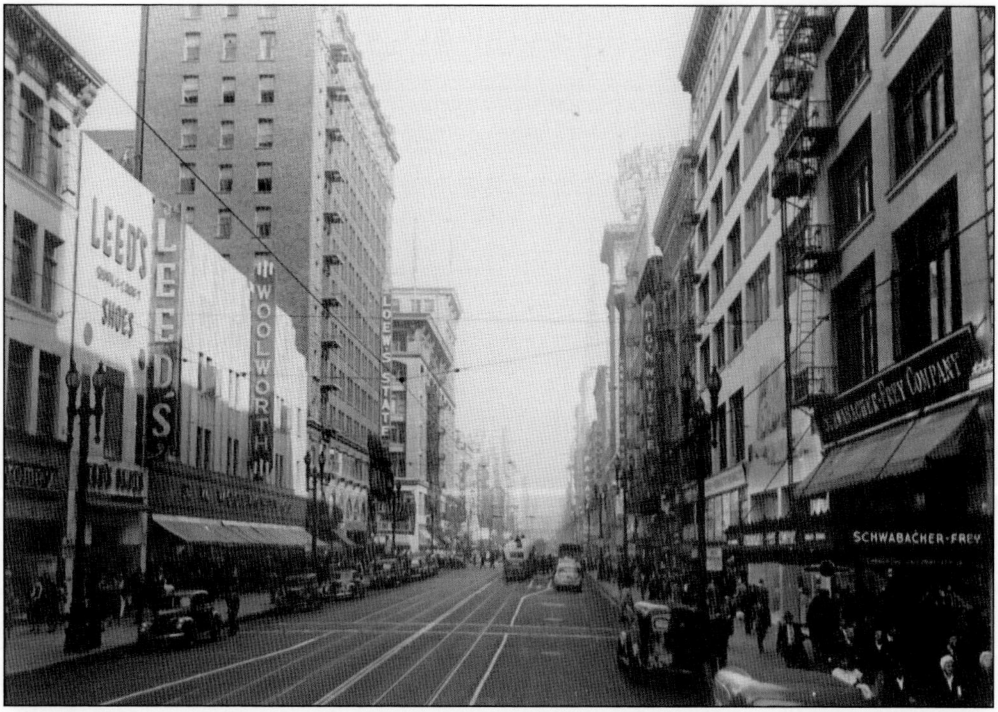

A Los Angeles street scene on Broadway in the 1940s shows the diverse retail shops close to the Pig 'N Whistle. Looking north toward Seventh Street, the signage for the Lankershim Hotel can be seen. Leeds, Jeromes, Woolworth, Loew's State Theatre, and Schwabacher-Frey are also visible. This Pig 'N Whistle location was one of the last to close in the downtown area.

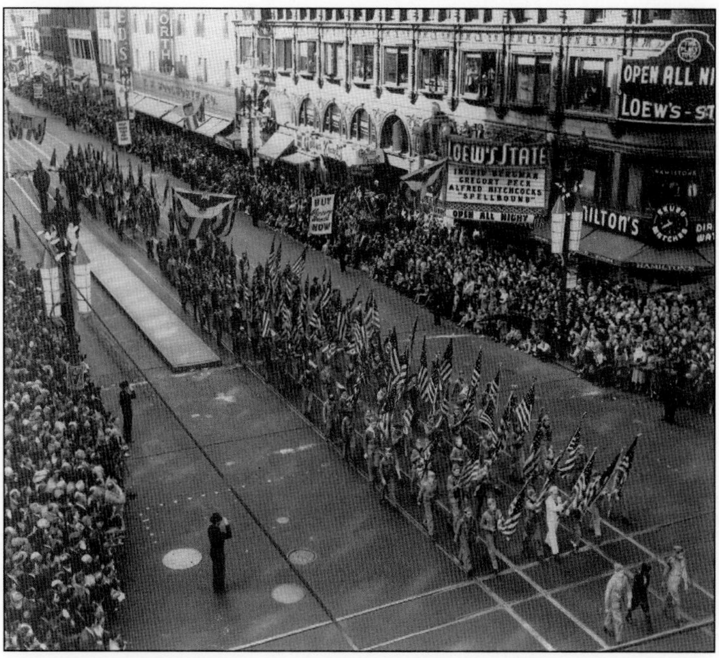

Boy Scouts march down Broadway in front of Loew's State Theatre on Armistice Day, November 12, 1945. The end of the war also marked the end of the downtown area's popularity. In 10 years, the migration to the suburbs closed many theaters as television eclipsed moviegoing. (Courtesy Security Pacific National Bank Collection/Los Angeles Public Library.)

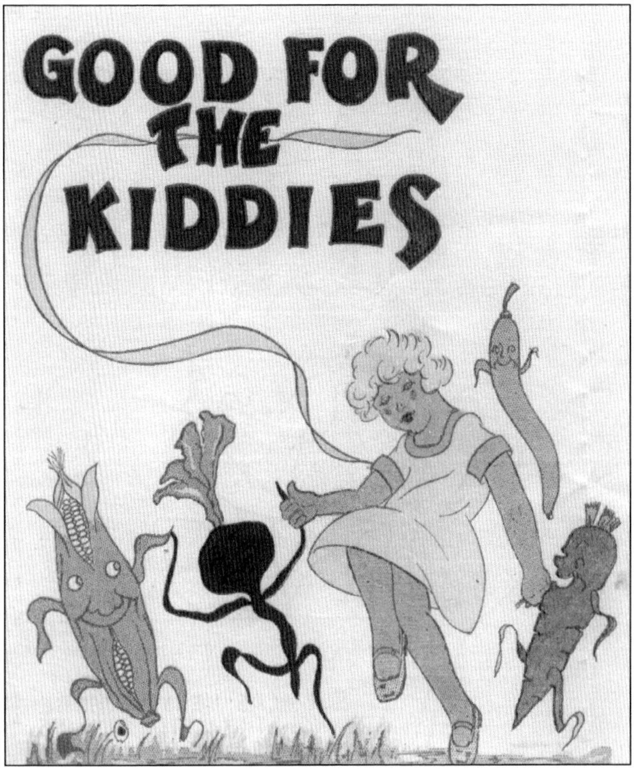

Sidney Hoedemaker felt that the children of restaurant patrons were important customers, too. He believed that many restaurants wrongly ignored them and that those who catered to the family trade should offer something that would make children feel special. Pig 'N Whistle menus and tableware were made with nursery rhyme–themed characters, dancing vegetables and of course, dancing pigs. In the industry trade magazine *Cooking for Profit*, Hoedemaker noted, "When there are young children in a family group, they should be served first, so that when the adults are served, these tots are ready for dessert." The 1930s menu at left listed an "Old Mother Hubbard" meal of a peanut butter sandwich, applesauce, and Ovaltine for 25¢.

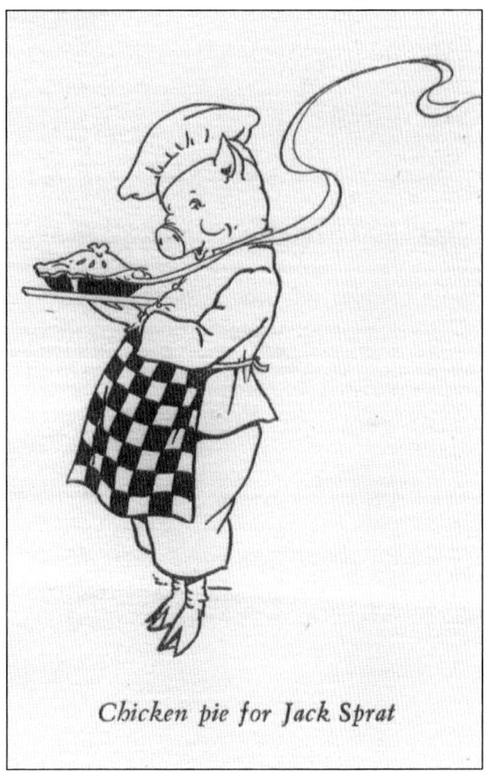

This child's menu could be used as a mask after dining. The pig seems to be inspired by the enormously popular and Academy Award–winning cartoon Walt Disney's *The Three Little Pigs* from 1933. In 1935, Warner Bros. introduced Porky Pig in their Merrie Melodies series of cartoons. This 1938 mask bears a slight resemblance to this famous swine as well.

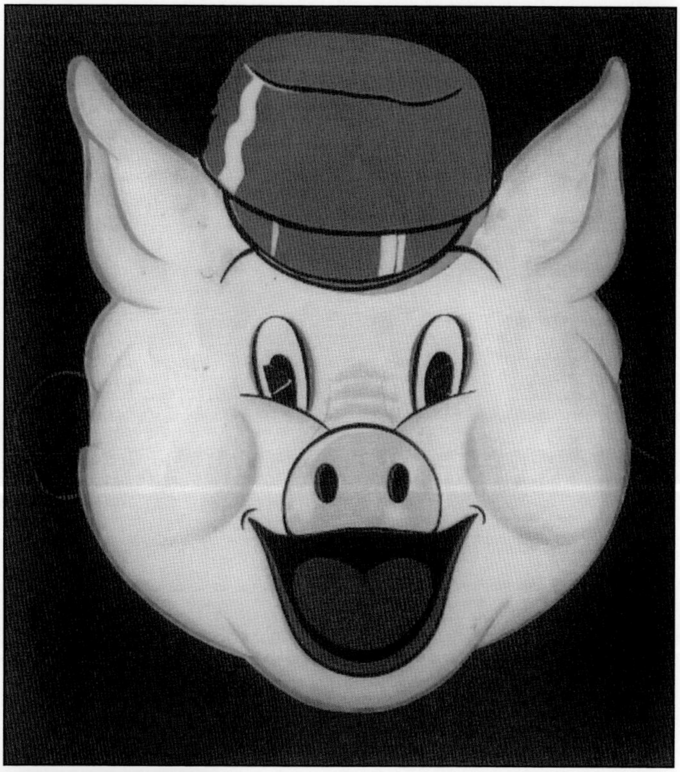

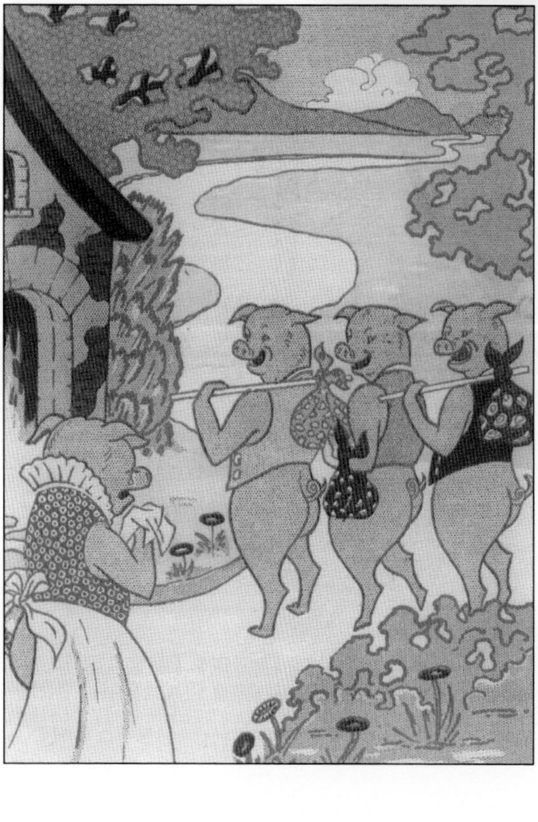

Here the fable of *The Three Little Pigs* is featured in a coloring book menu from the mid-1930s. The story itself was from 19th-century England; Disney made it more popular than ever. The Disney pigs had names and played musical instruments: Practical Pig played the piano, Fiddler Pig played the fiddle, and Fifer Pig played the flute.

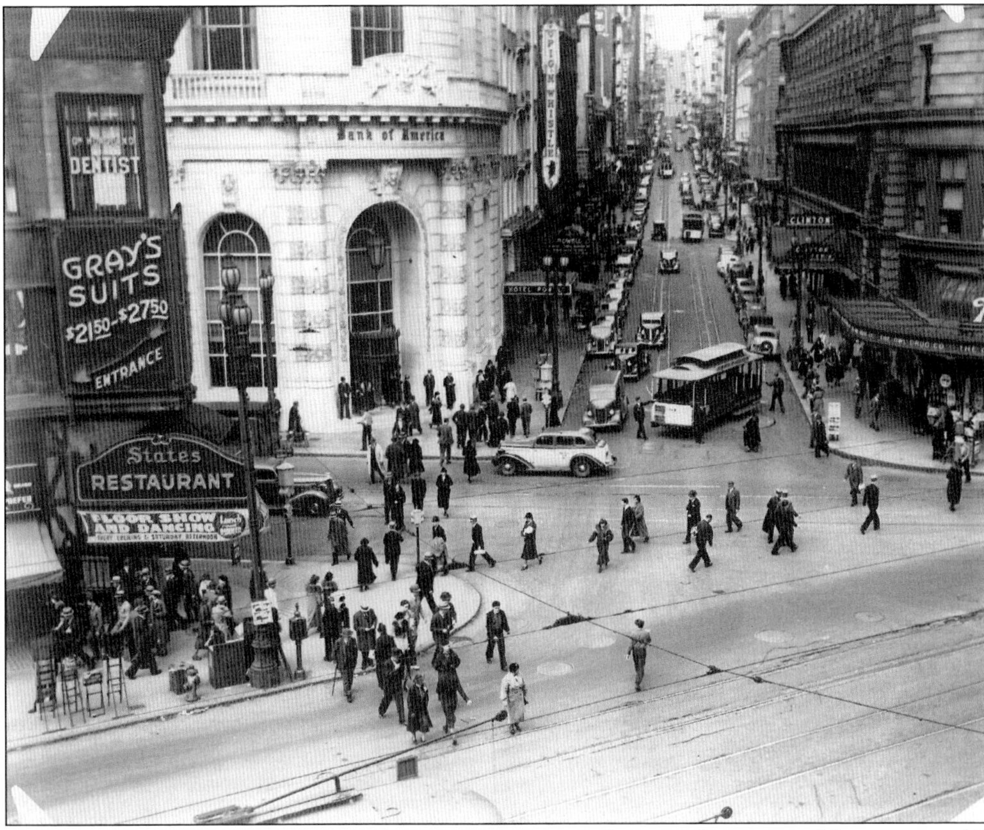

The intersection of Powell and Market Streets is where the Powell-Mason cable car turntable is located. The line has run since 1888—longer than any other transit line in the world. This intersection is bustling with activity; seen here in 1937, the States Restaurant is advertising "Floor Show and Dancing Every Night and Saturday Evening." The Pig 'N Whistle blade signage is seen at center. (Courtesy San Francisco Public Library.)

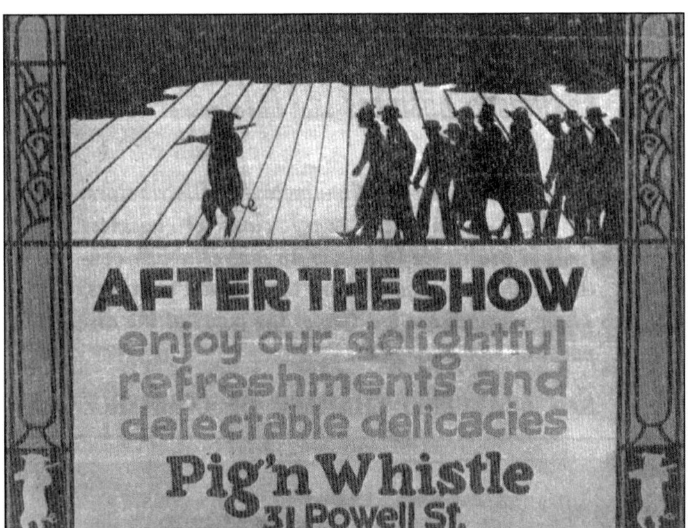

The San Francisco Pig 'N Whistle on Powell Street also attracted theater goers. The popular Alcazar Theatre, nearby at 260 O'Farrell Street, was destroyed in 1906 and rebuilt in 1911. This Art Deco–styled advertisement was featured in a 1925 *Playgoer* magazine. The address was 31 Powell Street, but eventually it branched out next door to 33 Powell Street. It was sometimes listed as 31–33 Powell Street.

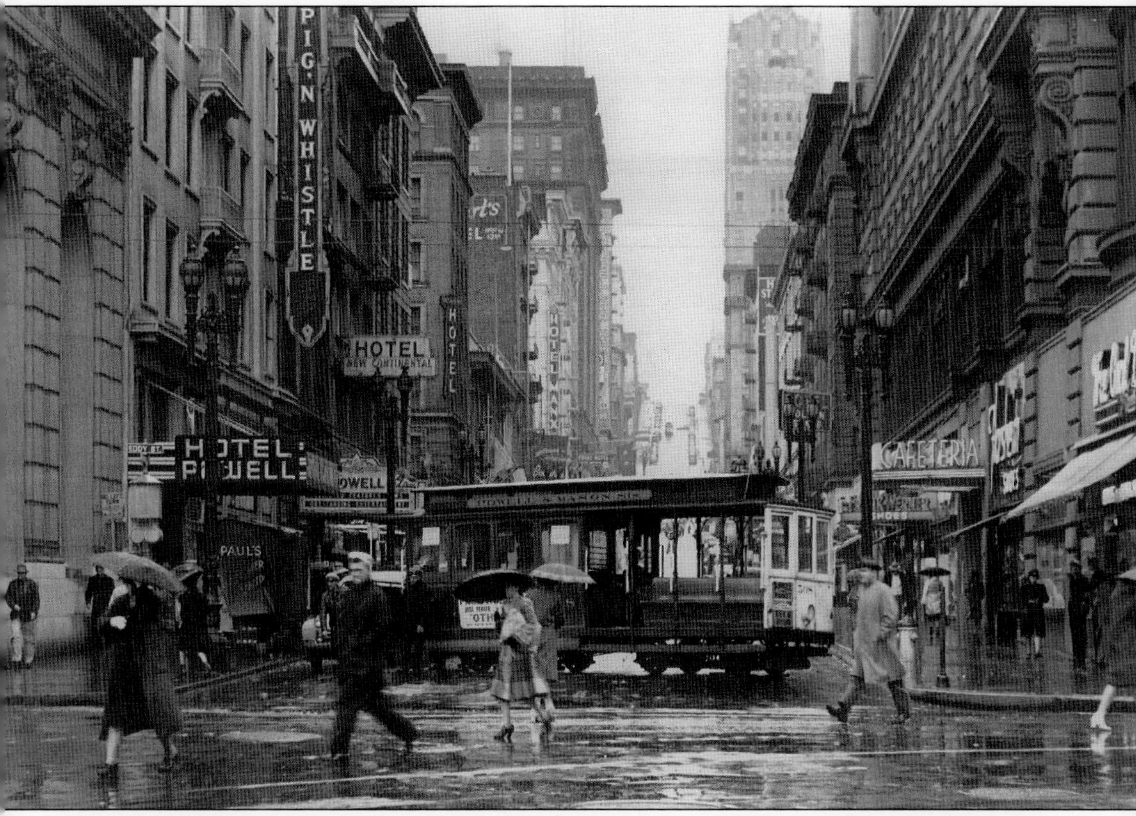

This photograph of a rainy afternoon on Powell and Market Streets on March 24, 1945, shows the Powell and Mason No. 508 cable car being turned around by hand. It is the most photographed cable car turntable in the world. Hotels that can be seen in the distance are the Powell, the New Continental, the Manx, the Crane, the Chancellor, and the Pasadena. Among the people dashing across the street is a sailor in his peacoat and Dixie Cup hat. An advertisement for Jose Ferrar in the stage production of *Othello* is visible on the cable car. The news copy for this photograph reads, "Here's one good ol' San Francisco corner that always seems to look the same. Seems like it always rains more at Powell and Market than anywhere else in town." (San Francisco Public Library.)

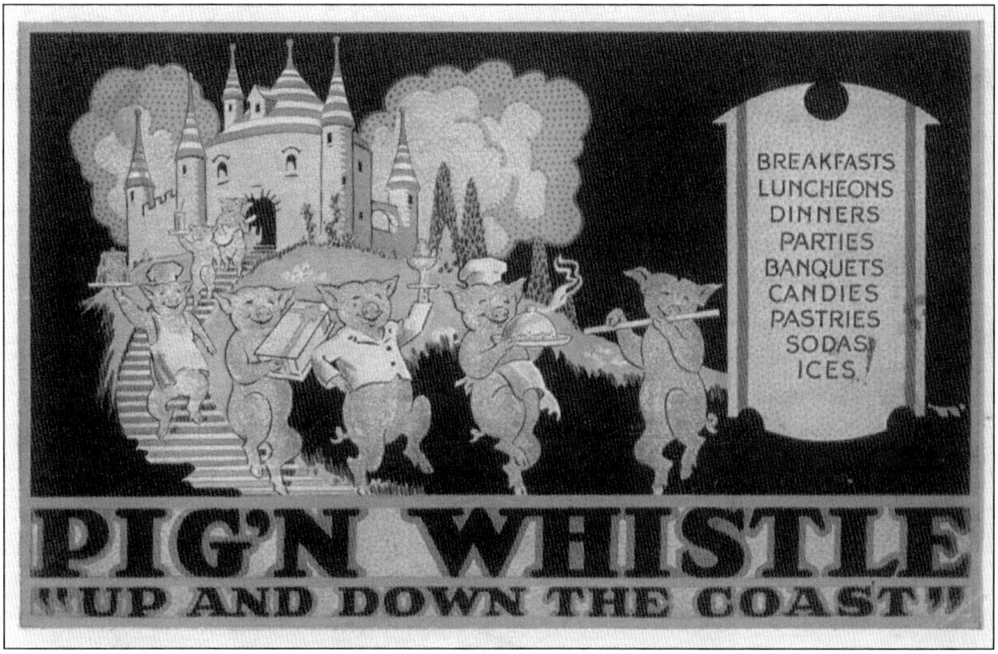

An advertising postcard from the mid-1930s shows a parade of pigs filing down from a castle on a hill. The text on the back reads, "That piping dancing little Pig with the jolly, come hither smile has all sorts of good things for your refreshment and entertainment." It was mailed from Pasadena in 1938 and is inscribed, "Precious Peggy. Do come to lunch!"

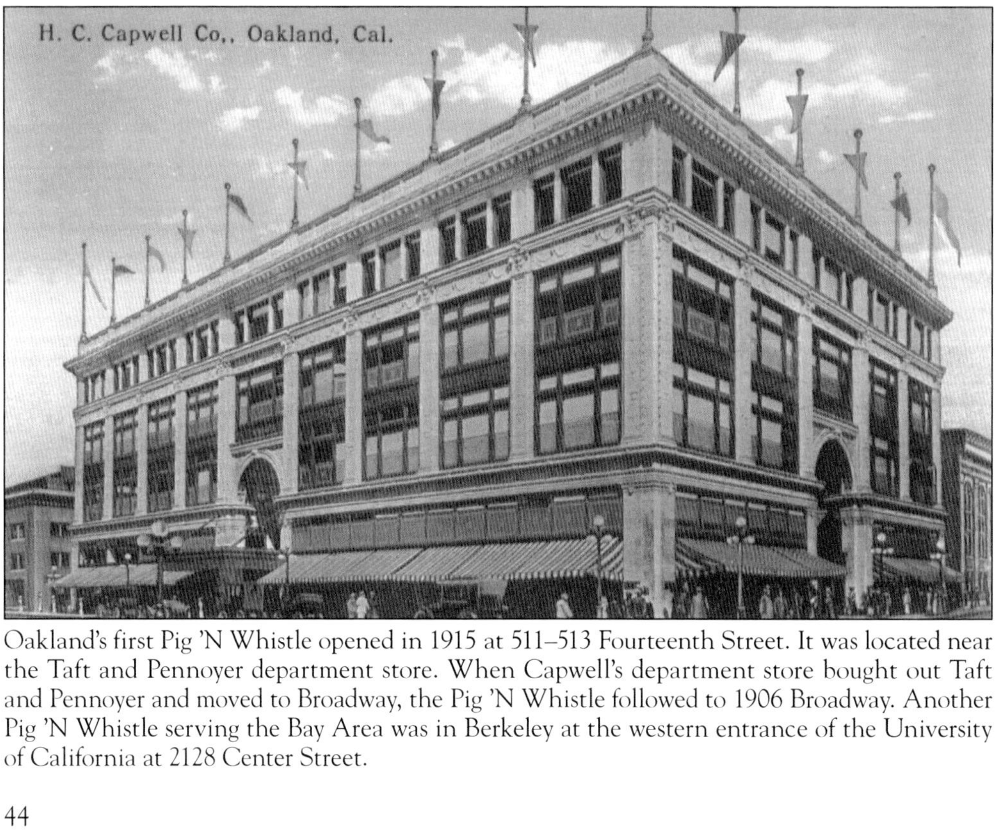

Oakland's first Pig 'N Whistle opened in 1915 at 511–513 Fourteenth Street. It was located near the Taft and Pennoyer department store. When Capwell's department store bought out Taft and Pennoyer and moved to Broadway, the Pig 'N Whistle followed to 1906 Broadway. Another Pig 'N Whistle serving the Bay Area was in Berkeley at the western entrance of the University of California at 2128 Center Street.

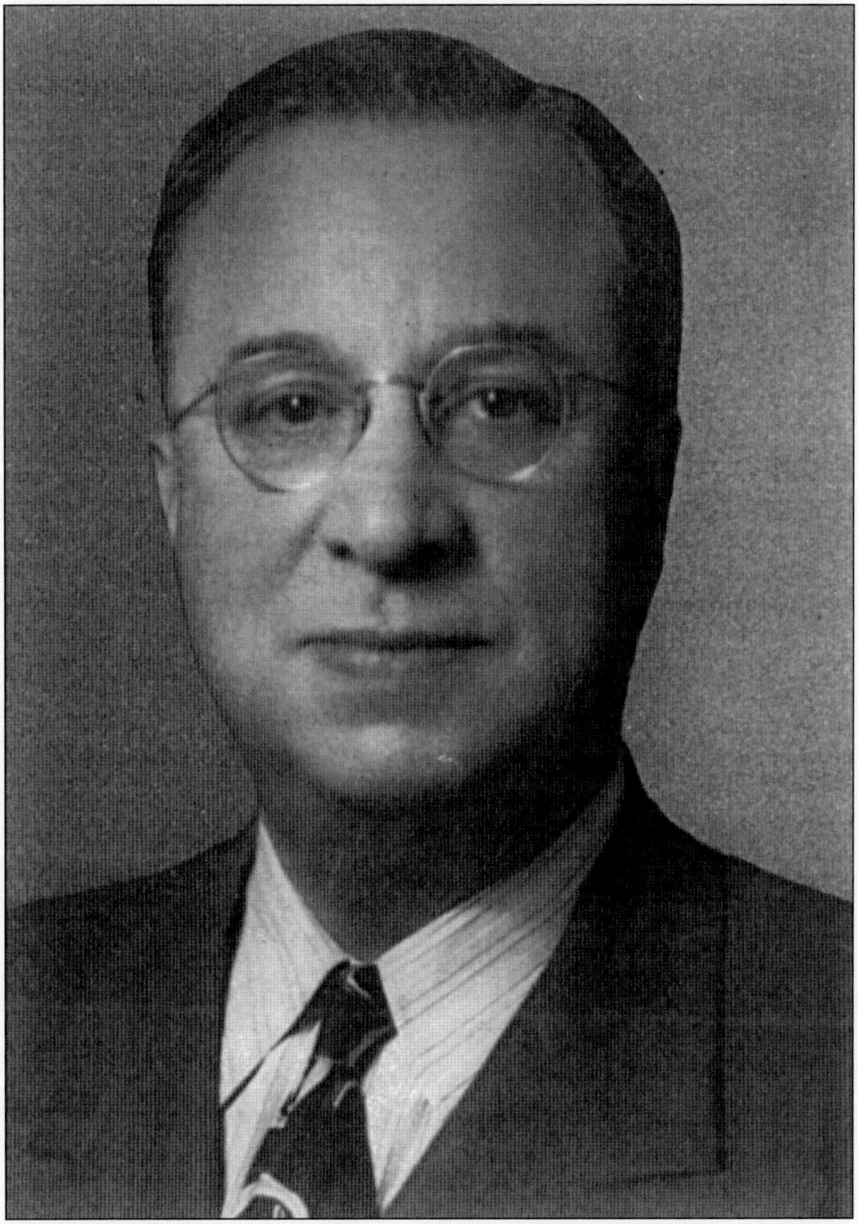

Sidney Hoedemaker was born in Amsterdam, Holland, in 1886. His father was a wealthy merchant, and Hoedemaker was educated in the best schools in the Netherlands. After learning to speak Dutch, French, and German, he was sent to London to learn English at age 16. At 18 years of age he took a vacation to the United States and came back year after year. In 1912, aged 26, he visited Texas and fell in love with a girl, Margaret Livingston, from San Antonio. They married, and Hoedemaker moved with his new bride to San Francisco. Until that point, he had not worked a day in his life. He was used to eating the best food and staying at the finest hotels while traveling from country to country. At this time in America, no matter how rich a man was, he was expected to do some type of work. Although the position was far beneath a man of his wealth, Hoedemaker briefly worked at a hamburger stand, then became a food checker at the Fairmont Hotel; by 1916, he was the assistant manager of the Palace Hotel. (Courtesy Eddie Hoedemaker.)

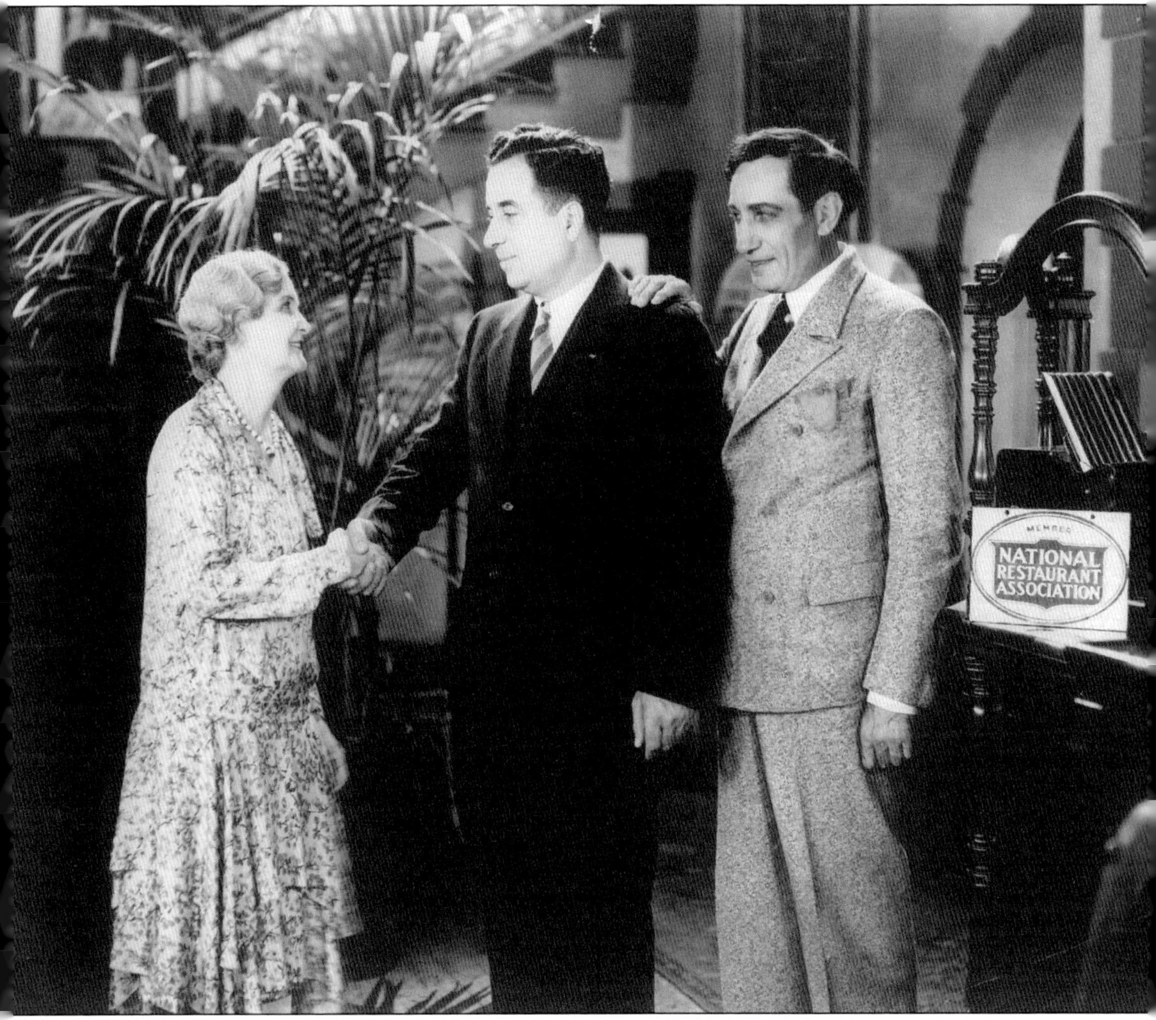

After World War I began, San Francisco's Palace Hotel manager Roy Carruthers recommended that assistant manager Hoedemaker take the job of organizing a mess hall for the navy. This experience taught him how to organize the feeding of many people, in a short amount of time, within a certain budget. After the war, he and his wife moved to Los Angeles, and he went into business for himself, establishing the Leighton Cafeterias. By 1927, there were 20 units within his chain. Pig 'N Whistle founder John Gage took note of the success Hoedemaker had and tapped him to join his corporation. He stepped in as general manager and vice president of the company. His accomplishments were recognized by both the Southern California Restaurant Association and the National Restaurant Association (NRA). He became president for both organizations and was the only person to be elected twice as president of the NRA. Pictured here in the center, he is accepting an award from the NRA by two unidentified members. (Courtesy Eddie Hoedemaker.)

The Los Angeles Biltmore Hotel opened in 1923. Pig 'N Whistle opened a candy shop inside the hotel in 1924. At this time the Biltmore was the largest hotel west of Chicago and had replaced the Alexandria as downtown's most popular hotel. In 1931, the Biltmore hosted the fourth Academy Awards ceremony, and it would go on to host the event seven more times (though not consecutively).

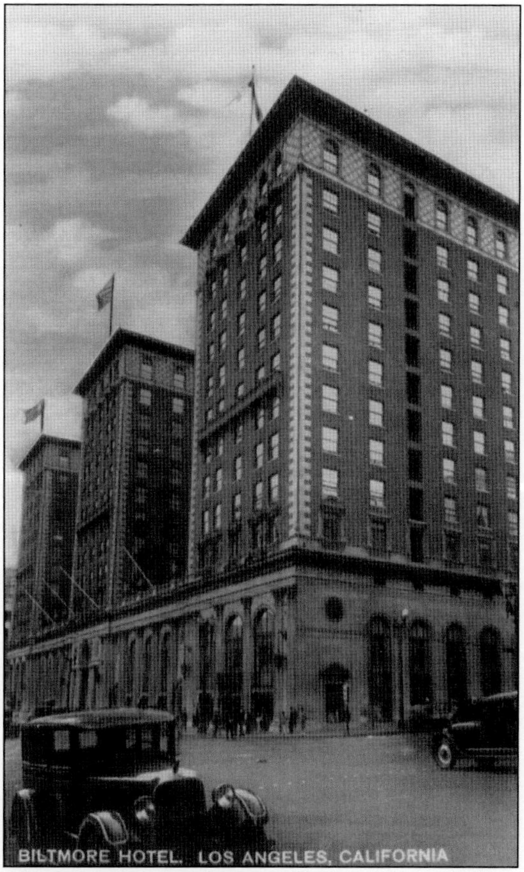

Pictured in 1930, the Biltmore Hotel can be seen nestled in Pershing Square, downtown Los Angeles's public park. Founded as La Plaza Abaja in 1866 by former mayor Cristobal Aguilar, it was renamed Pershing Square in 1918 for Gen. John Joseph "Black Jack" Pershing. (Courtesy Security Pacific National Bank Collection/Los Angeles Public Library.)

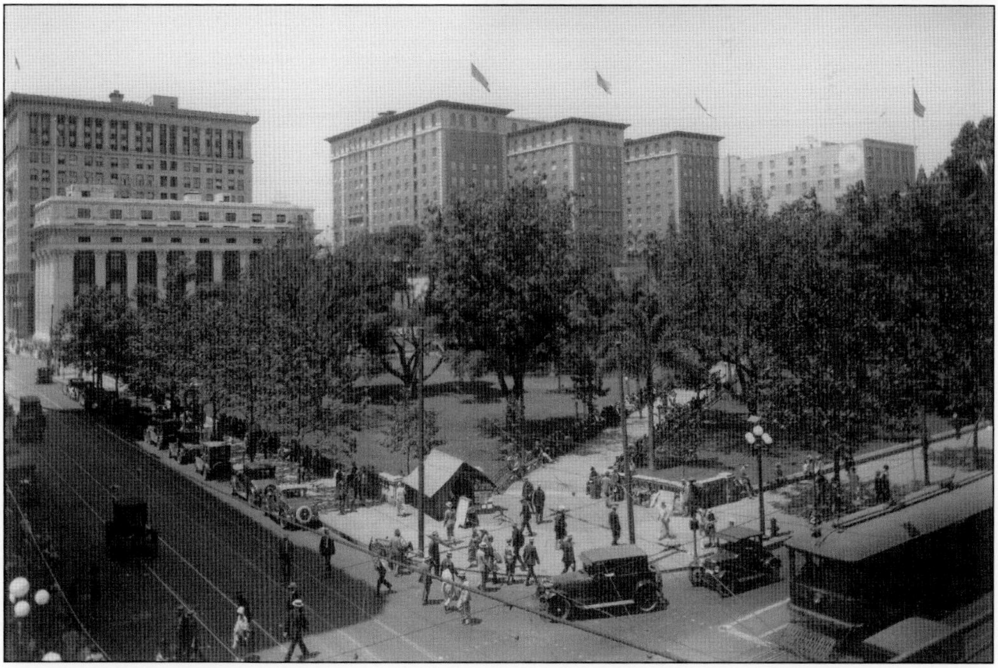

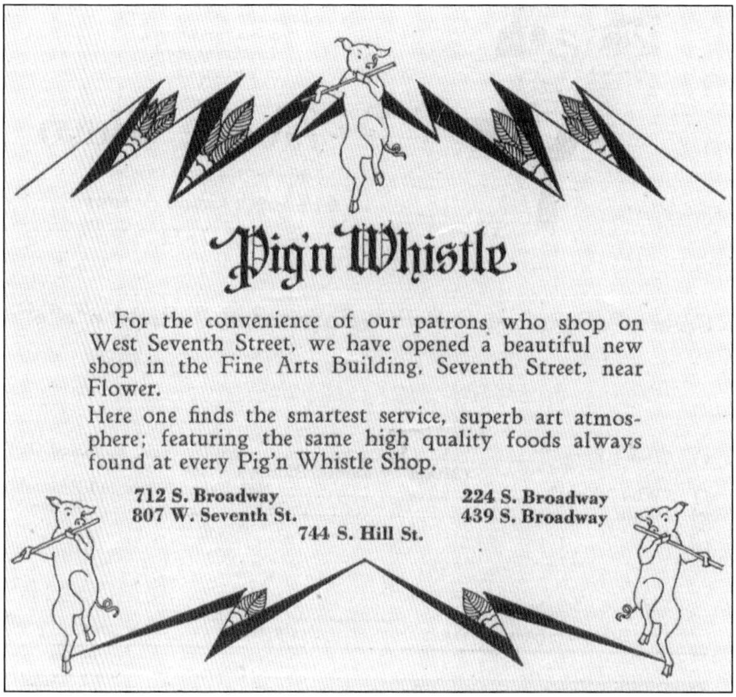

This advertisement from January 1927 announces a new Pig 'N Whistle opening in the Fine Arts Building at Seventh and Flower Streets. The Fine Arts Building was intended to house workers in the fine and applied arts, and was near Barker Brothers furniture store. A 15-year lease was signed by John Gage, but it remained in operation until 1947.

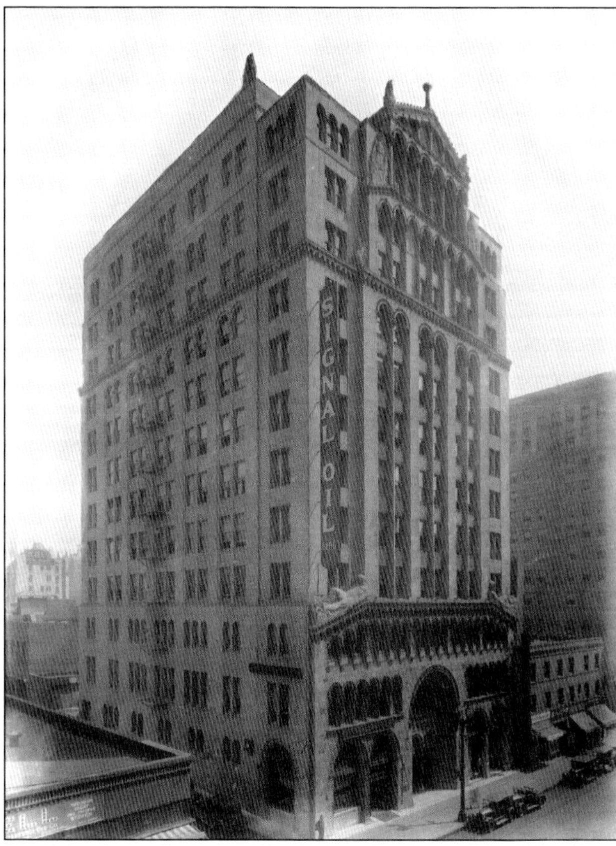

The Fine Arts Building was designed by architects Albert Walker and Percy Eisen of Walker and Eisen in 1926. It was later referred to as the Signal Oil Building when they were a tenant. Currently the building is owned by famed attorneys Mark Geragos and Brian Kabateck. Chris Breed and Alain Hajjar, current owners of the Hollywood Boulevard Pig 'N Whistle, are planning to restore the restaurant sometime in the future. (Courtesy Security Pacific National Bank Collection/ Los Angeles Public Library.)

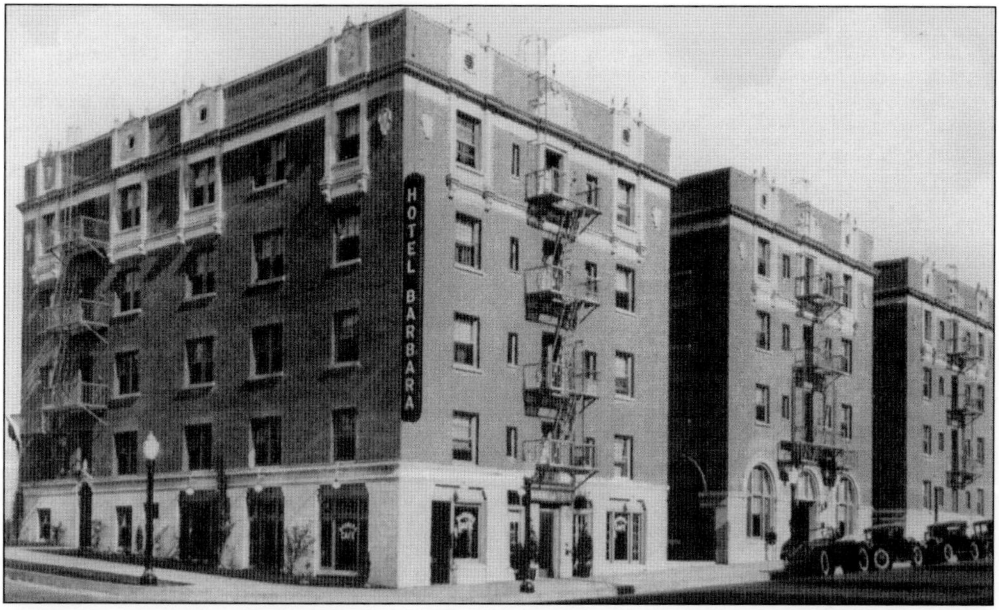

The Barbara Hotel at Sixth Street and Westlake Avenue was owned by famed pugilist Jack Dempsey. It had a Pig 'N Whistle café, and it was across the street from Westlake Park. In the 1880s, Westlake Park, Eastlake Park, and Echo Park were a series of reservoirs built for drinking water. The area around Westlake Park was known as the "Champs-Elysees of Los Angeles" and was surrounded by luxury hotels.

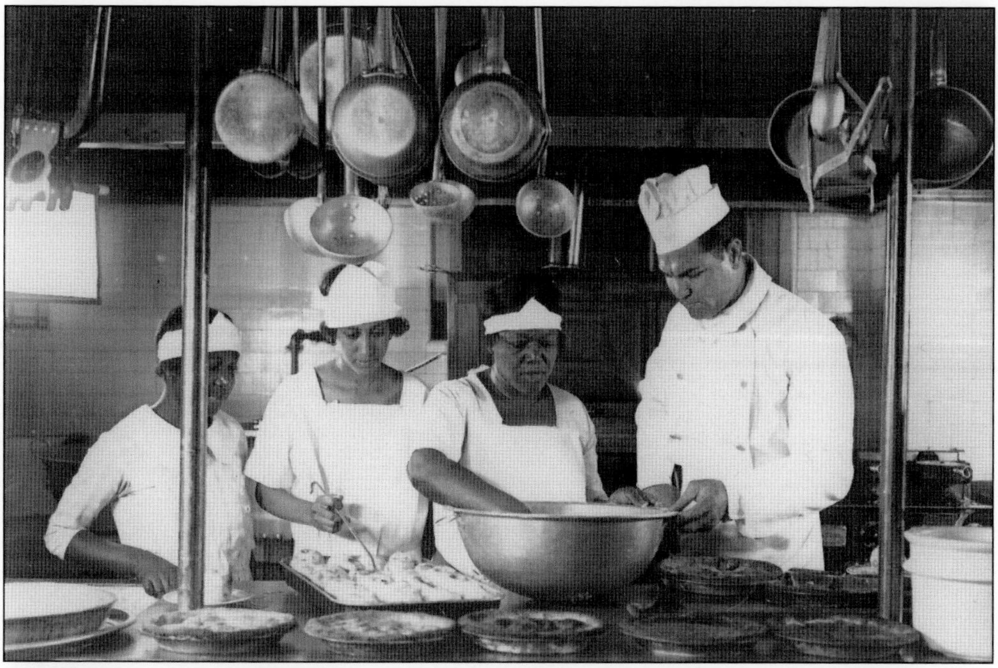

Jack Dempsey (right) helps make pies in his Pig 'N Whistle café around 1926. Dempsey was the heavyweight champion of the world when he bought the hotel in 1925. Born in Manassa, Colorado, he was nicknamed the "Manassa Mauler," though he boxed under the pseudonym "Kid Blackie" until 1916. (Courtesy Security Pacific National Bank Collection/Los Angeles Public Library.)

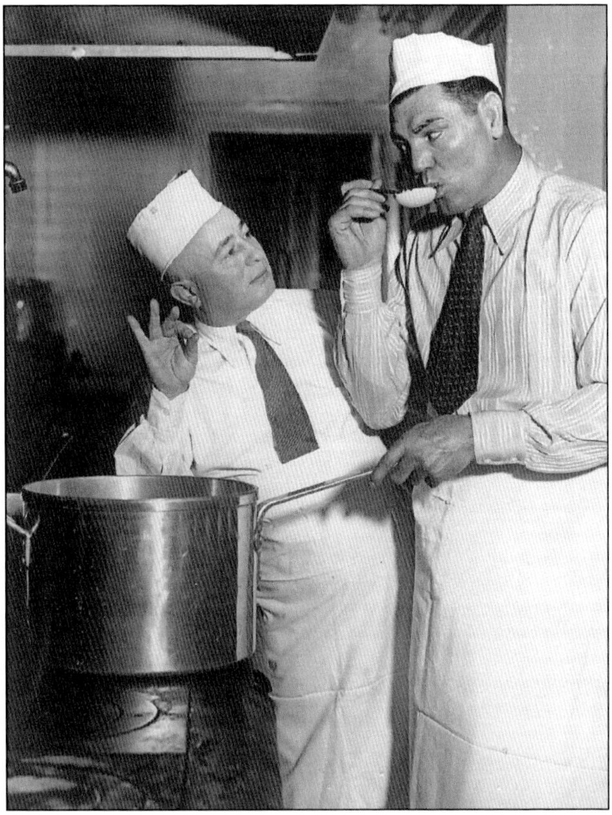

In 1932, Hungarian Eugene Stark (left) was head chef of the Barbara Hotel. Here he is pictured giving Jack Dempsey (right) a cooking lesson. In 1935, Dempsey would leave his Barbara Hotel for New York, where he opened Jack Dempsey's Broadway Restaurant in Times Square, opposite Madison Square Garden. (Courtesy Carroll Photo Service/ Herald Examiner Collection/ Los Angeles Public Library.)

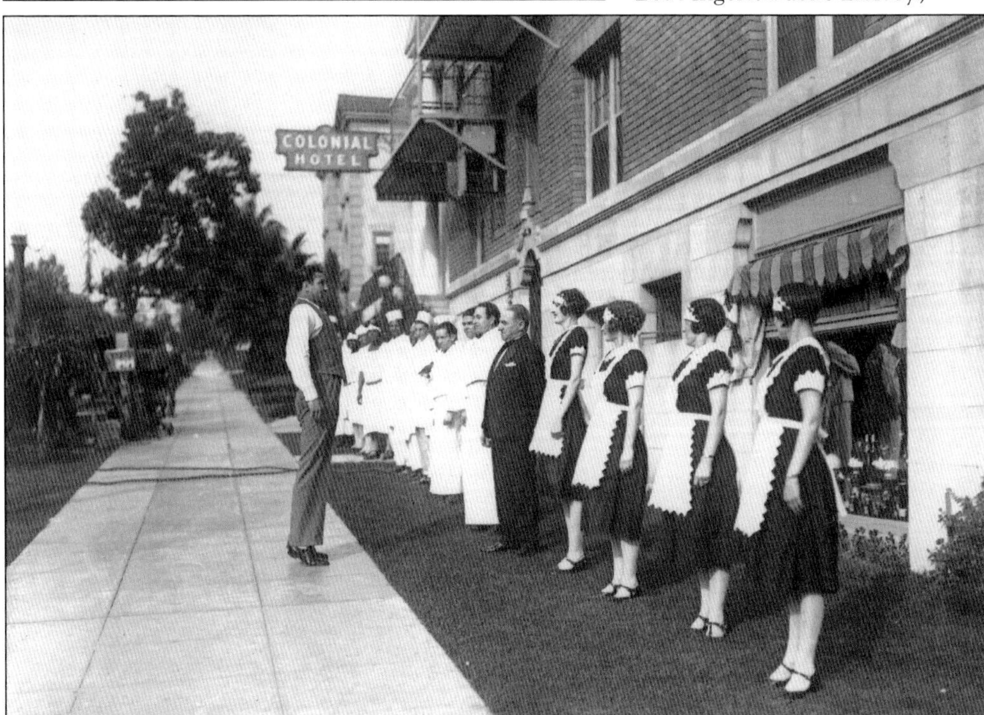

Jack Dempsey is exercising his staff on the lawn outside the Barbara Hotel. At this time, Dempsey was married to Estelle Taylor, a Hollywood silent film actress. The Dempseys stayed at the Barbara from time to time and had a private bar upstairs during Prohibition. (Courtesy Security Pacific National Bank Collection/ Los Angeles Public Library.)

The Hotel Lankershim was located on the southeast corner of Seventh Street and Broadway. It was designed by Robert B. Young and built in 1905 by one of the wealthiest landholders in the state of California, Col. James B. Lankershim. The Pig 'N Whistle had a café and bar in this hotel, which catered primarily to businessmen. (Courtesy Security Pacific National Bank Collection/Los Angeles Public Library.)

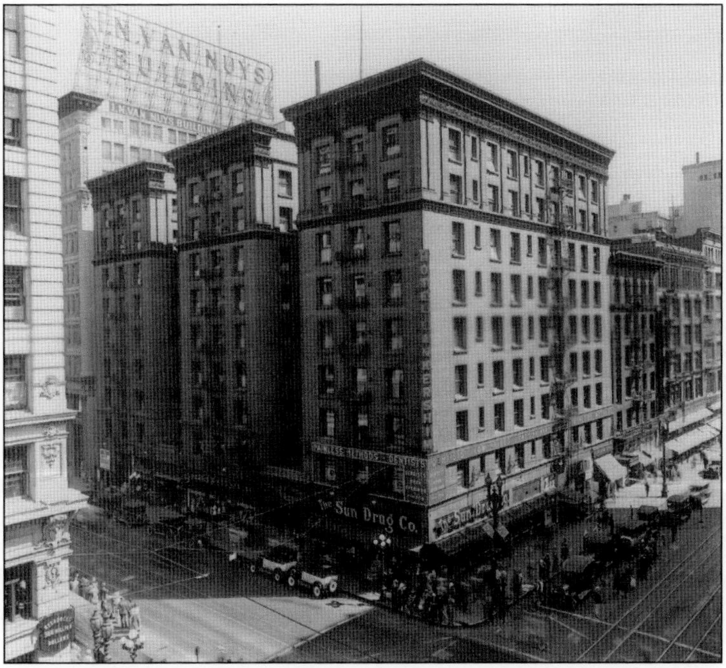

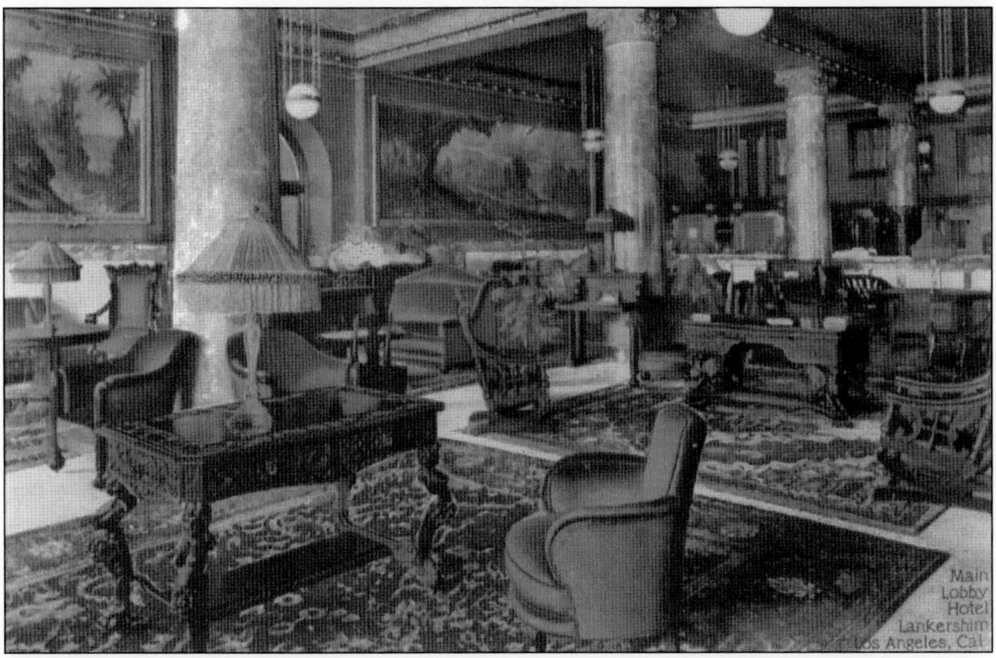

The lobby of the Hotel Lankershim is pictured here in 1913. The Lankershim was opulent, though not as grand as some of the other downtown Los Angeles hotels. The back of this card was mailed by a lawyer who wrote to his wife, "I am going on a case to Pasadena, about thirty minutes from here . . . a wealthy family." The Lankershim Hotel would be destroyed by fire in 1970.

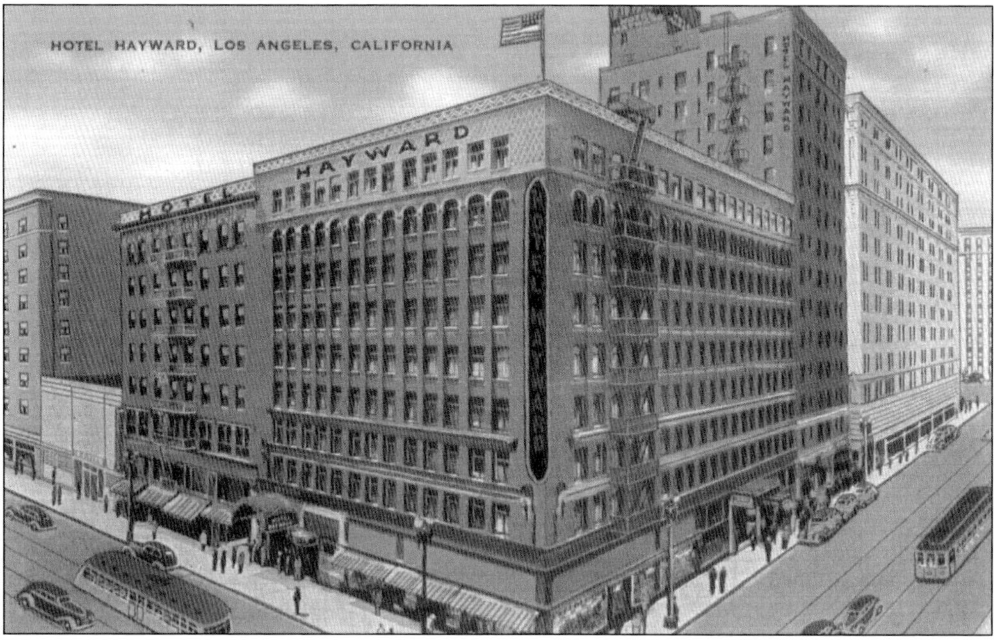

The Hayward Hotel was another downtown Los Angeles hotel to house a Pig 'N Whistle. This location was a full café and remained in operation from 1929 to about 1940. An advertising postcard describes it as serving "the heart of the theatrical district." Like the Alexandria, the Hayward added an annex to provide more rooms in 1925.

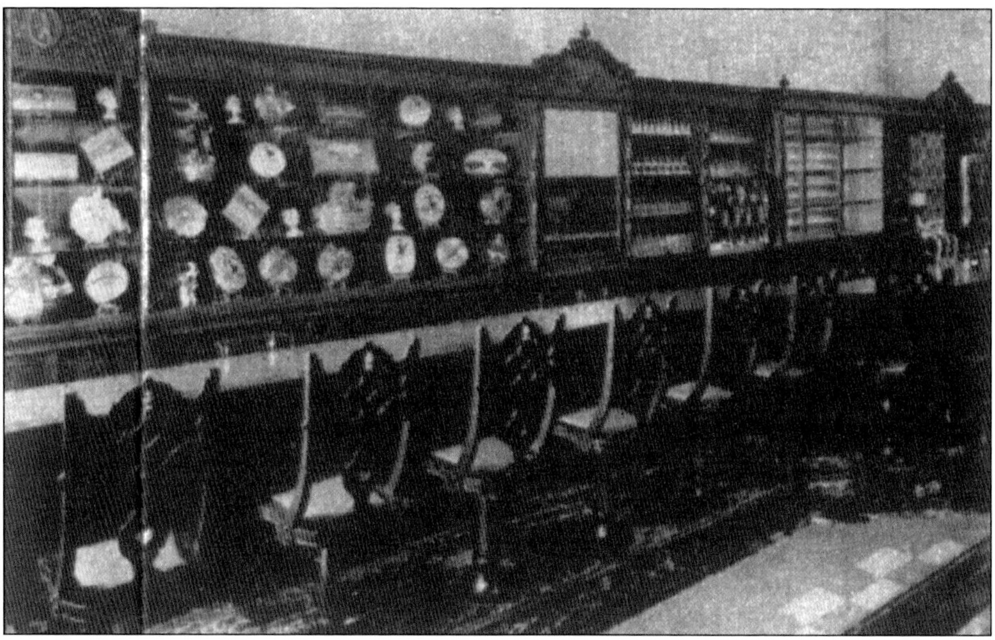

"Get the Hayward Habit," this brochure from 1929 proclaims. Pictured is a detail from the Pig 'N Whistle's candy counter and soda fountain. The Hayward, located down the street from the Alexandria Hotel, is located on Sixth and Spring Streets. Like the Lankershim Hotel, it catered to businessmen; in 1933, a Pig 'N Whistle menu for a shoe salesmen's convention held at the hotel was printed on a leather shoe insole.

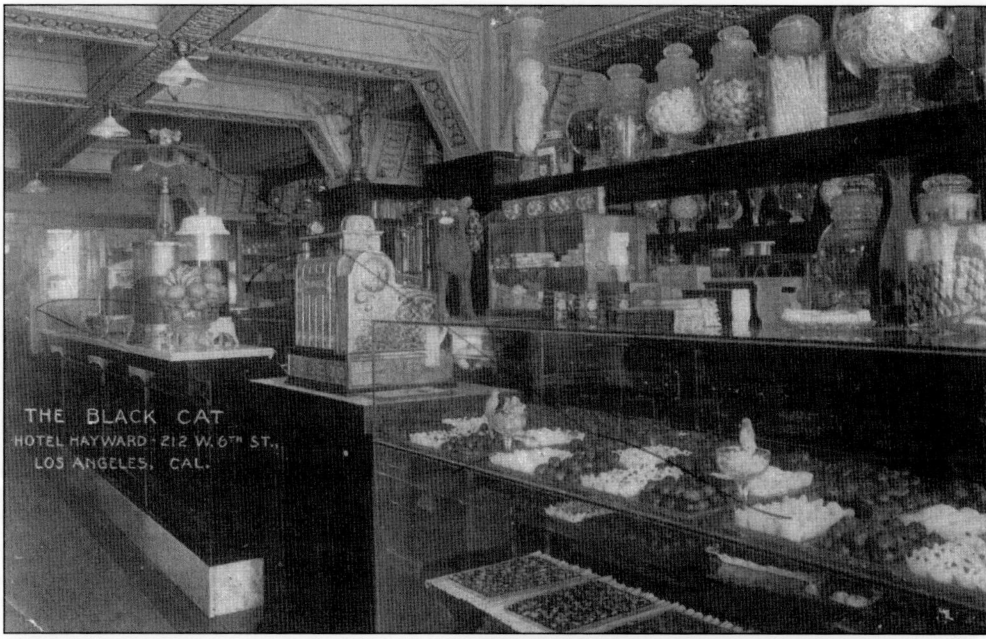

The Black Cat candy shop was located in the Hayward Hotel at 212 West Sixth Street. This candy shop predates the Pig 'N Whistle's occupancy, but gives an idea as to what one could find in a 1920s confectionary store. Notice the birds perched on the glasses inside the case and the stuffed black cat by the cash register.

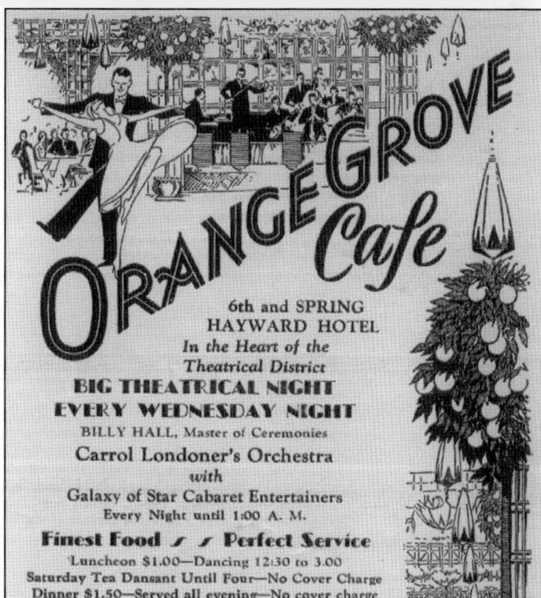

The Orange Grove Café, located in the Hayward Hotel, was akin to the Ambassador's Coconut Grove, but certainly did not match it in elegance or popularity. Most hotels had ballrooms with popular dance bands performing nightly. Dancing lessons were offered in many of them, and dance schools were everywhere.

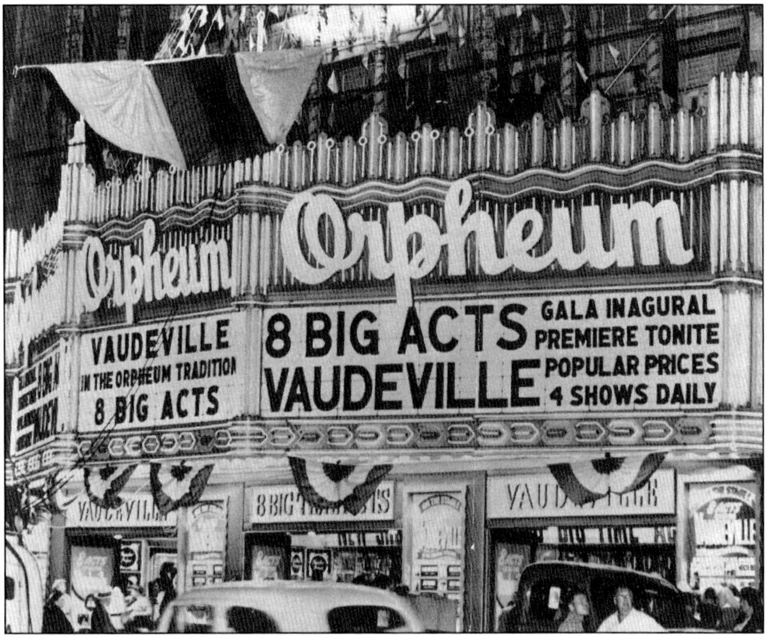

The Orpheum Theatre, known as the theater that "died a thousand deaths," found its fourth and final home at 842 South Broadway in 1926. Pig 'N Whistle was next door at 844 South Broadway, where it remained until 1942. (Courtesy Security Pacific National Bank Collection/ Los Angeles Public Library.)

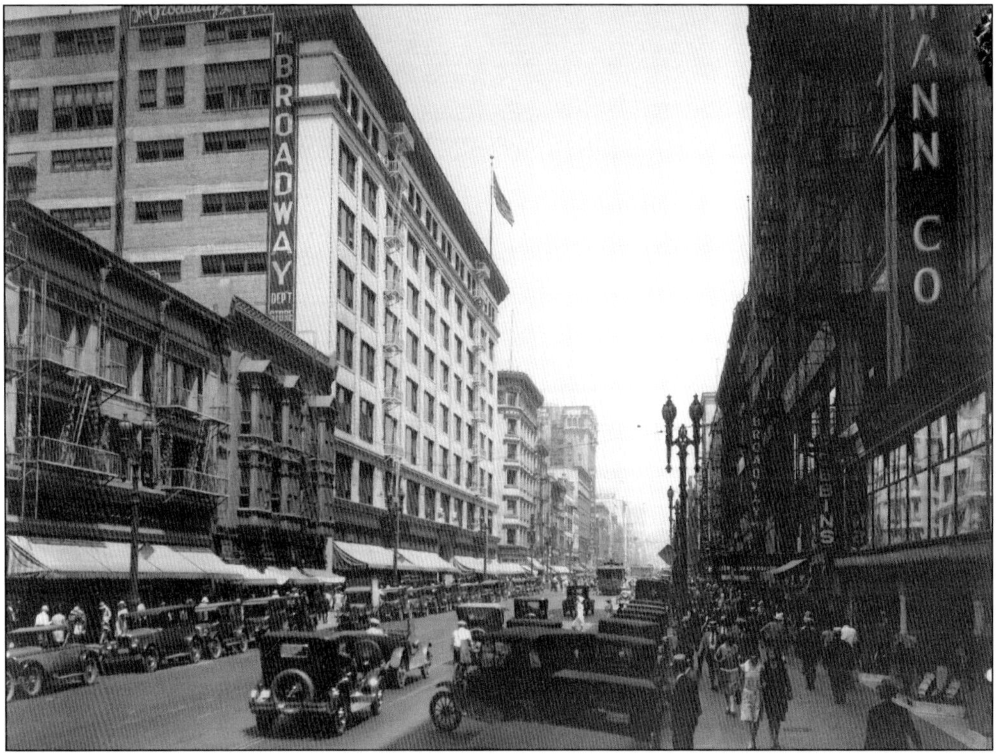

The downtown Los Angeles intersection of Broadway and Fourth Street was home to The Broadway department store. Founded in 1896 by Arthur Letts Sr., this 1915 structure was a shopping destination for many years. Arthur Letts Sr. went on to found Holmby Hills, an exclusive Los Angeles neighborhood that is part of the "Platinum Triangle," which also includes Bel Air and Beverly Hills. (Courtesy Security Pacific National Bank Collection/Los Angeles Public Library.)

The Pig 'N Whistle at 439 South Broadway was located near The Broadway department store, at 427 South Broadway. Pictured here is a 1920s business card for the manager of the candy department. This shop was a full café; beautiful children's menus were printed for the location, which remained popular from 1924 until it closed in 1939.

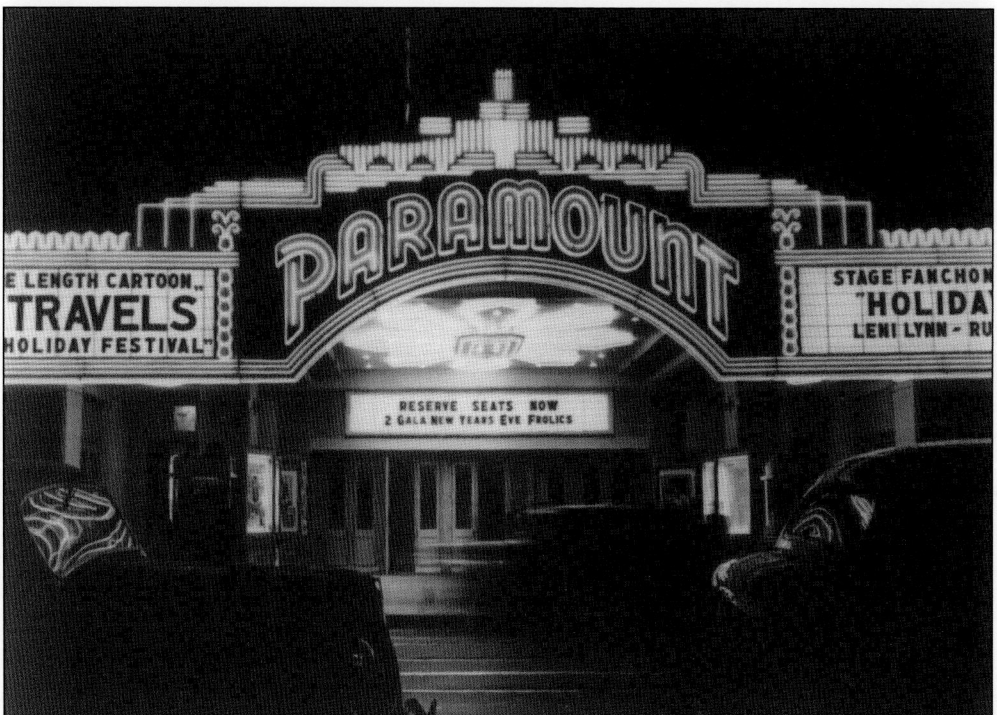

The Paramount Theatre was a prime spot for a Pig 'N Whistle. Sidney Hoedemaker put one near the Los Angeles and the San Francisco branches. Here is the Los Angeles Paramount Theatre in 1939, across the street from the Pig 'N Whistle at 318 West Sixth Street. In 1963, the theater was demolished, and the Pig 'N Whistle closed its doors in 1968. (Courtesy Security Pacific National Bank Collection/Los Angeles Public Library.)

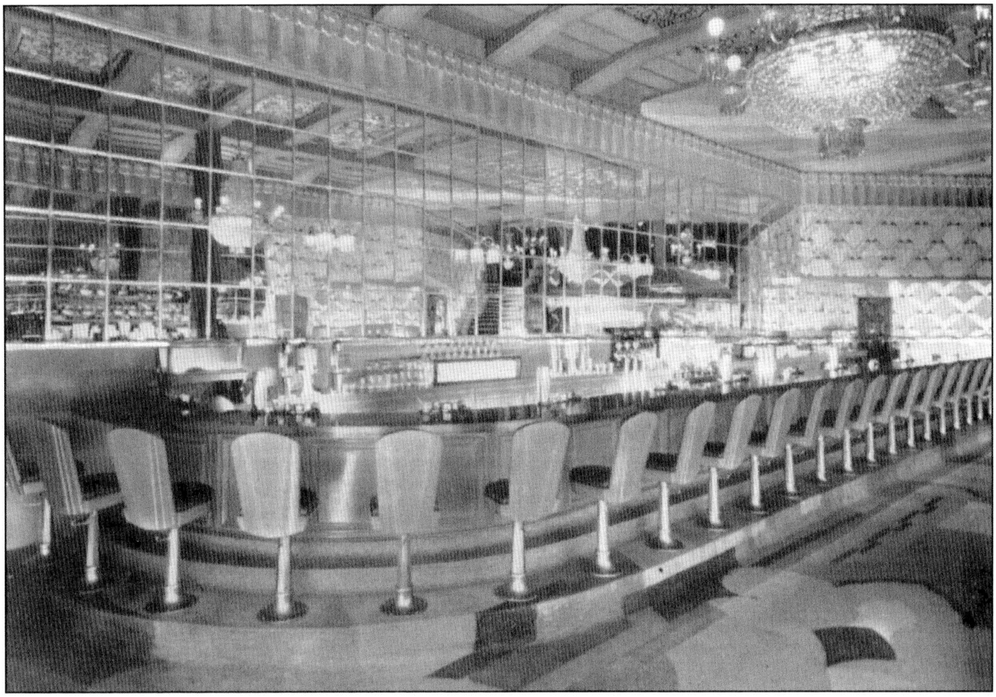

Like its Los Angeles counterpart, the Paramount Theatre in San Francisco was serviced by a nearby Pig 'N Whistle. Located in the city's "Movie Row," which also included the Orpheum (1926) and the Fox (1929) theaters, this location at 1032 Market Street had a 10-year run. Later in 1966, arson destroyed the Paramount at 1066 Market Street. The soda fountain pictured was built in 1931 by United-American.

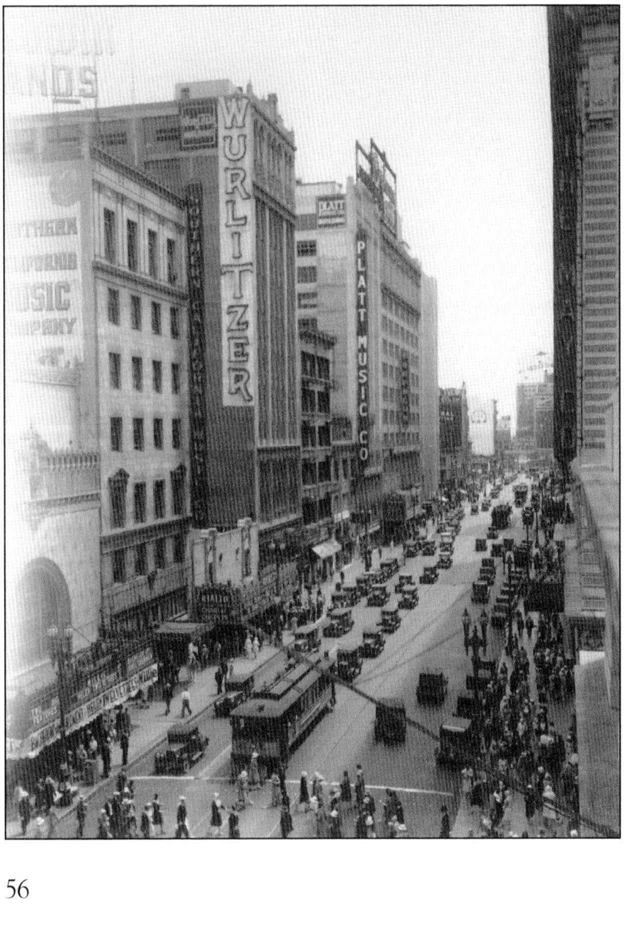

Broadway between Eighth and Ninth Streets was the heart of music publishing in Los Angeles; seen here are the Southern California Music Company, Platt Music Company, and the Rudolph Wurlitzer Company. In the 1920s and 1930s, there were four Pig 'N Whistles and a Melody Lane near this intersection. (Courtesy Security Pacific National Bank Collection/Los Angeles Public Library.)

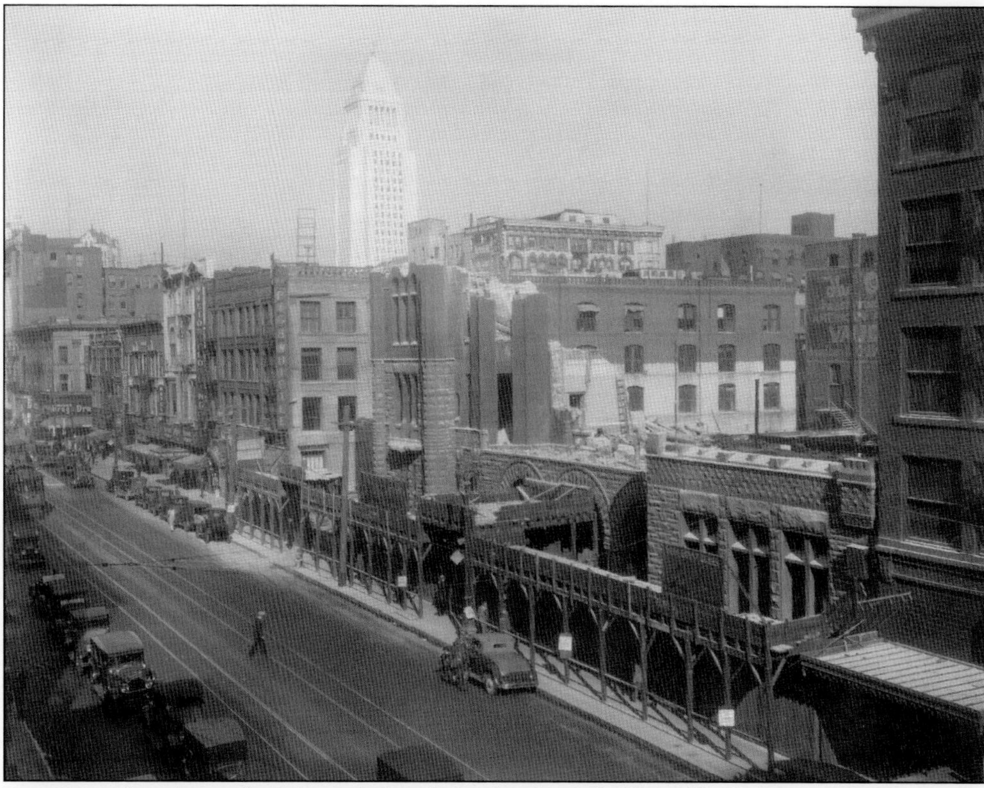

By 1928, a fourth city hall (seen behind the third city hall) had been built, and the smaller building at 226 South Broadway had to be demolished. The older furnishings were auctioned off on January 10, 1928, and the 40-year-old structure was torn down soon after. The Pig 'N Whistle at 224 South Broadway also closed its doors in 1928. (Courtesy Security Pacific National Bank Collection/Los Angeles Public Library.)

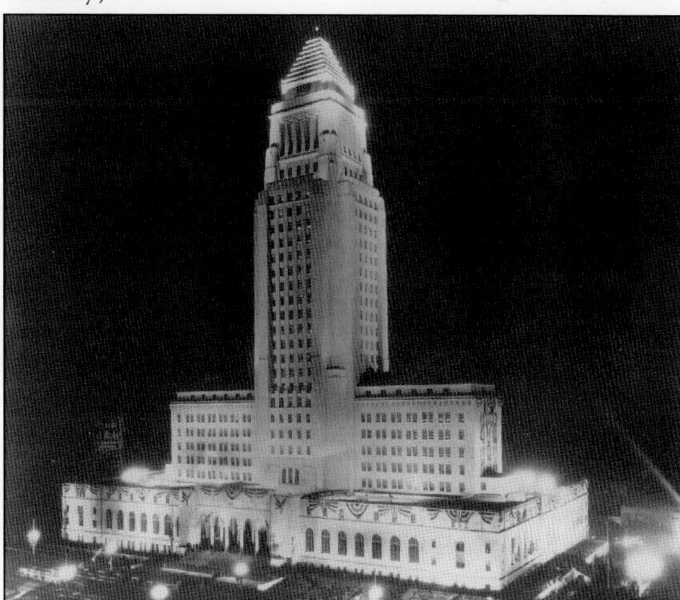

John Parkinson designed Los Angeles's fourth and current city hall, which opened in 1928 at 200 North Spring Street. At one time it was the tallest structure in downtown; today it has been eclipsed by much higher structures. A popular symbol of Los Angeles for over 80 years, it has been used or recreated in many films and television shows. (Courtesy Security Pacific National Bank Collection/Los Angeles Public Library.)

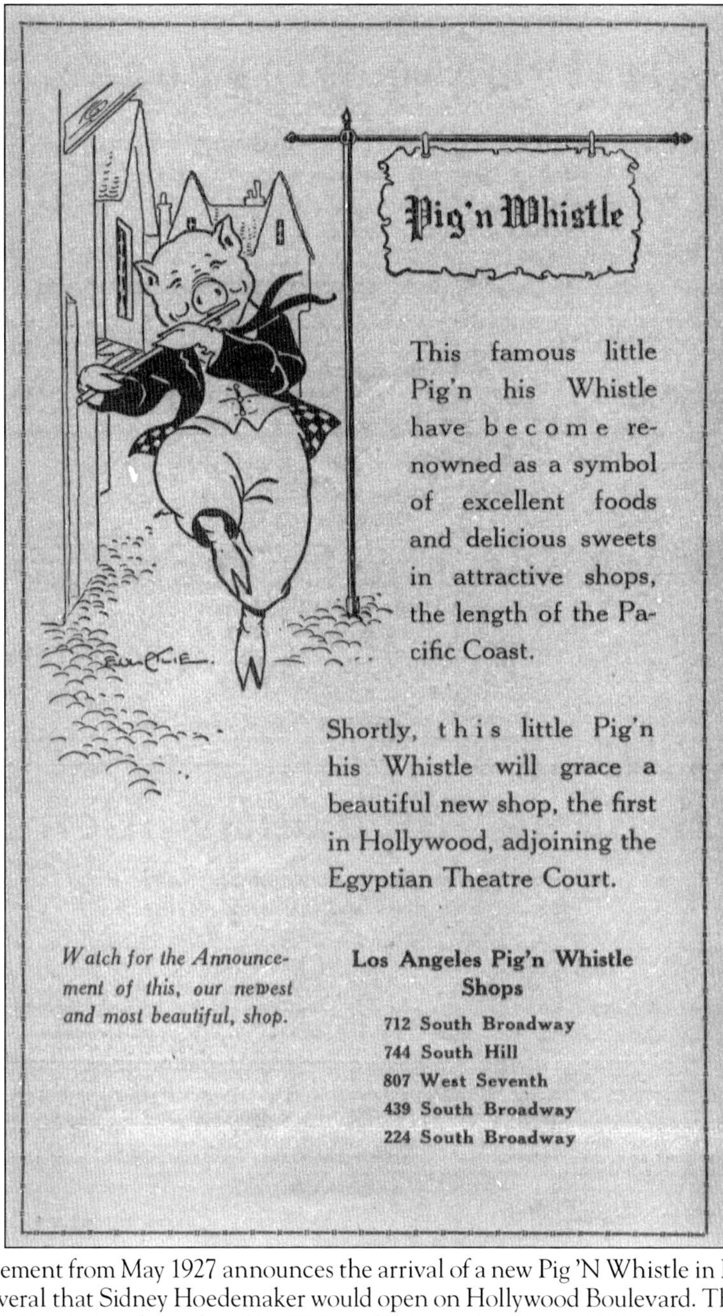

This advertisement from May 1927 announces the arrival of a new Pig 'N Whistle in Hollywood—the first of several that Sidney Hoedemaker would open on Hollywood Boulevard. The downtown location at 224 South Broadway closed by 1928, and this new location at 6714 Hollywood Boulevard promised to be the "newest and most beautiful shop." It was to adjoin the Grauman's Egyptian Theatre, which was built by Sid Grauman in 1922. In 1918, Grauman built the Million Dollar Theatre in downtown Los Angeles, and by the time of this ad, he had also opened the Chinese Theatre at 6925 Hollywood Boulevard. There were several popular theaters in Hollywood for the Pig 'N Whistle to serve, like the Hollywood Playhouse on Vine Street just north of Hollywood Boulevard. Many patrons of this Pig 'N Whistle were also guests next door at the Christie Hotel at 6724 Hollywood Boulevard.

Four

Hooray for Hollywood!

West-northwest of downtown Los Angeles, Hollywood was the center of motion picture making. By the 1920s, Hollywood had four major motion picture studios: Paramount, Warner Bros., RKO (Radio-Keith-Orpheum), and Columbia. Hollywood's first major hotel, the Hollywood Hotel, had been built in 1902 at 6811 Hollywood Boulevard, on the corner of Hollywood Boulevard and Highland Avenue. Several major motion picture theaters existed in Hollywood by 1927 as well as a major department store, The Broadway, on Hollywood Boulevard. It was only natural for the Pig 'N Whistle, which became incorporated in 1926 after nearly 20 years of California success, to be a part of this exciting and vibrant city.

The first planned Hollywood shop was located at 6714 Hollywood Boulevard, next door to Grauman's Egyptian Theatre, adjoining its forecourt. The site at 6718 Hollywood Boulevard was being used as the office for the J. L. Olsen Company, a real estate firm that eventually moved to the corner of Hollywood and Cherokee Street. Architects Octavius Morgan, John Walls, and Stiles Clements of Morgan, Walls, and Clements were asked to design the café, and it opened on July 21, 1927. There was a Wurlitzer organ installed within a balcony overlooking the dining room, and pipe organ concerts were given for the entertainment of the patrons.

In 1924, the Hollywood Roosevelt Hotel opened at 1637 North Vine Street, and Hollywood and Vine became one of the busiest intersections in Hollywood. The hotel was a destination for many radio and movie personalities. Sidney Hoedemaker wanted a Pig 'N Whistle to be represented on this famous corner, so a café was opened on the ground floor of the hotel in 1928. Announcements were mailed to offices in the nearby Taft and Guaranty Buildings, which housed the offices for many prominent show business agencies. While not as popular as the Egyptian's location (it had to compete with the second Brown Derby location, which opened in 1929 across the street), it enjoyed success until 1938, when Hoedemaker planned a bigger and better restaurant on the corner of Hollywood and Vine.

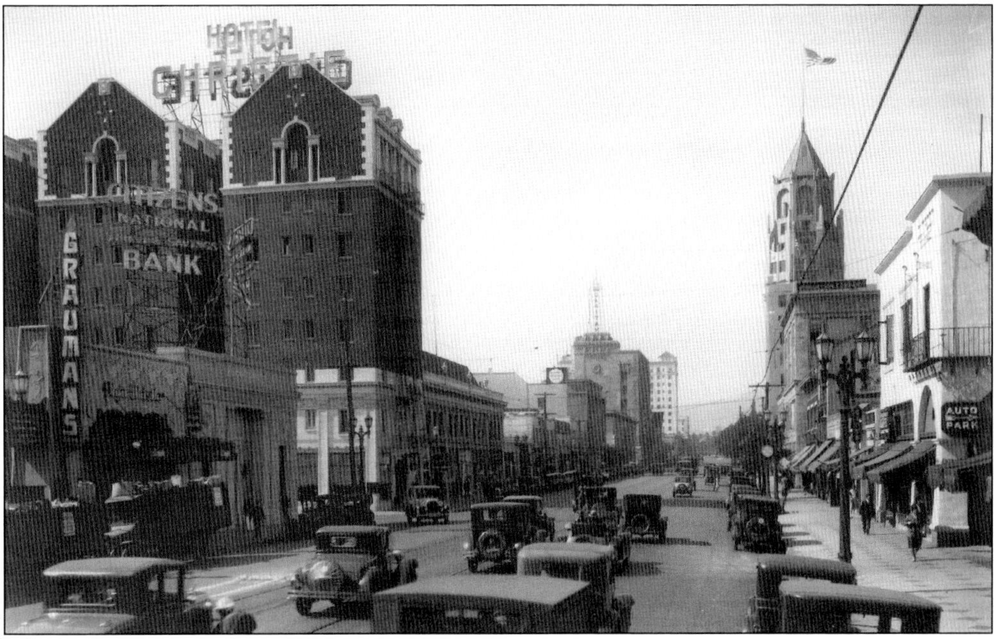

Looking west from Grauman's Egyptian Theatre, the Pig 'N Whistle is next door to the Citizen's National Trust and Savings Bank and the Hotel Christie. A 1927 menu from this location is inscribed, "We had dinner at the Pig 'N Whistle in Hollywood next door to the Egyptian Theatre; the boys wanted to see Buster Keaton in *College*, so we went in." (Courtesy Security Pacific National Bank Collection/Los Angeles Public Library.)

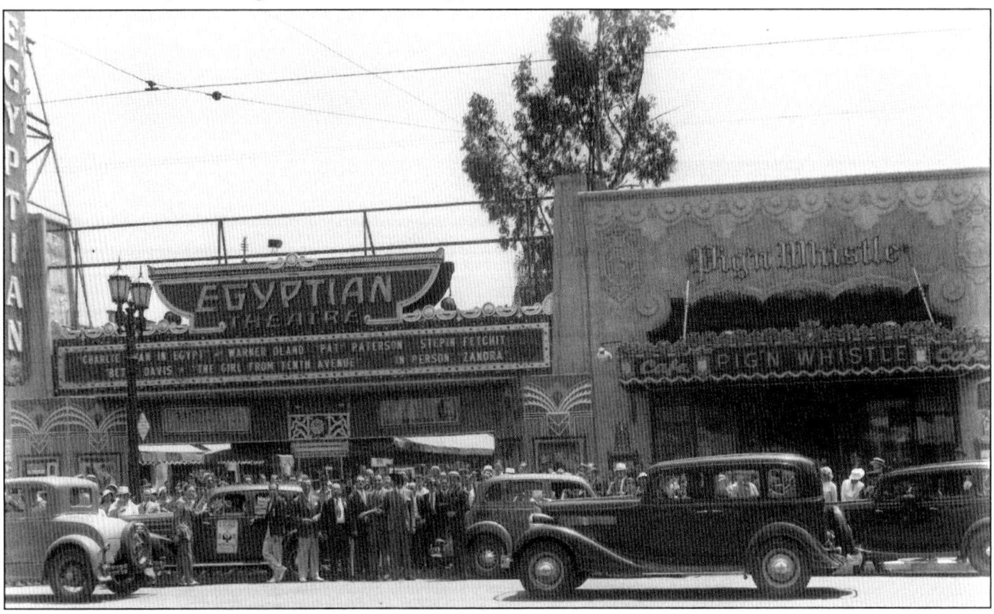

A crowd gathers in front of the Egyptian Theatre for the double feature of *Charlie Chan in Egypt* with Warner Oland, Pat Paterson, and Stepin Fetchit and Bette Davis in *The Girl from Tenth Avenue*. Both pictures were released in June 1935. Also on the marquee is "In Person Zandra." The Pig 'N Whistle is referenced in the 1974 film *Chinatown*. (Courtesy Security Pacific National Bank Collection/Los Angeles Public Library.)

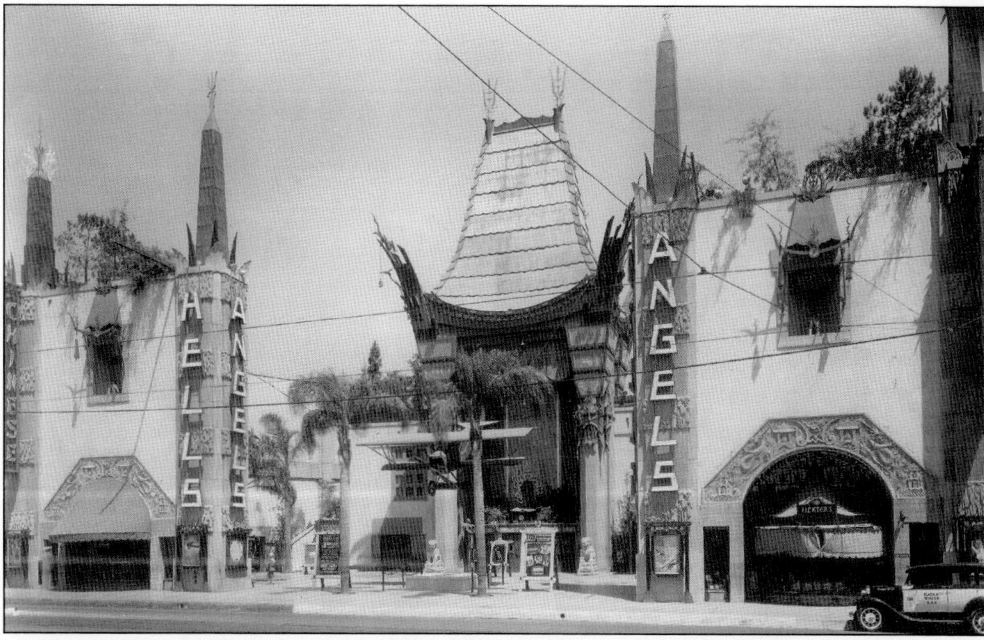

Grauman's Chinese Theatre is advertising *Hell's Angels*, a picture so expensive it made no profit upon first release. Financed and directed by Howard Hughes, it cost $4 million and was released in May 1930, with tickets sold at $11 each ($140 today). There is a replica of a biplane flying through the courtyard. (Courtesy Security Pacific National Bank Collection/Los Angeles Public Library.)

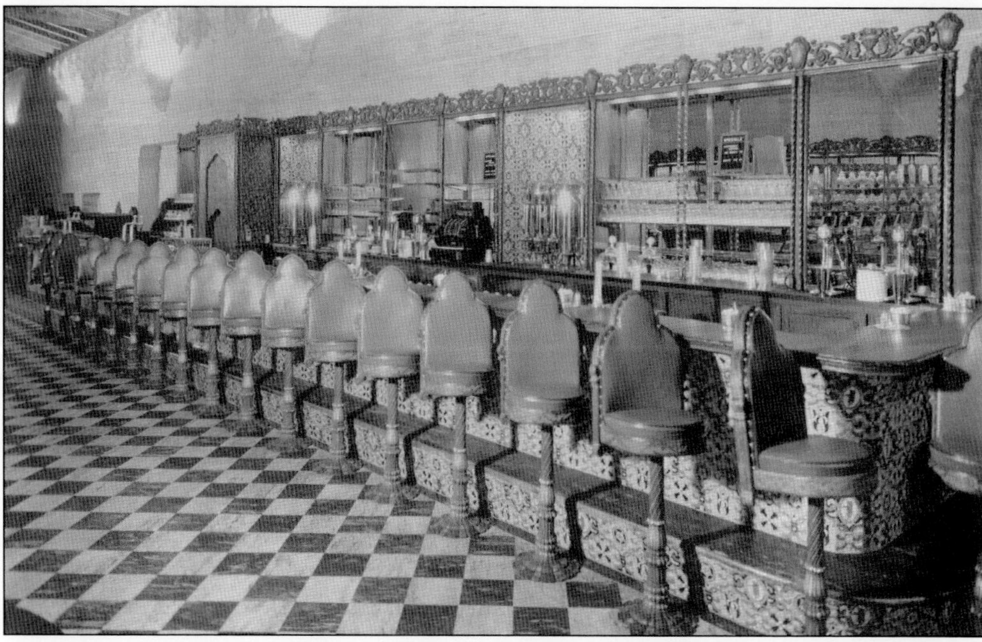

An interior shot of the Pig 'N Whistle café at 6714 Hollywood Boulevard shows the soda fountain and its beautiful ornamental iron stools. When it closed in 1952, the interior was to be gutted and demolished. Restaurant owner Carmen Miceli rescued the stools and many fixtures, incorporating them into his Miceli's restaurant around the corner at 1646 Las Palmas Avenue, where they are still in use today. (Courtesy Bison Archives.)

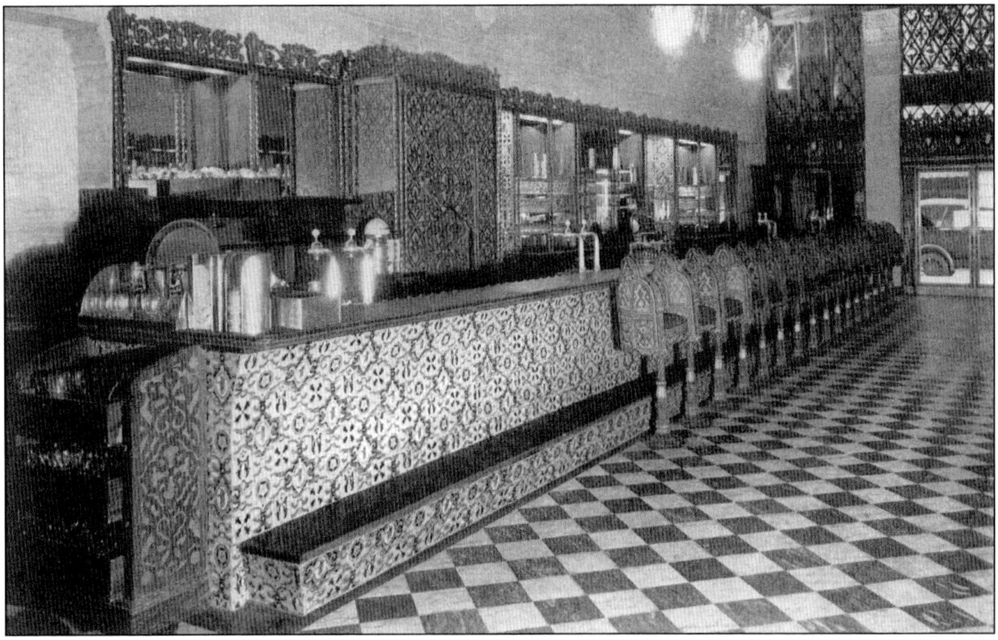

An opposite view of the Pig 'N Whistle's soda fountain at 6714 Hollywood Boulevard shows the water stand, where glasses and trays were kept next to the waitresses' station. The beautiful decorative tile was made by Gladding, McBean, and Company, according to *Architectural Digest* in 1928. (Courtesy Bison Archives.)

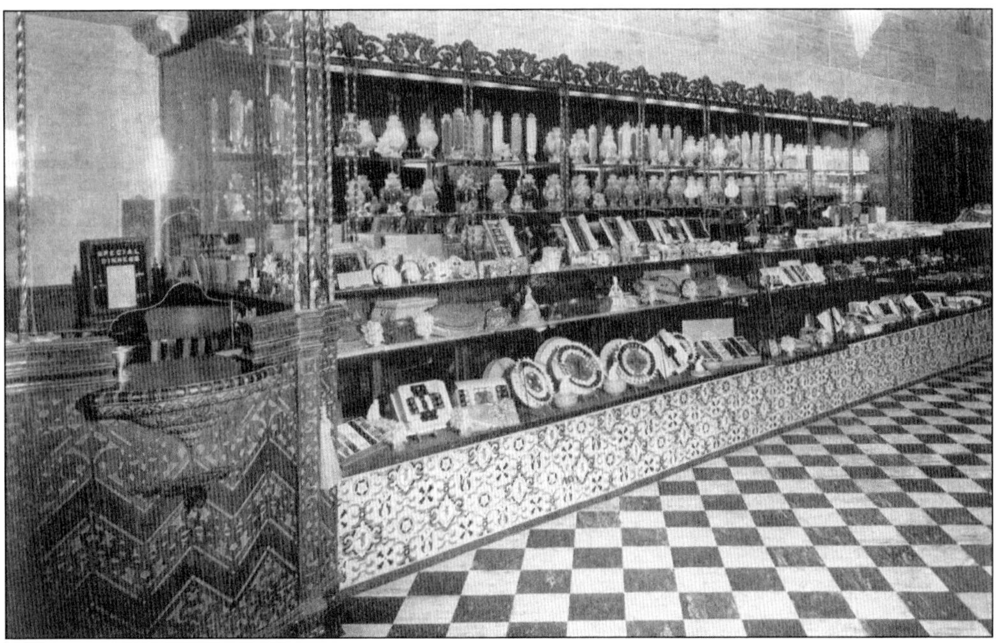

The candy counter was one of the most attractive features of the Pig 'N Whistle. All of the candy was made downtown on Wall Street in the Pig 'N Whistle's own candy factory. Seen here next to the cashier's booth, it offers all kinds of chocolates, glace fruits, and various types of hard candy sold by the pound or in attractive gift boxes and figurines. (Courtesy Bison Archives.)

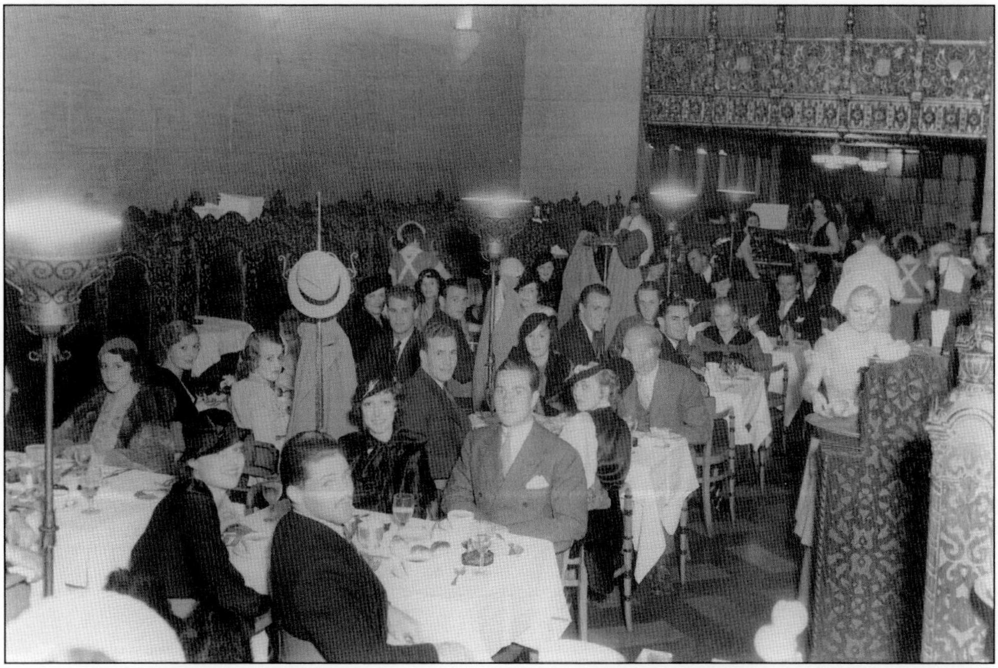

A pipe organ concert is being given by an unidentified woman and her accompanying vocalist, who is also unidentified. The Wurlitzer pipe organ was normally played up on the balcony; however, there was an elevator system installed by Llewellyn Iron Works in the back to move it down to the ground floor for more intimate entertainment. (Courtesy Bison Archives.)

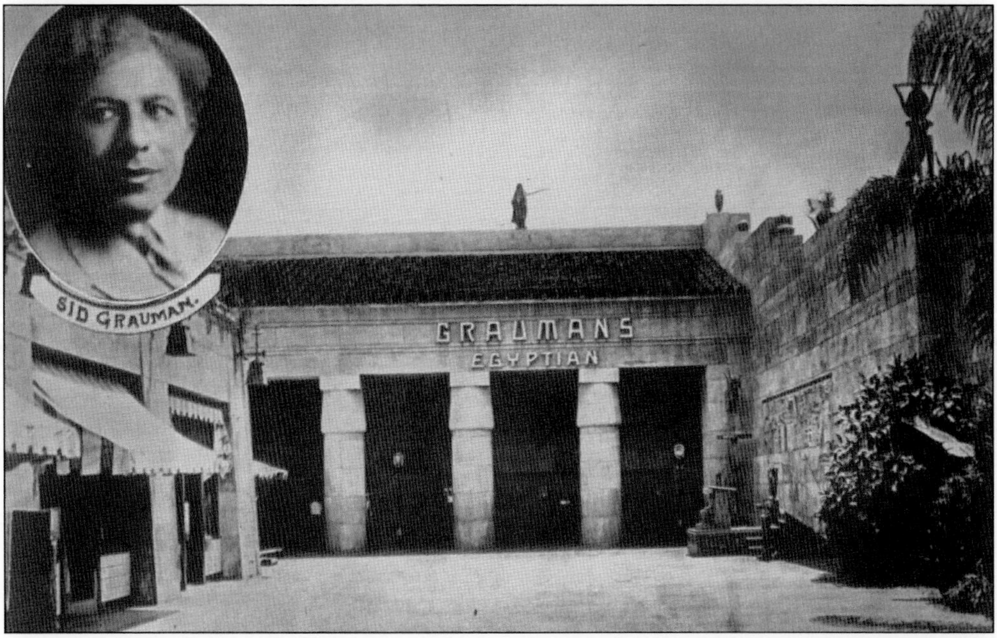

Sid Grauman built three major theaters in the Los Angeles area, the first being the Million Dollar Theatre on Broadway in 1918. The second was the Egyptian Theatre (pictured above), which opened in 1922. His last, and most famous, was the Chinese Theatre in 1927. The Egyptian held the first-ever Hollywood movie premiere in 1922, for *Robin Hood* starring Douglas Fairbanks.

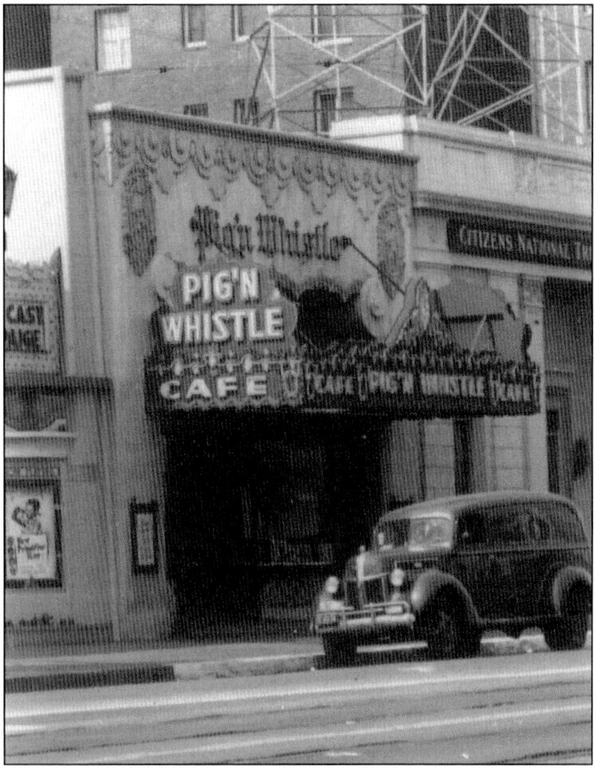

The Pig 'N Whistle's electric sign could be seen from far down the block; here it is in 1944. There was "ample parking at the Christie Hotel" that could be validated with a guest check, according to the menu. There was also free parking on the street, unheard of in today's Hollywood. The film being shown next door at the Egyptian Theatre in this photograph is *Her Primitive Man*. (Courtesy Bison Archives.)

By 1951, the renovated Egyptian Theatre looked completely unrecognizable to what it had been a few years back. The marquee announces, "Caruso Sings Tonight," which was a promotion for *The Great Caruso*, starring Mario Lanza. Looking slightly out of date, its neighbor the Pig 'N Whistle would close within a year. (Courtesy Bison Archives.)

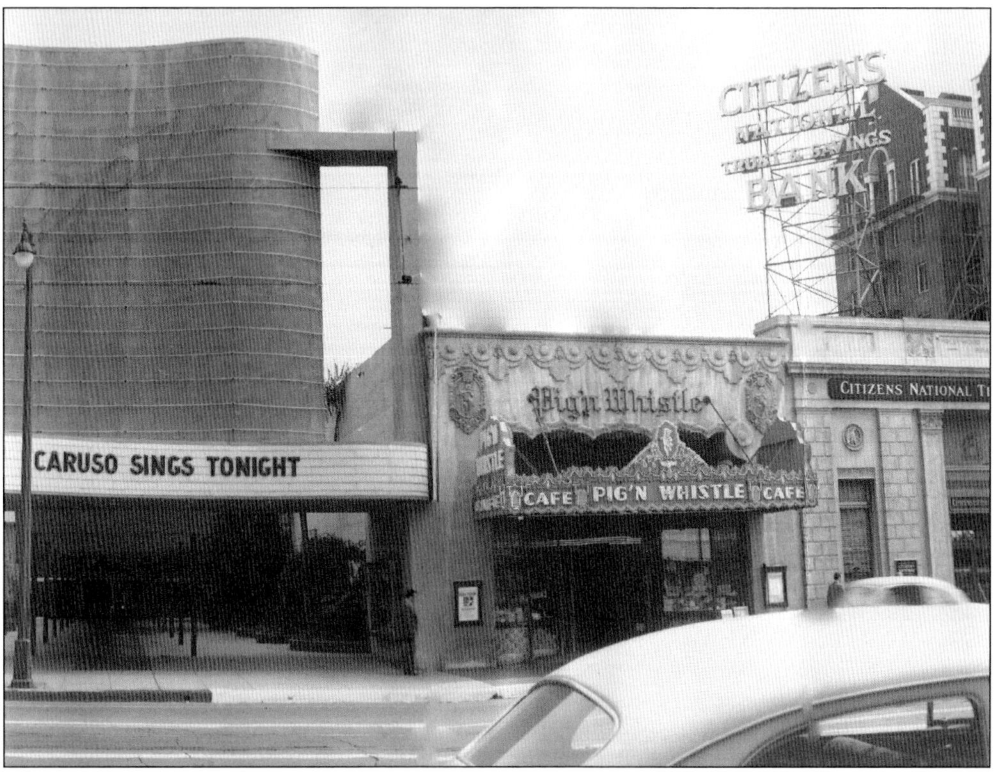

A Mother's Day menu from 1939 offers a special coconut layer cake decorated with a candy rose for one dollar. This pre–World War II menu from the 6714 Hollywood Boulevard location offers a variety of entrées, including sauerbraten with potato pancakes, braised ox joints, and Hungarian goulash with spatzle.

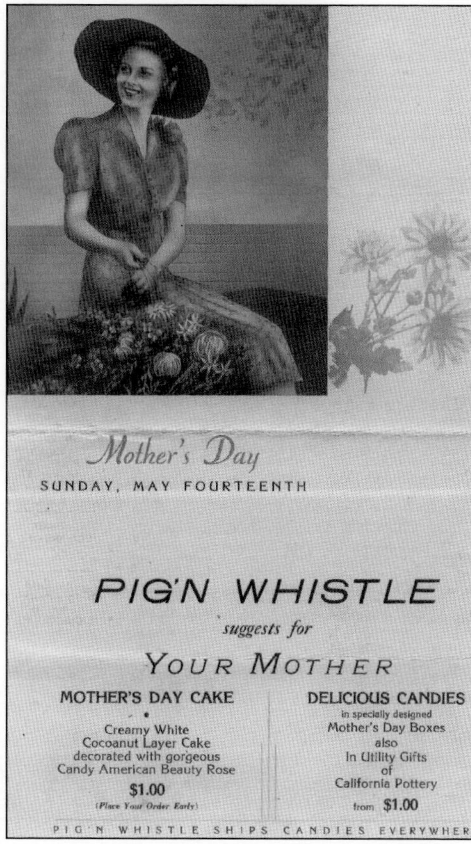

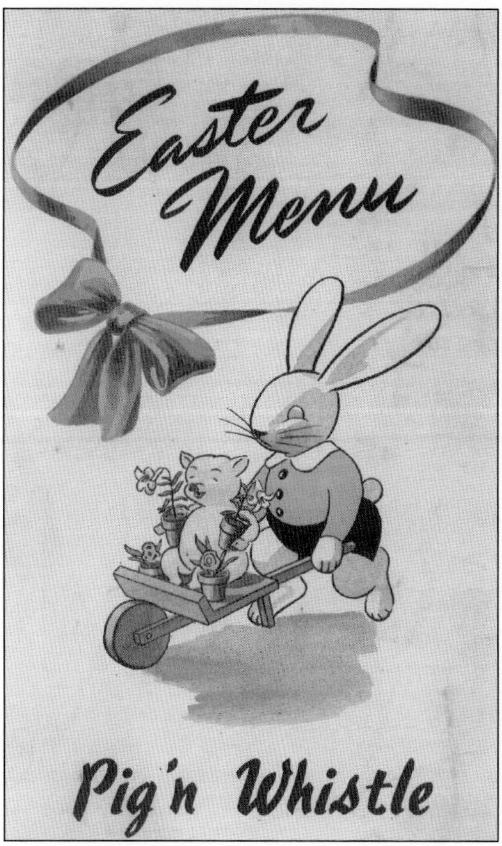

Another holiday menu from the 6714 Hollywood Boulevard location commemorates Easter Sunday 1944. The offerings on this menu reflect wartime rationing, as they are drastically different from what was offered five years earlier. Gone are the elaborate entrées and large fountain menu; the special for the day was chicken croquettes or leg of rabbit.

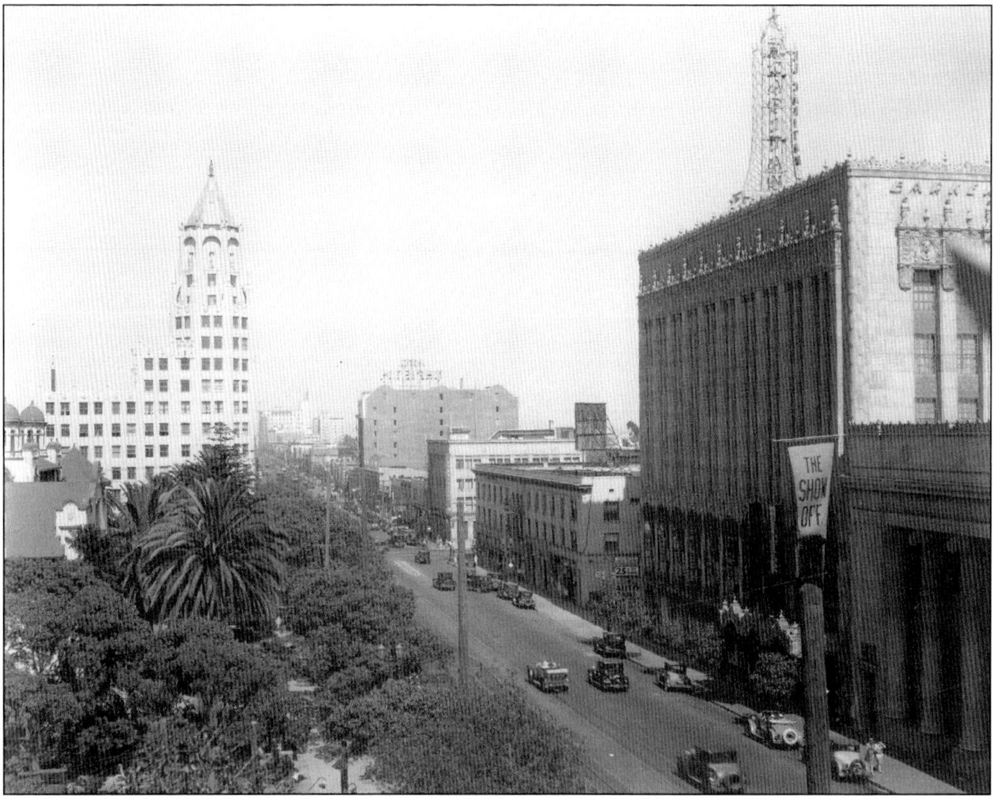

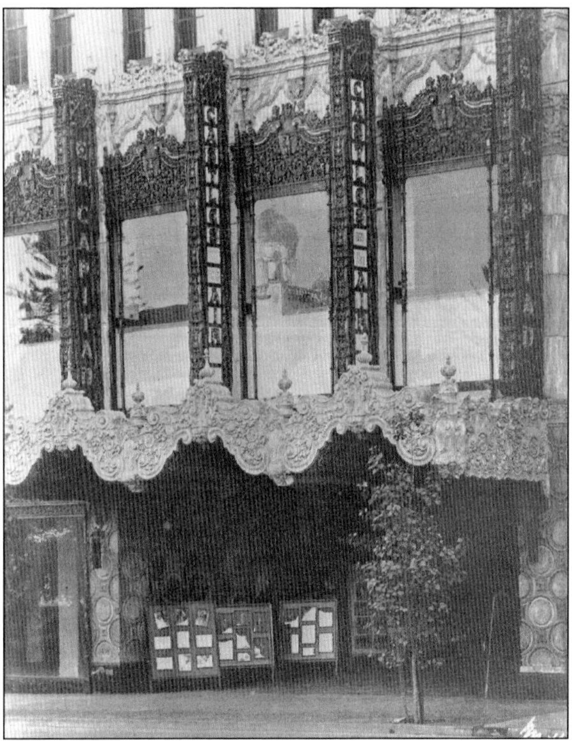

In this view of Hollywood Boulevard looking east, the El Capitan Theatre can be seen at right. The large building at left is the Pacific-Southwest Trust and Savings building, designed in an Art Deco Gothic style by architects Meyer and Holler. The El Capitan is advertising the movie *The Show Off* in this 1935 photograph. (Courtesy Security Pacific National Bank Collection/ Los Angeles Public Library.)

The El Capitan Theatre in Hollywood had a Pig 'N Whistle next door at 6902 Hollywood Boulevard. The theater was designed by Morgan, Walls, and Clements and opened in 1926. The El Capitan Pig 'N Whistle opened in 1929 and remained there until 1938. (Courtesy Security Pacific National Bank Collection/ Los Angeles Public Library.)

Although a photograph of the El Capitan Pig 'N Whistle has not been found, there are records of a Duo Art player piano being installed in 1929. A fountain menu from this location features a Franklin Pangborn Sundae, which was vanilla ice cream and pineapple sherbet topped with caramel and chocolate sauce, slices of pineapple, and pecans. (Courtesy Security Pacific National Bank Collection/Los Angeles Public Library.)

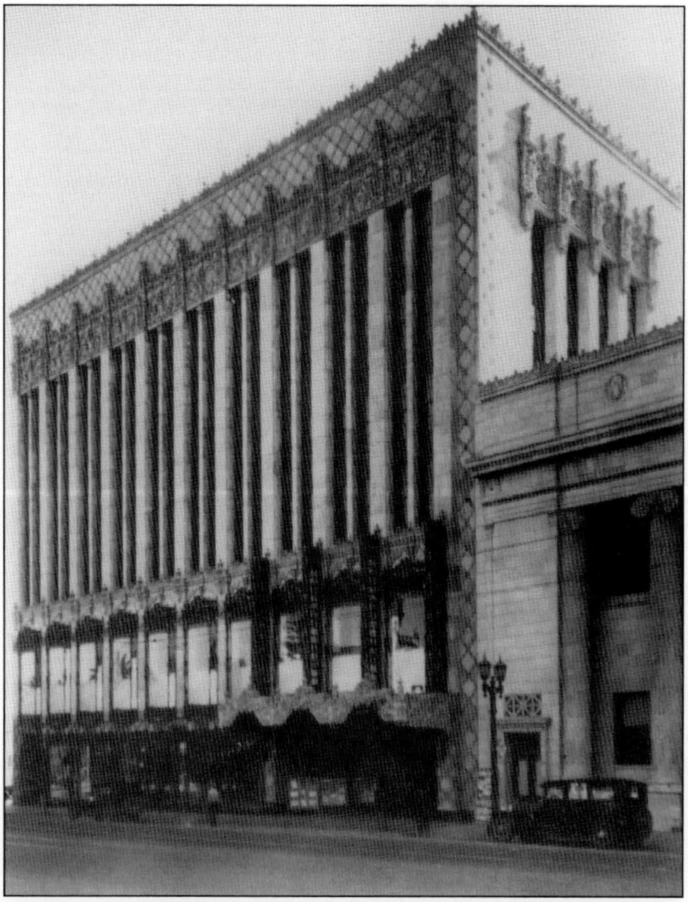

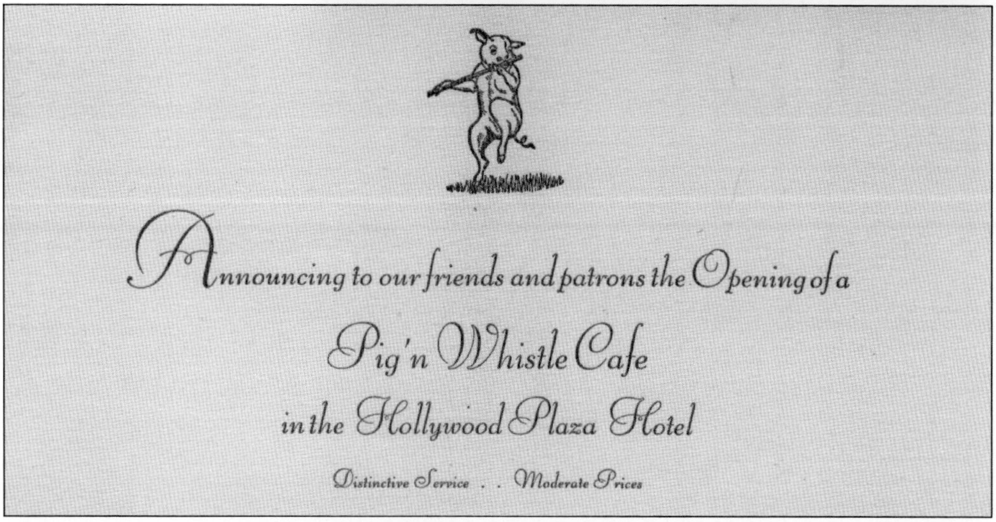

Announcing to our friends and patrons the Opening of a

Pig'n Whistle Cafe

in the Hollywood Plaza Hotel

Distinctive Service . . Moderate Prices

This invitation was mailed to Pig 'N Whistle patrons as well as those in the surrounding offices of the Hollywood Plaza Hotel. After enjoying a successful year in Hollywood, the next step was to branch out; two more shops were opened by 1929. The Pig 'N Whistle Corporation also mailed out letters inviting select guests to open charge accounts.

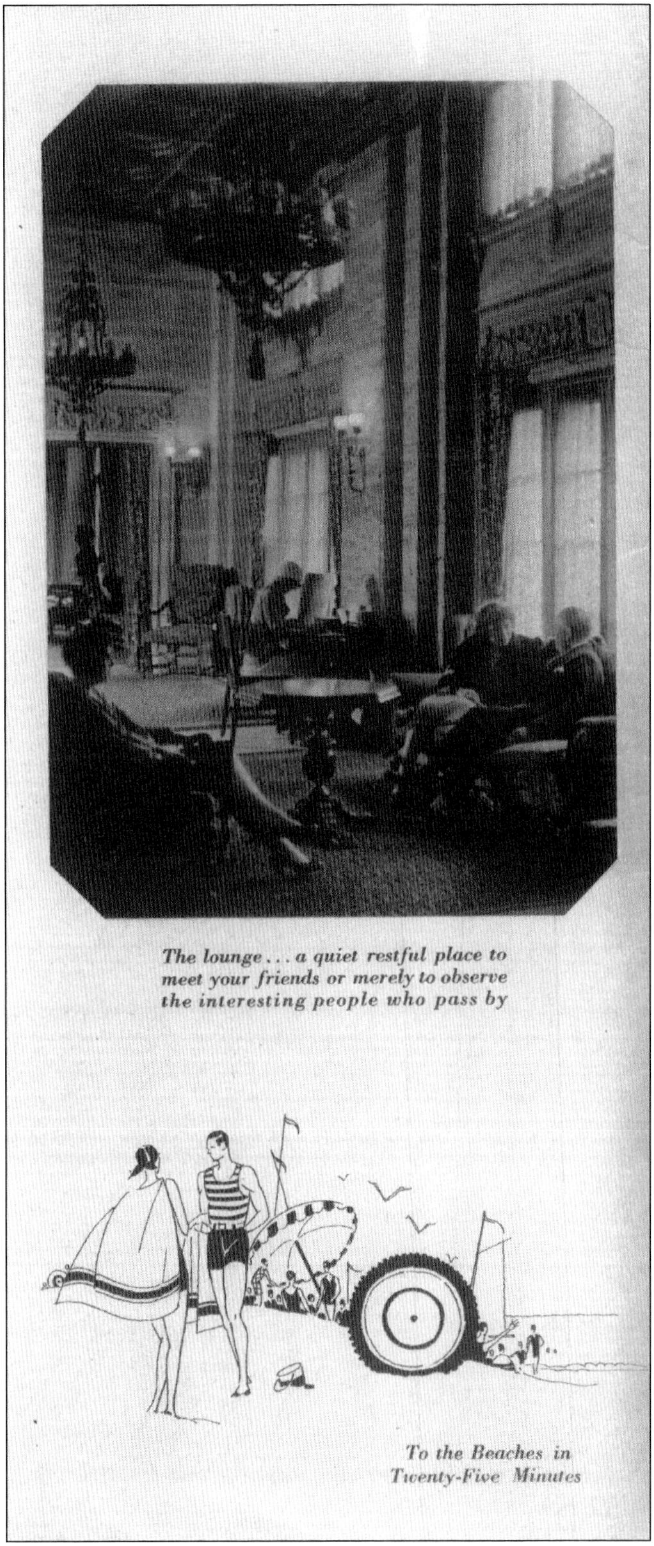

A pamphlet from 1928 describes the Hollywood Plaza Hotel as being Hollywood's social center. It advertised, "You will see the people of Hollywood—the moving picture people and the celebrated faces—when you visit this great hotel." Pictured is the lounge, described as "a quiet and restful place" where one could "observe the interesting people who pass by."

The Hollywood Plaza Hotel was one of many hotels in the area that catered to movie and radio stars. Built in 1924, it was designed by the architectural firm of Walker and Eisen at 1633 North Vine Street. Competing for business in the area were the Knickerbocker, the Roosevelt, the Christie, and the Hollywood hotels. (Courtesy Security Pacific National Bank Collection/ Los Angeles Public Library.)

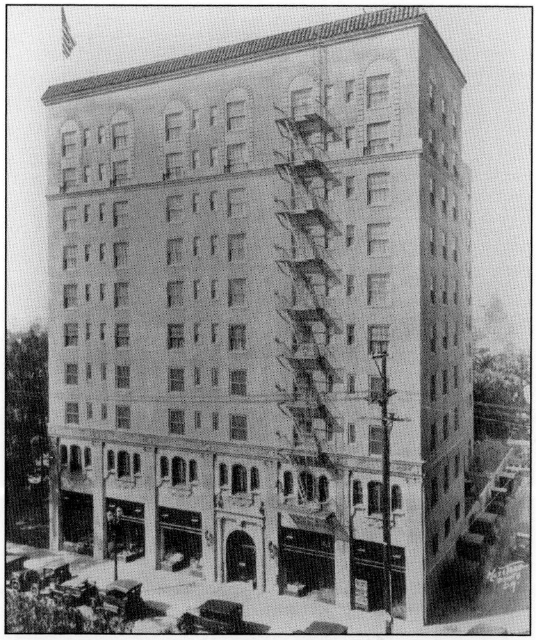

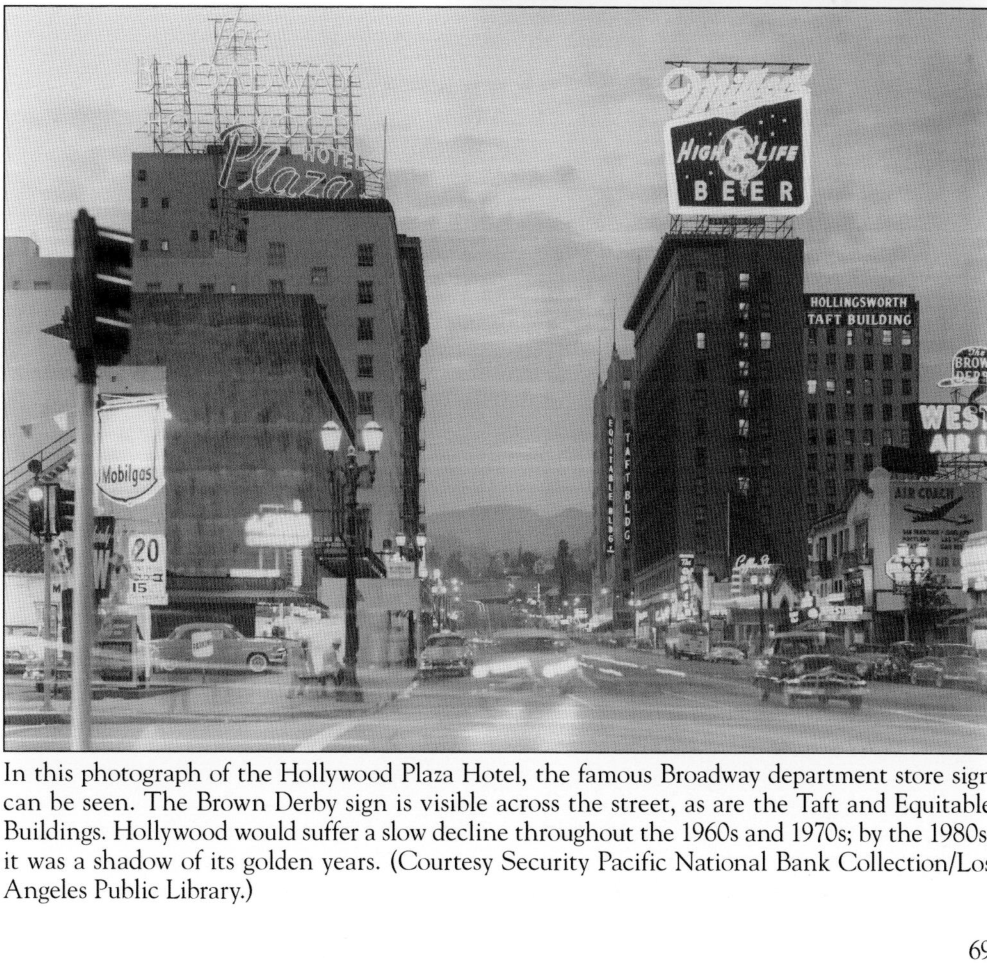

In this photograph of the Hollywood Plaza Hotel, the famous Broadway department store sign can be seen. The Brown Derby sign is visible across the street, as are the Taft and Equitable Buildings. Hollywood would suffer a slow decline throughout the 1960s and 1970s; by the 1980s, it was a shadow of its golden years. (Courtesy Security Pacific National Bank Collection/Los Angeles Public Library.)

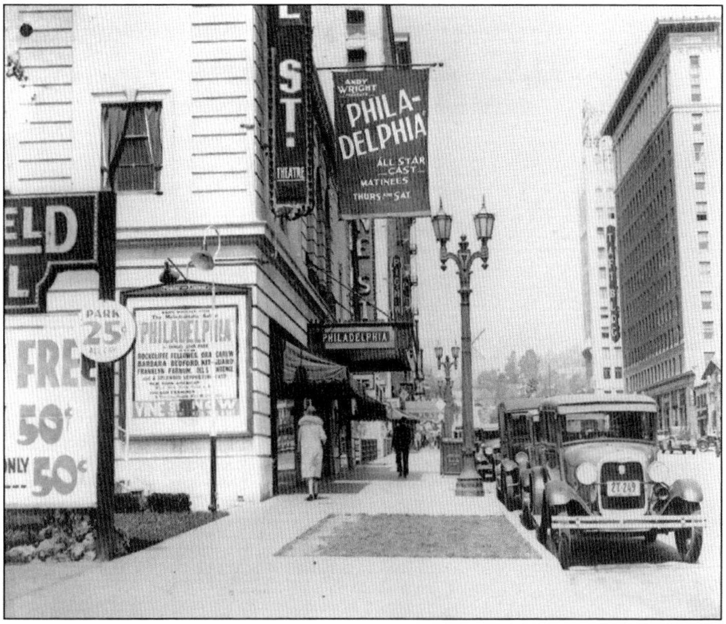

Looking north on Vine Street from the Vine Street Theatre, the Pig 'N Whistle sign can be seen at center on the Hollywood Plaza Hotel, just below the flag outside the theater advertising, "Andy Wright presents Philadelphia." The Taft Building is also visible at right. The Taft was built in 1923 by architects Walker and Eisen and housed many entertainment offices. (Courtesy Security Pacific National Bank Collection/Los Angeles Public Library.)

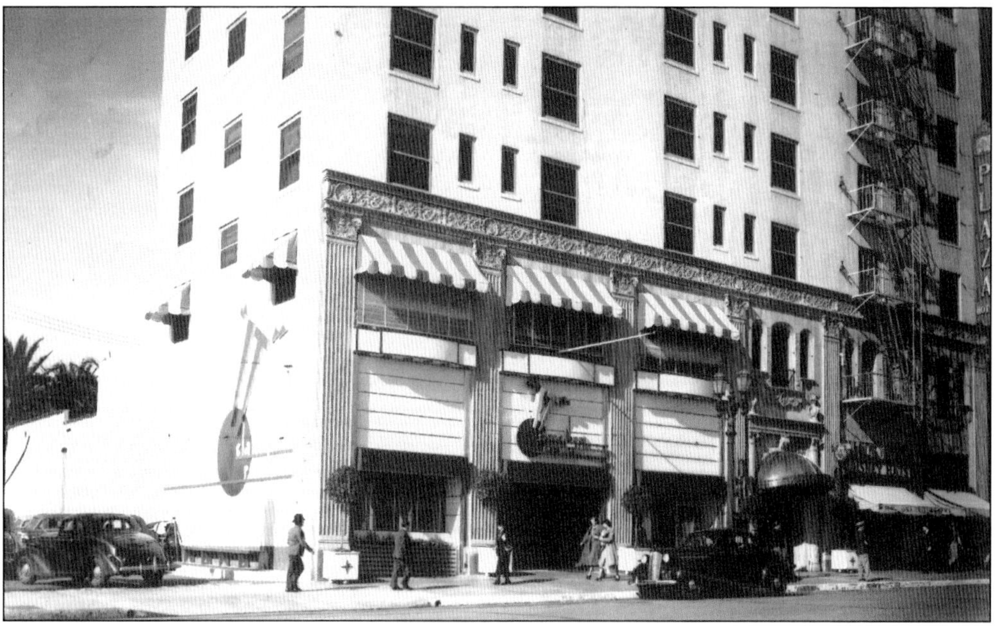

By 1936, the Pig 'N Whistle café was gone from the Hollywood Plaza Hotel and replaced by Clara Bow's It Café. In the 1920s, Clara Bow was one of the top female box office stars and was one of the first big movie celebrities to attach his or her name to a Hollywood restaurant. By 1927, she was known as the "It Girl" and embodied the carefree flapper persona; however, her popularity had waned by the early 1930s due to public scandals, and she suffered a mental breakdown at age 25. She later married cowboy star Rex Bell, and they had two children together. Bell partnered with her in this business venture, and his name can also be seen on the restaurant sign. The café was short-lived, as the inner circles of Hollywood never accepted Bow and regarded her as a disgrace to the community. She suffered from more mental illness, and eventually the couple moved to Las Vegas. (Courtesy Security Pacific National Bank Collection/Los Angeles Public Library.)

Five

Melody Lane

Sidney Hoedemaker, vice president and general manager of the Pig 'N Whistle Corporation, expanded the chain in 1927 by acquiring an established downtown café on Hill Street called Neve's Melody Lane. Neve's was near the music publishing companies and was a popular hangout for musicians and radio personalities. Hoedemaker dropped "Neve's" as part of the name, and it became simply Melody Lane. A Wurlitzer organ in the back offered diners daily concerts. When Prohibition was partially repealed in March 1933, Pig 'N Whistle and Melody Lane soon added beer and wine to the menu and began building cocktail lounges within their units.

During the 1930s, Wilshire Boulevard's Miracle Mile was a stretch of Art Deco and Streamline Moderne buildings that were accessible by automobile. Hoedemaker opened a Pig 'N Whistle in the Ralph's shopping center in 1929, and it served the Wilshire District for eight years. John Gage passed away in 1938, and Hoedemaker became president of the corporation. Several Pig 'N Whistles were closed in favor of the newer and more modern Melody Lane. In 1938, a Melody Lane opened at Wilshire Boulevard and Detroit Street in the Miracle Mile. Soon other Melody Lanes followed at the intersections of Hollywood Boulevard and Vine Street and Wilshire Boulevard and Western Avenue, and by the 1940s, the cities of Beverly Hills and Long Beach both added a new and modern Melody Lane restaurant.

When the United States entered World War II, it changed, among other things, the way Americans ate. Dining out became more of a luxury, and strict rationing was enforced. Many Pig 'N Whistles were closed in the early 1940s. Los Angeles and San Francisco were flooded with servicemen, and many had never seen the big cities before. Sending a souvenir menu home with a few lines inscribed to a loved one back home was sometimes the last thing a soldier or sailor did before heading off to an unknown destination.

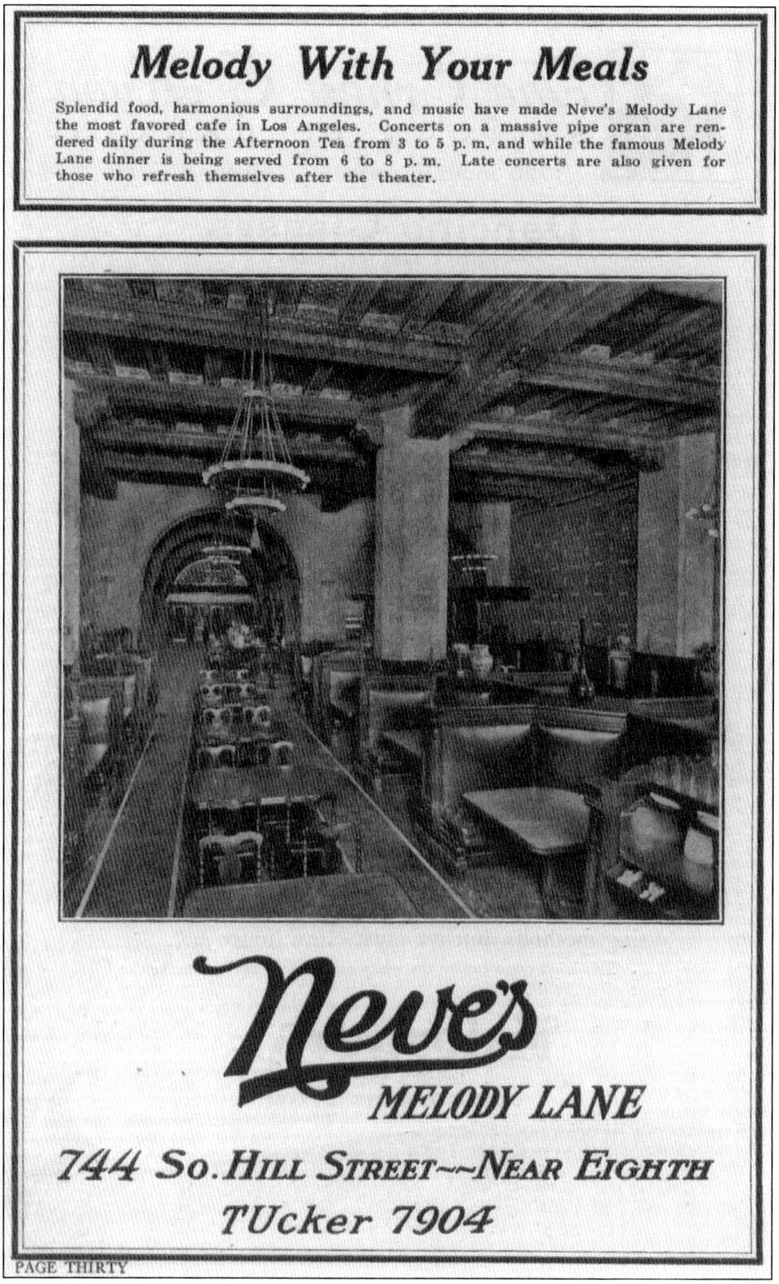

Neve's Melody Lane was located at 744 South Hill Street and was very popular with the music publishing crowd. It had a Wurlitzer pipe organ on a balcony for giving concerts, a feature that Sidney Hoedemaker would replicate later in his 1927 Hollywood Pig 'N Whistle. Pig 'N Whistle Corporation bought Neve's in 1926, changed the name to "Melody Lane," and added the same menu as the Pig 'N Whistle. A cocktail lounge was added in 1934. At the time of purchase, Neve's Melody Lane was described in *Greater California, the Wonderland* as having "rare architectural construction with the superlative of artistry in embellishment, elegance, and taste of equipment and decorations, all of which represent an investment of approximately a quarter-million dollars. In respect to the cuisine, the service is by the most competent French, Italian, and Swiss chefs."

An interior scene of the main dining room at Melody Lane on Hill Street shows eight waitresses serving the busy crowd. There are many waiting to be seated in the lobby near the soda fountain, and no less than five waitresses behind the fountain counter. This photograph was taken around 1943 at the height of the restaurant's popularity. (Courtesy Bison Archives.)

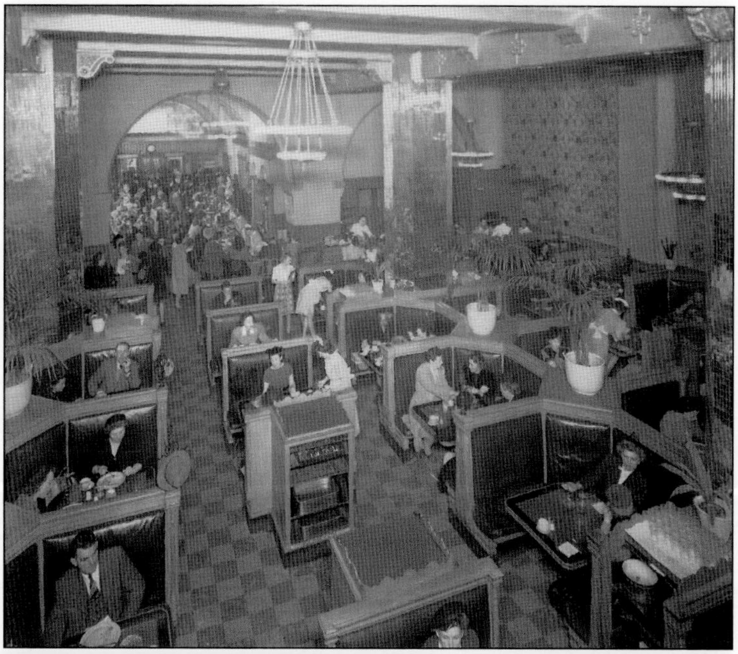

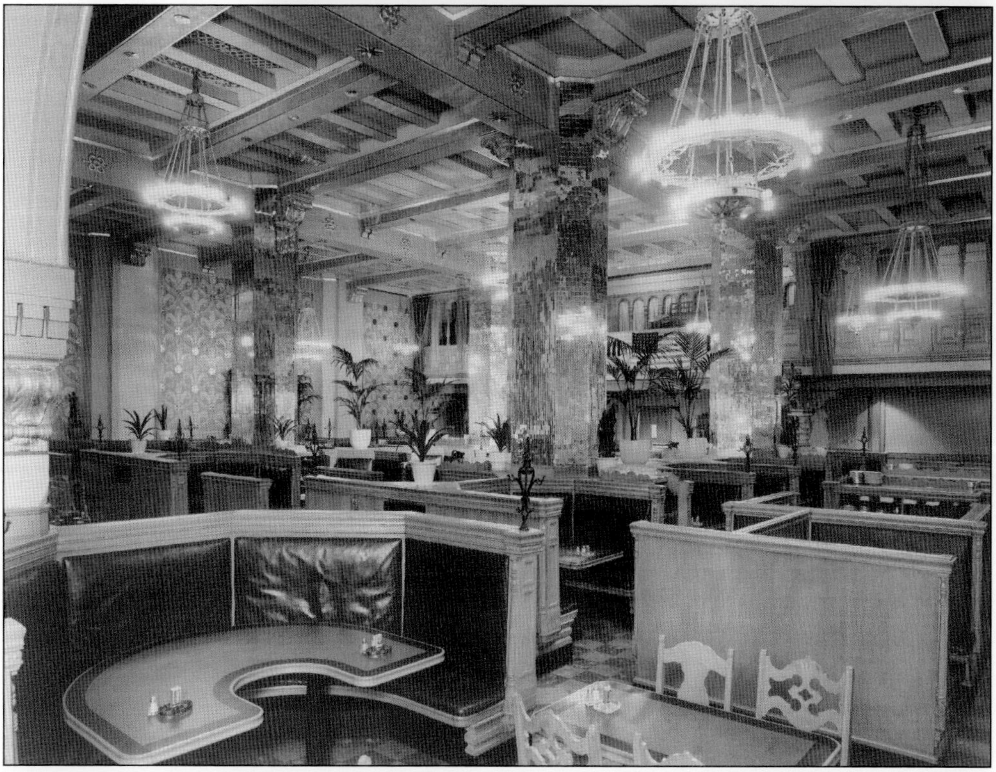

This interior scene of the first Melody Lane on Hill Street shows the high-backed booths that provided diners more privacy and the mirrored columns that added a soft, reflective glow from the ornate chandeliers above. The Wurlitzer pipe organ can be seen on the balcony, which is adorned by the American flag. (Courtesy Bison Archives.)

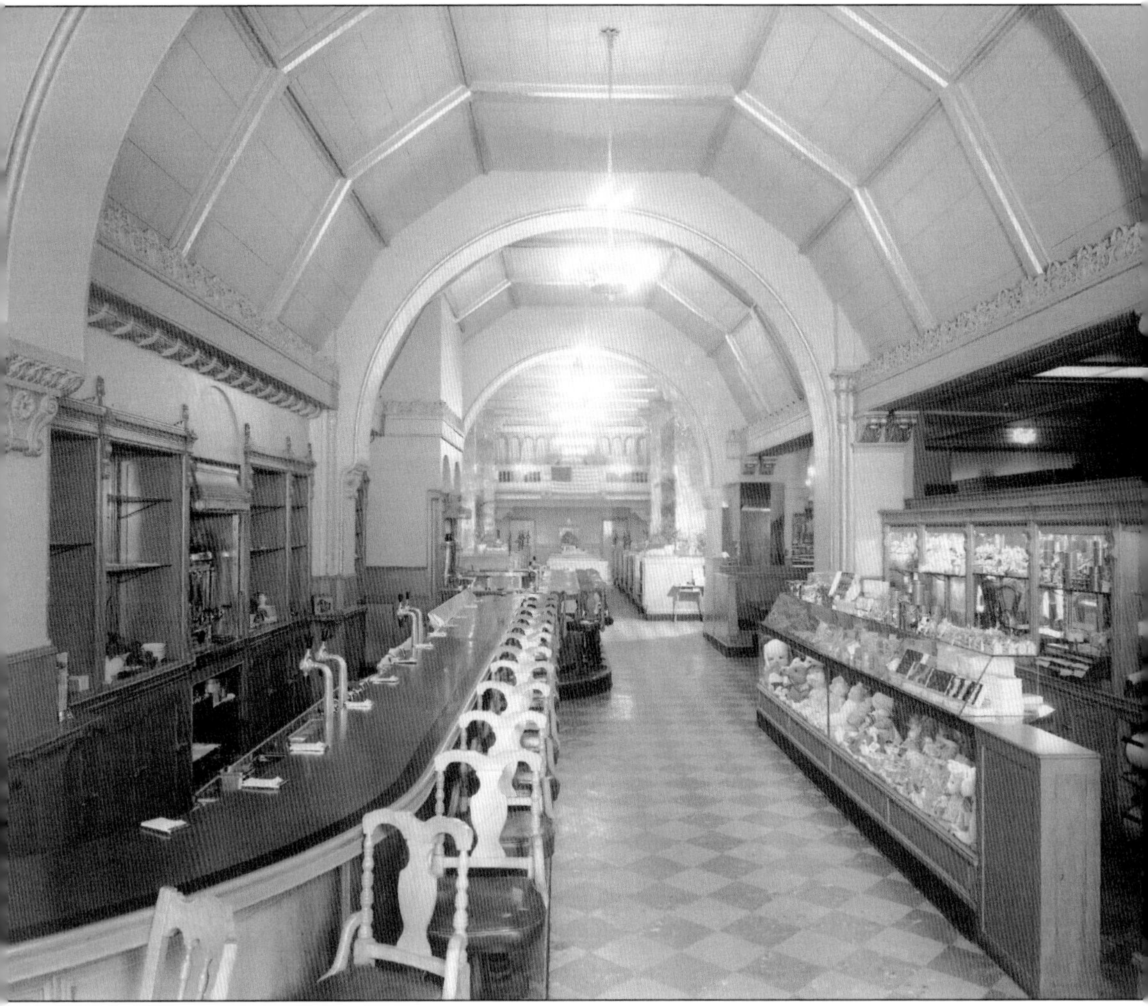

A 1943 shot of the entrance to Melody Lane on Hill Street shows the soda fountain at left, with waitress order books placed near each seat. The Wurlitzer pipe organ can be seen on its balcony, the American flag prominently displayed. According to Ken Rosen, current owner of the Pig 'N Whistle Wurlitzer from the 6714 Hollywood Boulevard location, these two organs were very similar. The Melody Lane Wurlitzer was purchased from the Rudolph Wurlitzer Company in North Tonowanda, New York, in February 1925. After Melody Lane closed its doors, the organ was owned by Dr. Phillip Stocker of Riverside, California, for nearly 40 years before being sold to a pipe organ museum in Germany, where it now resides completely intact. To the right, the candy counter has a wide variety of chocolates for sale as well as a collection of stuffed animals and baby dolls. (Courtesy Bison Archives.)

Children were still important customers at Melody Lane like they were at the Pig 'N Whistle. Details of a children's menu from the 1930s are shown here; there are "pretty girls in frilled caps" amongst the music notes. Using good manners is always a lesson worth learning, the little poem below instructs: "Hearts, like doors, will open with ease, to very, very, little keys. And don't forget that two of these are 'I thank you,' and 'If you please.' " The back of this kid's menu advertises the different locations for the cocktail lounges: "Only for the grown-ups who brought you to the house of the Little Pigs!"

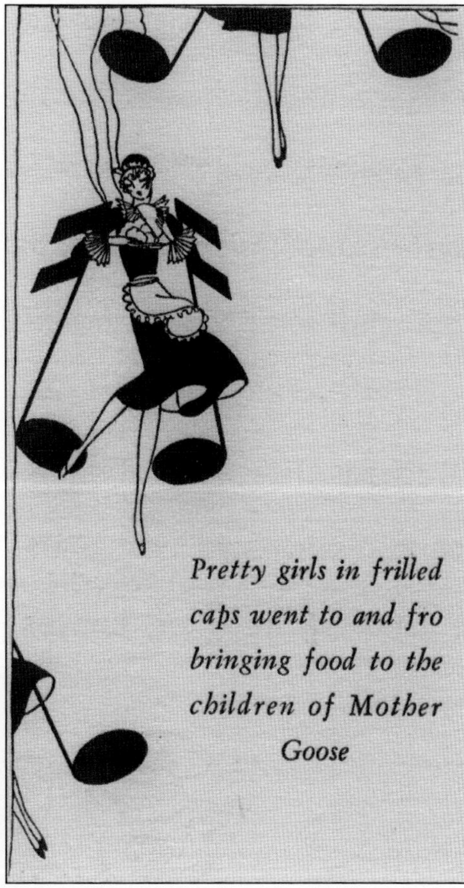

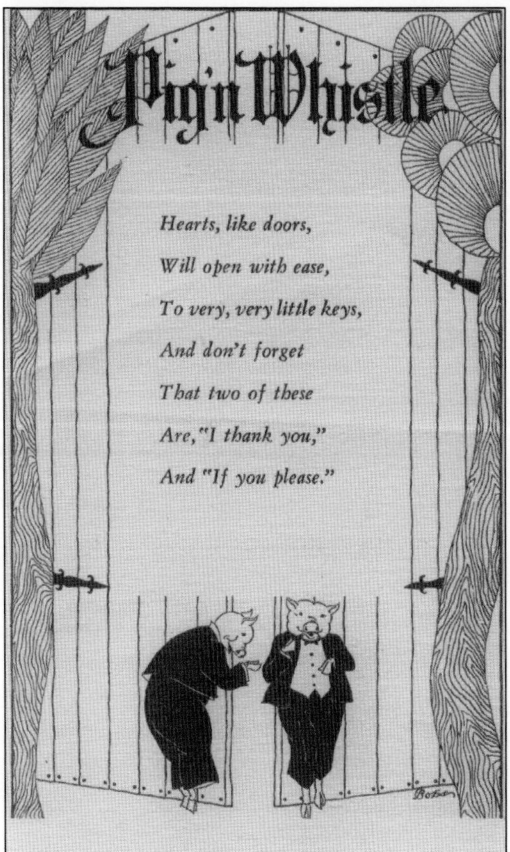

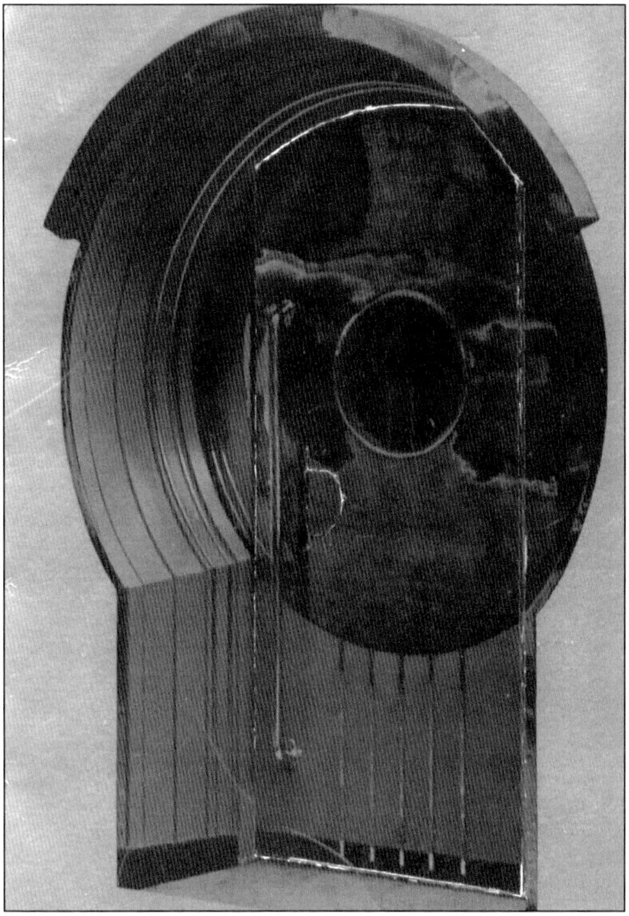

The keyhole-shaped door of Melody Lane was featured on the invitations to the opening of Melody Lane's cocktail bar, "A Pig 'N Whistle Enterprise." This invitation once held a golden key that entitled the recipient to a free 25¢ cocktail. It reads, "For an hour or two for good fellowship for a tete-a-tete, for an informal business chat . . . we suggest the quiet, pleasant surroundings of Melody Lane Lounge."

The cocktail lounge for Melody Lane was added next door at 746 South Hill Street. This 1934 postcard depicts the Streamline Moderne style of the bar and lounge. These elements are reflected in the design of the chairs, tables, shelves, and circular mirror behind the bar. Melody Lane opened to much success and was one of the first restaurants in Los Angeles to add a cocktail lounge.

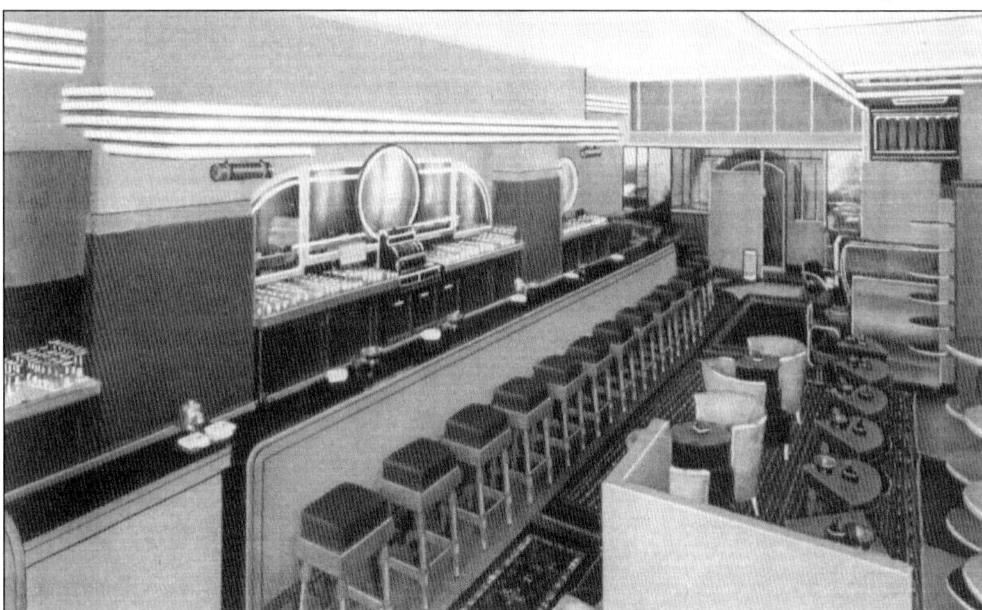

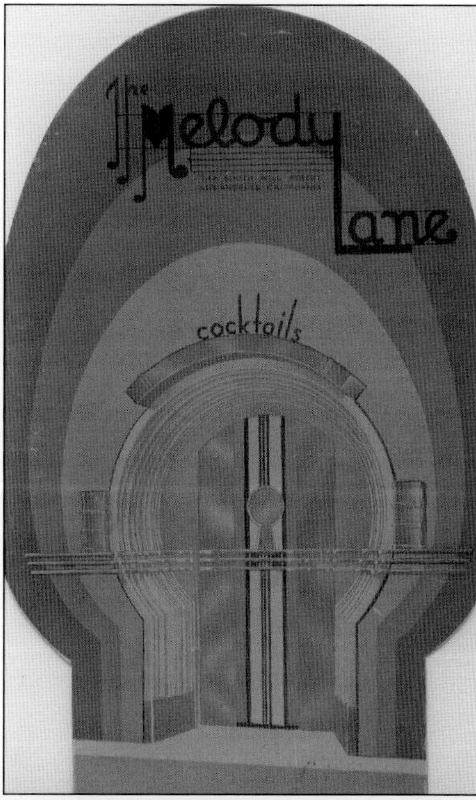

Melody Lane's keyhole design of the bar's front door also mirrors the design of the popular 1933 Philco 16B Baby Grand Cathedral radio. California tax was added onto liquor prices, roughly adding up to a penny or two. A bottle of Eastside beer is priced at 14.6¢ and would have cost 15¢; champagne is 58¢, and an Orange Blossom cocktail is 24¢.

Below is a detail of the Melody Lane cocktail lounge's exterior. The Pig 'N Whistle added cocktail lounges to most of their units after 1934. The Lankershim Hotel Pig 'N Whistle had "The 222," the Fine Arts Building had "The Whistling Pig," and the Pig 'N Whistle on Sixth Street in downtown had "The 322." Later when a Pig 'N Whistle opened on 440 South Hill Street near the Subway Terminal Building, the cocktail lounge was named "The Oasis."

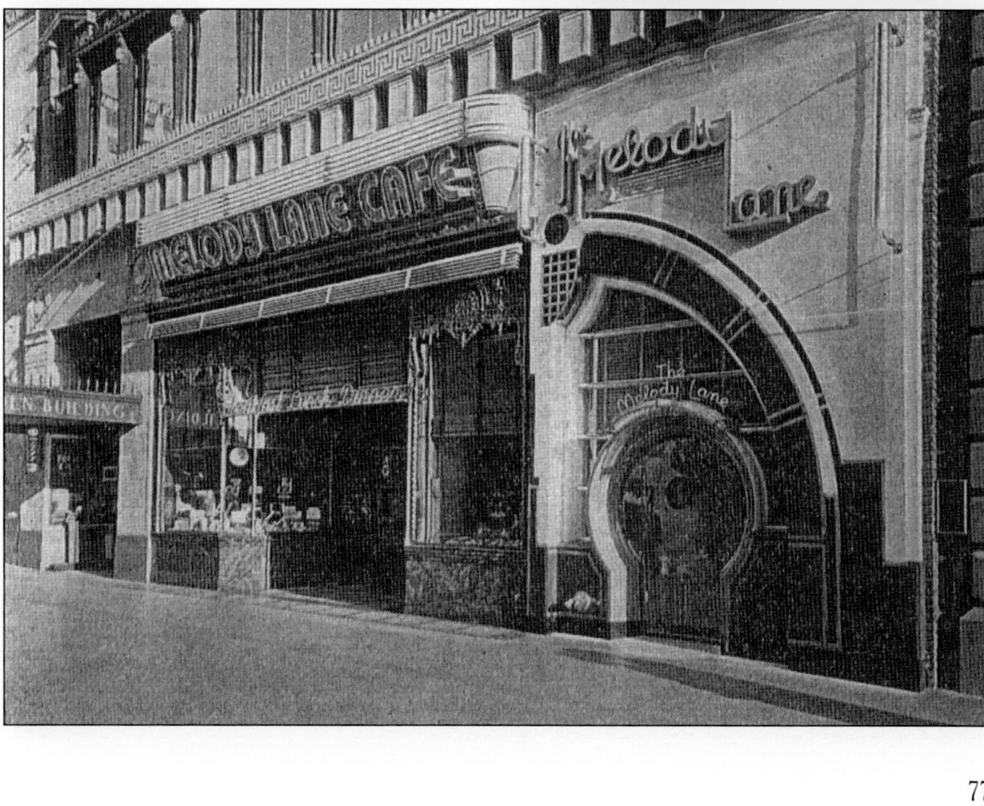

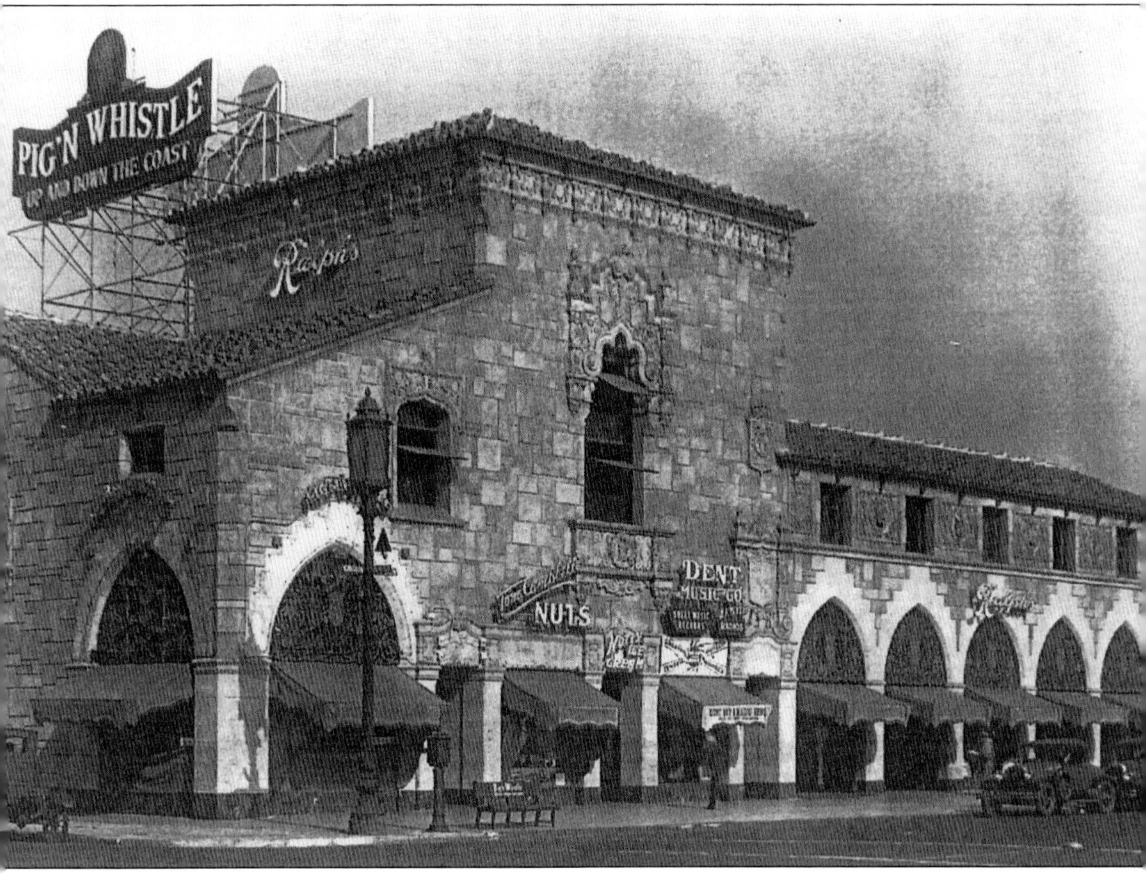

The Pig 'N Whistle was a part of the Ralph's shopping center on Wilshire and Hauser Boulevards from 1929 to 1938. This Spanish Colonial Revival arcade building was designed by Morgan, Walls, and Clements in 1926 and also housed the Dent Music Company and Tom Campbell's Nut Shop. In 1933, during the depths of the Depression, a Dinner De-Luxe cost $1. It included a cup of Pig 'N Whistle Supreme Cream soup, seafood cocktail, salted Jordan almonds, half of a broiled lobster, potatoes au gratin, buttered carrots and peas, a salad, hot mince pie with brandy sauce, a large glass of draught beer, a cup of sherbet, and for 50¢ more, a manhattan or martini cocktail with a bottle of Burgundy or sauterne wine. The Pig 'N Whistle on Wilshire and Hauser Boulevards closed in 1938, coinciding with the opening of a second Melody Lane at Wilshire Boulevard and Detroit Street the same year.

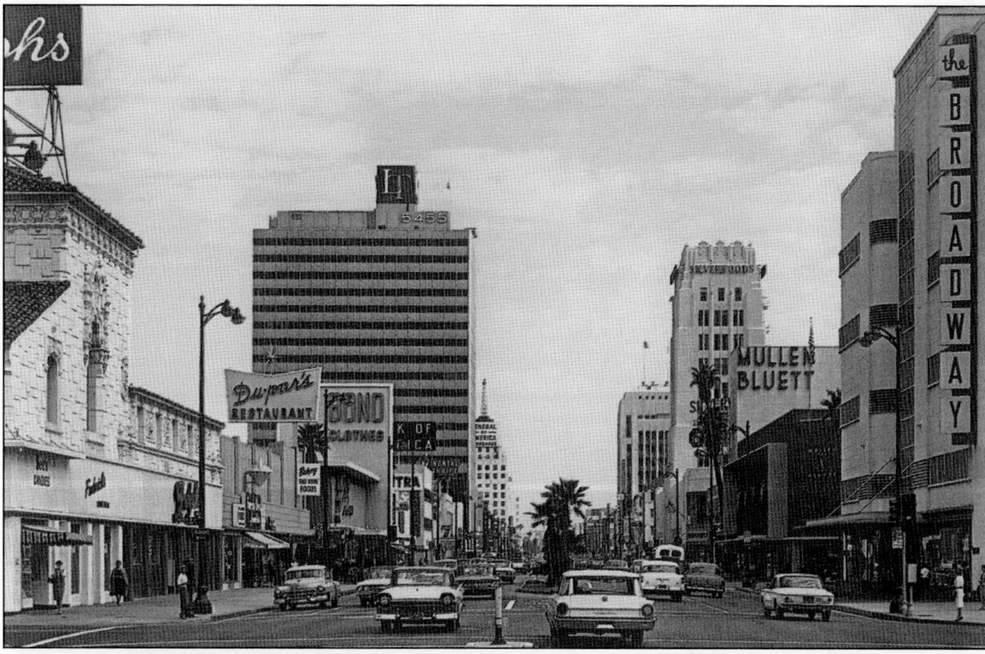

The Pig 'N Whistle on Wilshire and Hauser Boulevards was replaced by See's Candies by the 1960s. Du-Par's Restaurant, named for founders James Dunn and Ed Parsons, can be seen on the left. They had a regular pinochle game with Sidney Hoedemaker in the 1950s, along with Bob's Big Boy founder, Bob Wian, and founder of Los Angeles's Clifton's Cafeteria chain, Clifford Clinton. (Courtesy Eric Lynxwiler.)

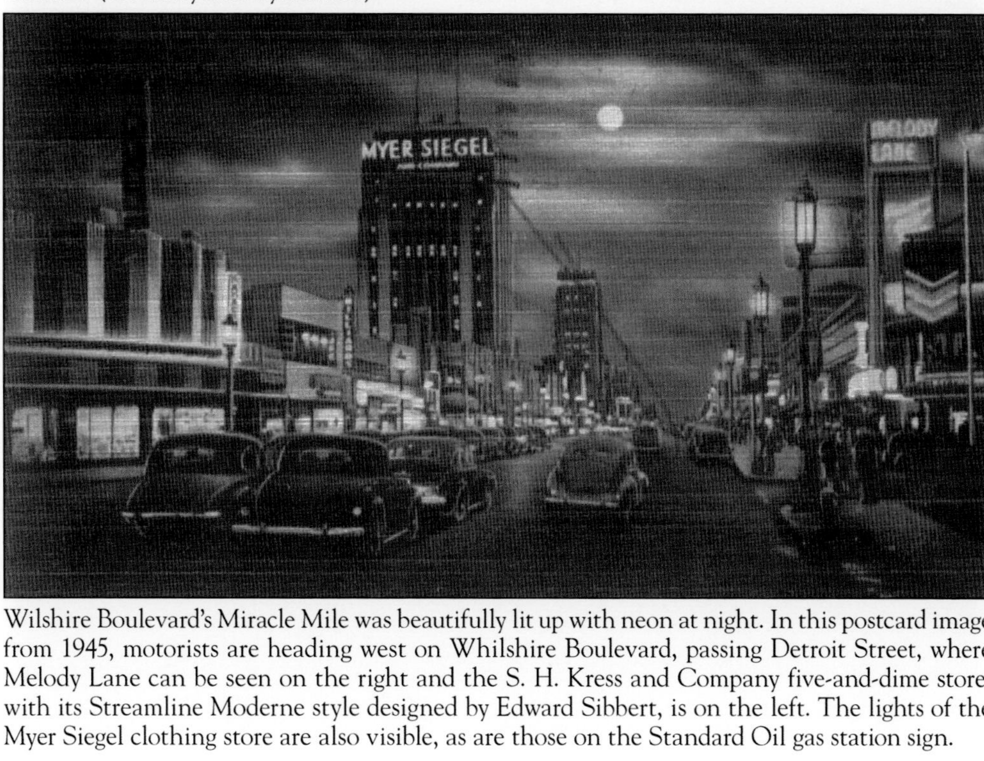

Wilshire Boulevard's Miracle Mile was beautifully lit up with neon at night. In this postcard image from 1945, motorists are heading west on Whilshire Boulevard, passing Detroit Street, where Melody Lane can be seen on the right and the S. H. Kress and Company five-and-dime store, with its Streamline Moderne style designed by Edward Sibbert, is on the left. The lights of the Myer Siegel clothing store are also visible, as are those on the Standard Oil gas station sign.

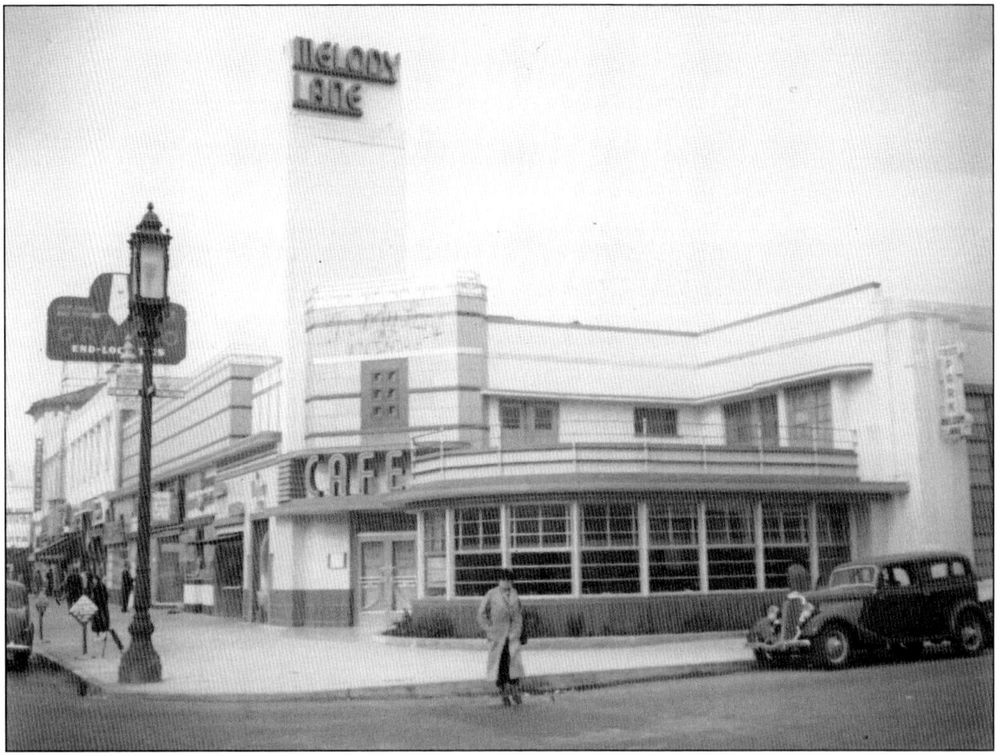

The Melody Lane on the corner of Wilshire Boulevard and Detroit Street was built in the Streamline Moderne style of architecture in 1938. The style emphasized aerodynamic curved forms and long horizontal lines. Like the Melody Lane cocktail bar on Hill Street, the Melody Lane on Detroit Street was free from unnecessary ornamentation and had a clean, functional design. (Courtesy Security Pacific National Bank Collection/Los Angeles Public Library.)

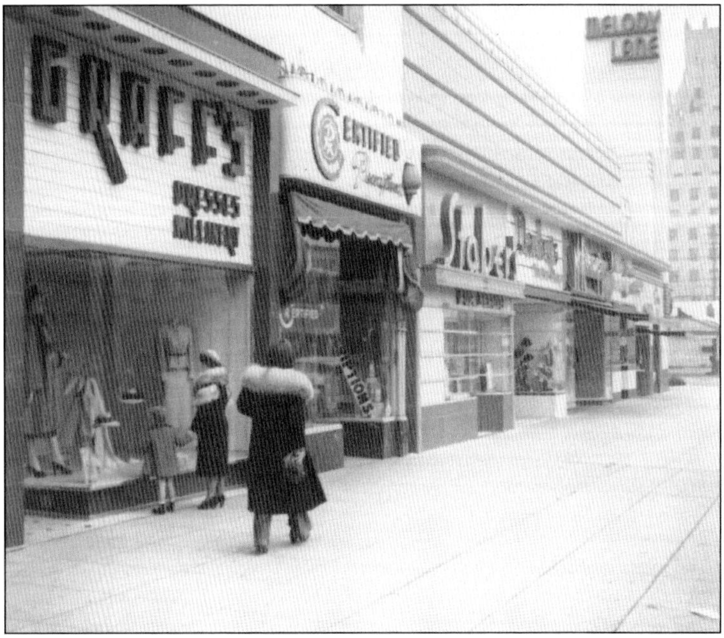

There were many exclusive shops near Melody Lane on Wilshire Boulevard and Detroit Street where attractive window displays caught the attention of passersby; Wilshire Boulevard rivaled Broadway as a window-shopping destination during the Depression. On this block is a Certified Prescription drugstore and Staber's Furs. (Courtesy Herman Schultheis/ Los Angeles Public Library.)

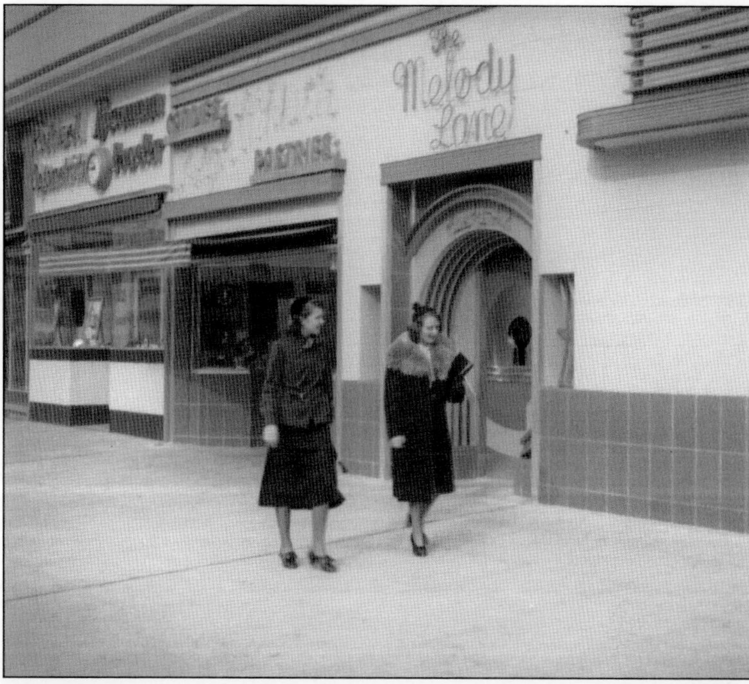

A close-up of the Melody Lane on Wilshire Boulevard and Detroit Street shows the Pig 'N Whistle candy shop's neon sign and that of the cocktail lounge next door. The huge keyhole-shaped door was a design feature for all Melody Lanes. (Courtesy Security Pacific National Bank Collection/ Los Angeles Public Library.)

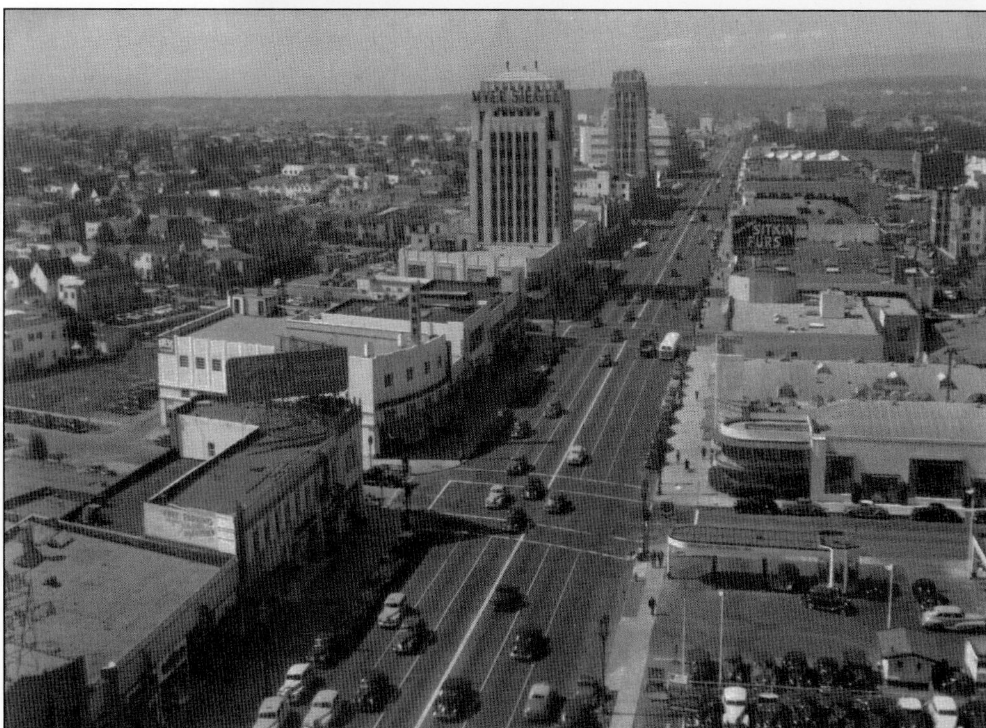

This view looking west on Wilshire Boulevard shows the Miracle Mile as it looked in 1948. A postcard describes it as the "Fifth Avenue of the West. One of the heaviest traveled thoroughfares in the world; it is studded with many smart shops, restaurants and hotels." Melody Lane is visible on the right. (Courtesy John D. "Snappy" Goodrich.)

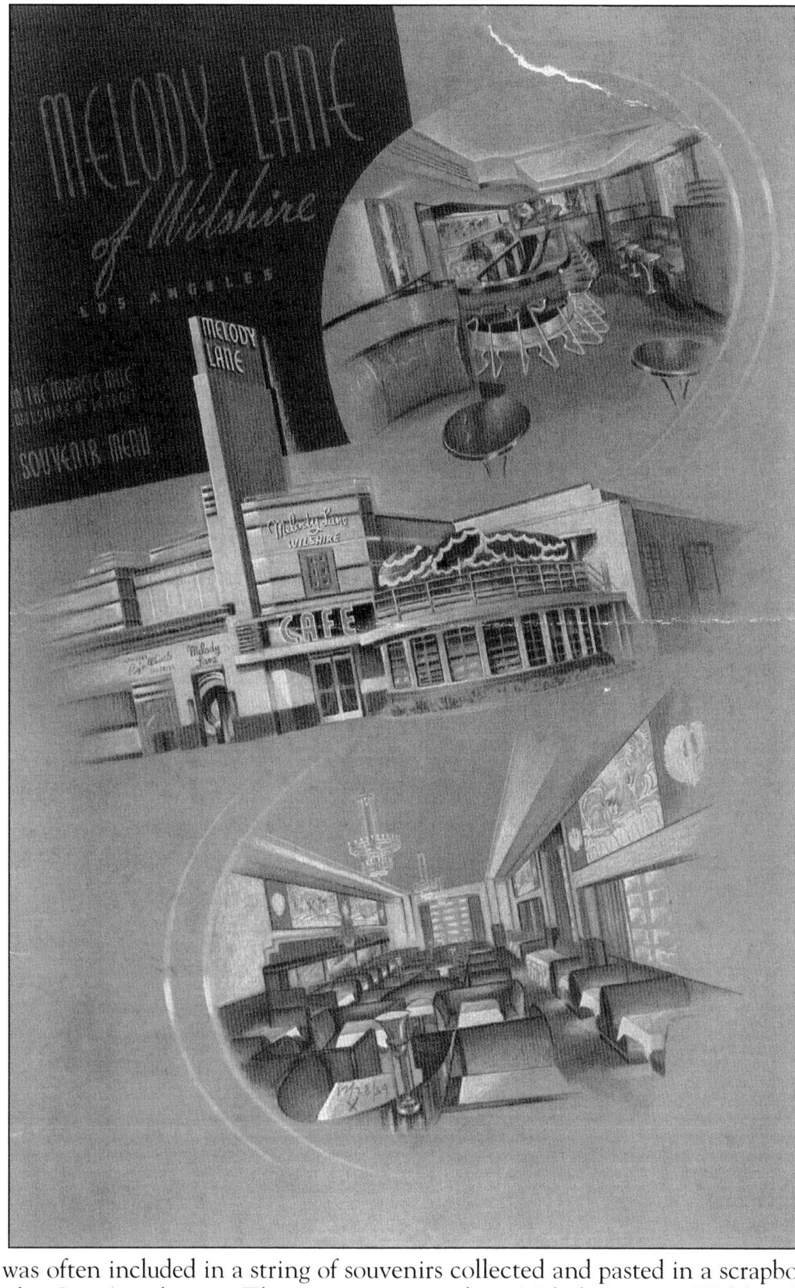

A menu was often included in a string of souvenirs collected and pasted in a scrapbook from a Hollywood or Los Angeles trip. This souvenir menu from Melody Lane on Wilshire Boulevard has an inscription from December 1939: "Dinner De-Luxe . . . 12/28/39 at 7:15 PM after broadcast at NBC." A program for the *Babe of Bethlehem* presented by the English Lutheran Church and a tour pamphlet for NBC Studios on Sunset Boulevard and Vine Street was glued inside the menu. The exact booth that the vacationer sat in is marked in pencil with an "X," and the date is on the front cover. During summer months, the outdoor patio was used, and diners sat under brightly colored umbrellas looking out at the motorists on Wilshire Boulevard. A menu from 1940 bears the following inscription: "Topping a gay morning atop the Melody Lane—Eleanora, dear, I've enjoyed this initiation into Los Angeles' shopping!"

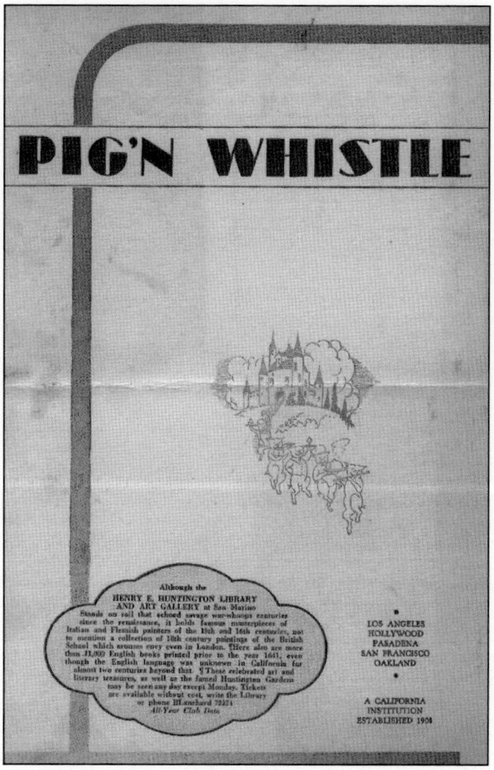

These 1937 menus are from the Melody Lane on Hill Street and the Pig 'N Whistle in the Fine Arts Building on Seventh Street. Pre–World War II menus had an astounding selection: T-bone steaks, New York steaks, French lamb chops, Louisiana shrimp, and a wide variety of fancy ice cream sundaes. These menus included interesting facts about Southern California, for example that "California gold was first discovered in England in 1831, when flakes of gold were found on the roots of California tree specimens brought back by Scotch botanist David Douglas." The Pig 'N Whistle menu also gave the reader information on the Henry E. Huntington Library and Art Gallery in San Marino, a popular tourist destination.

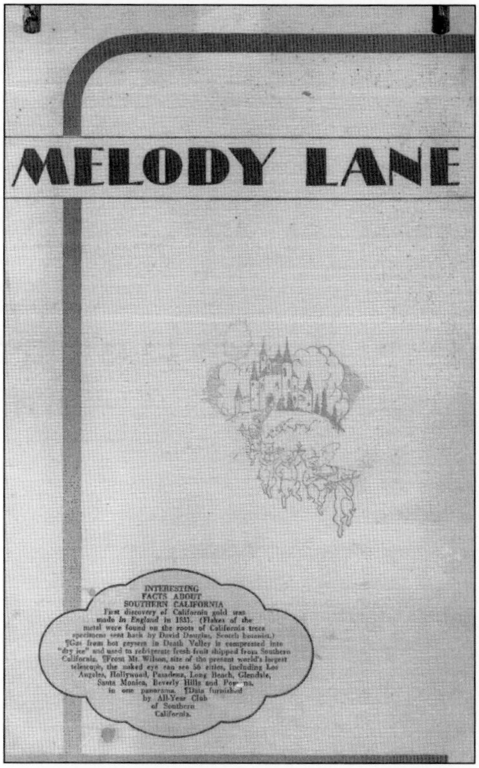

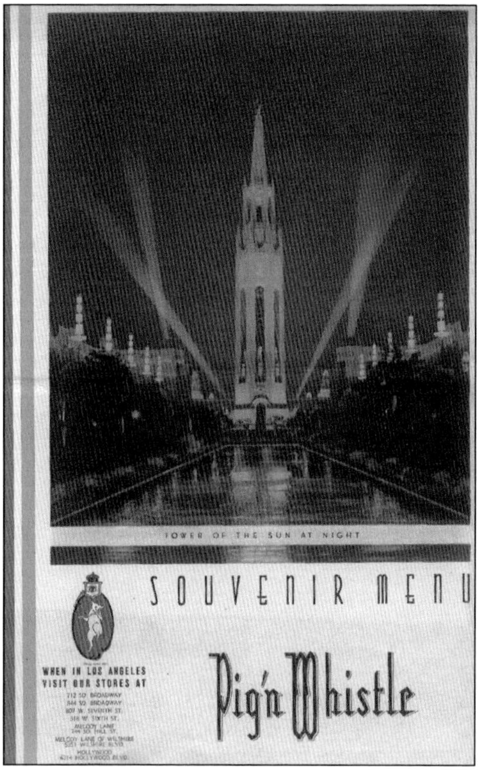

In 1939, San Francisco held a world's fair–like exposition called the Golden Gate International Exposition, which showcased the Pacific Ocean and celebrated the recent building of the San Francisco–Oakland Bay Bridge and the Golden Gate Bridge. The man-made Treasure Island (named after the book by Robert Louis Stevenson) that was the fair site later became a naval base when the United States entered World War II. The theme of this fair was "Pageant of the Pacific," and Pacifica, goddess of the ocean, and the Tower of the Sun were symbols of the exposition. Pig 'N Whistle built a location in the Palace of the Fine Arts and stayed open from 1939 until 1940.

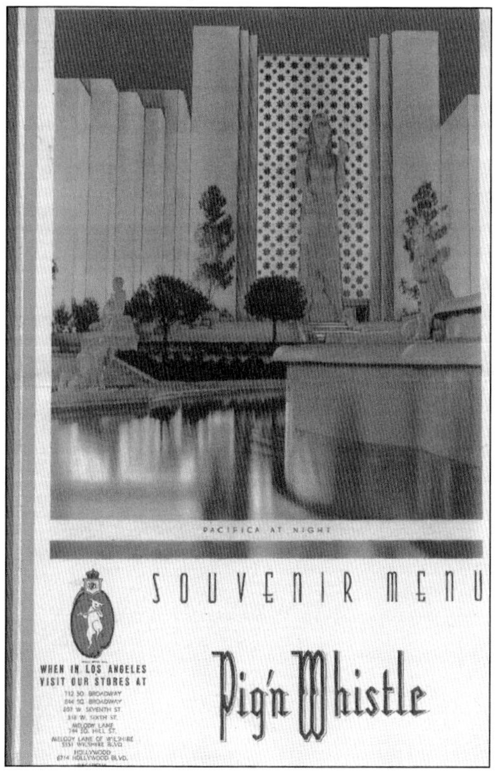

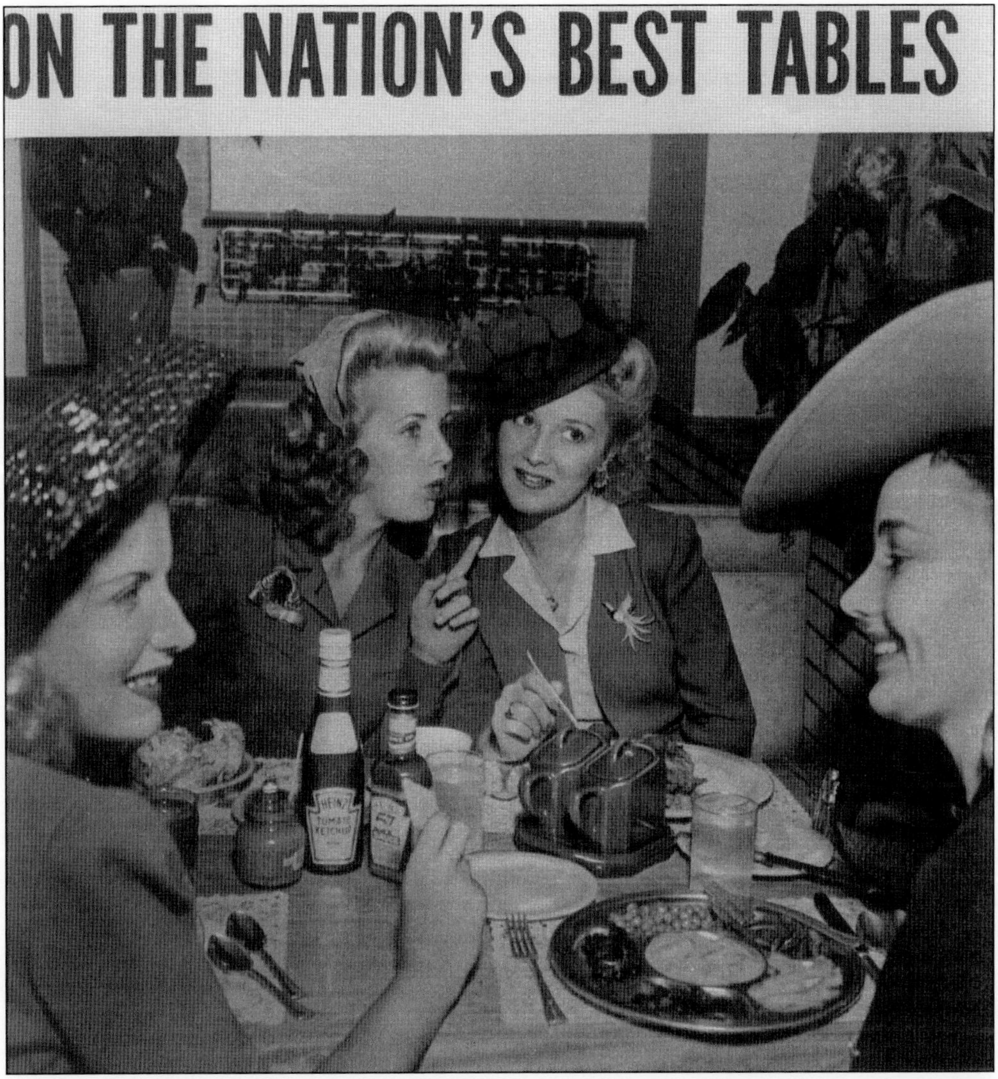

In 1942, a new Melody Lane opened at 3800 Wilshire Boulevard at Western Avenue. It was near the beautiful Art Deco Wiltern Theatre at 3790 Wilshire Boulevard and about a mile west from the 1929 Art Deco Bullocks Wilshire Building. This October 1942 advertisement for Heinz condiments shows the interior of Sidney Hoedemaker's first drive-in restaurant, a Wayne McAllister–designed café. It read, "On the Nation's Best Tables: Latest and loveliest of the twenty-three restaurants operated by Sidney Hoedemaker, president of the Pig 'N Whistle chain. Patronized, as the picture indicates, by some of the most beautiful girls in Hollywood, this attractive eating place complements its delicious foods with racy Heinz condiments." Divided plates, as seen on the table, were used to easily portion out food; the teapots used on all of Melody Lane's tables were from the Hall China Company. Pictured on the table is Hall's "Tea for Two" set.

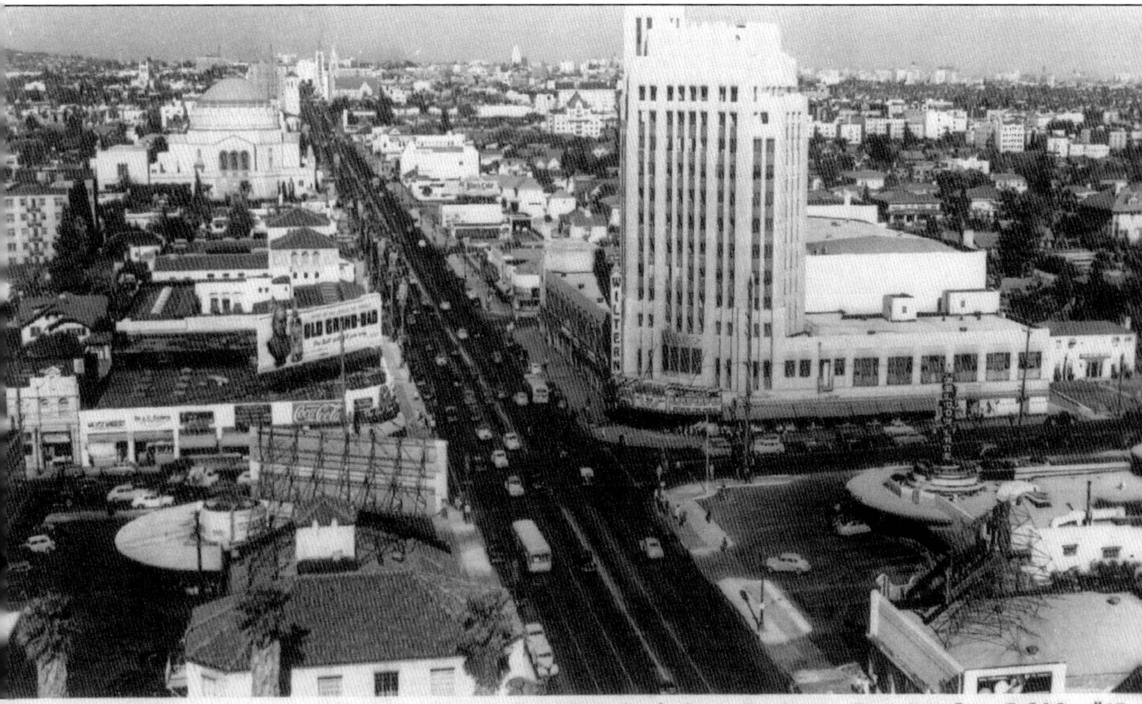

Wilshire Boulevard, busy shopping center. Looking East from Western. Los Angeles, Calif. #43.

Looking east from Western Avenue, this Melody Lane is located across from the Wiltern Theatre on the southwest corner of Wilshire Boulevard. The Wiltern was designed in 1929 and opened in 1931 as the Warner Bros. Western Theatre. The early years of the Depression forced it into closure, but it reopened in the mid-1930s as the Wil-Tern. Very soon after, it dropped the hyphen and became the Wiltern, as it is still known today. The Wiltern is no longer a movie house, but a venue where top-rated music and comedy acts perform. Here in 1944, when it was still a movie theater, *Between Two Worlds* starring John Garfield is showing. A billboard for Old Grand-Dad bourbon can be seen atop the Owl Drug Store on the northeast corner, where the Los Angeles Metro Rail station is now currently located.

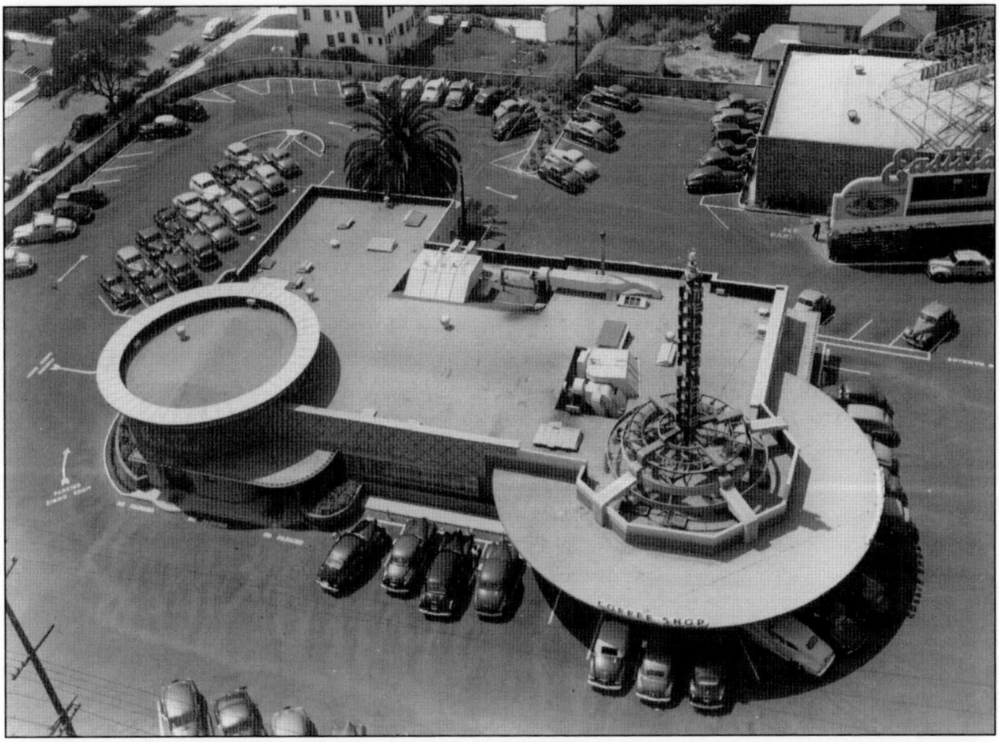

Two views of Melody Lane on Wilshire Boulevard and Western Avenue illustrate the curved lines of architect Wayne McAllister's 1942 Streamline Moderne design. In the above photograph, an overhead shot shows the Starlite Room cocktail lounge in the smaller circular section at left. The crowded drive-in at right has a "Melody Lane" neon spindle sign rising from the center. The Pig 'N Whistle candy and pastry shop was located in the rear, detached from the main restaurant. In the below photograph, Melody Lane is seen from across Western Avenue. There are signs advertising such brands as Ranier Ale, Eastside Beer, Roma Sherry, Canadian Club, and Par-T-Pak ginger ale, "America's Party Drink." (Above, Courtesy Security Pacific National Bank Collection/Los Angeles Public Library; below, Bison Archives.)

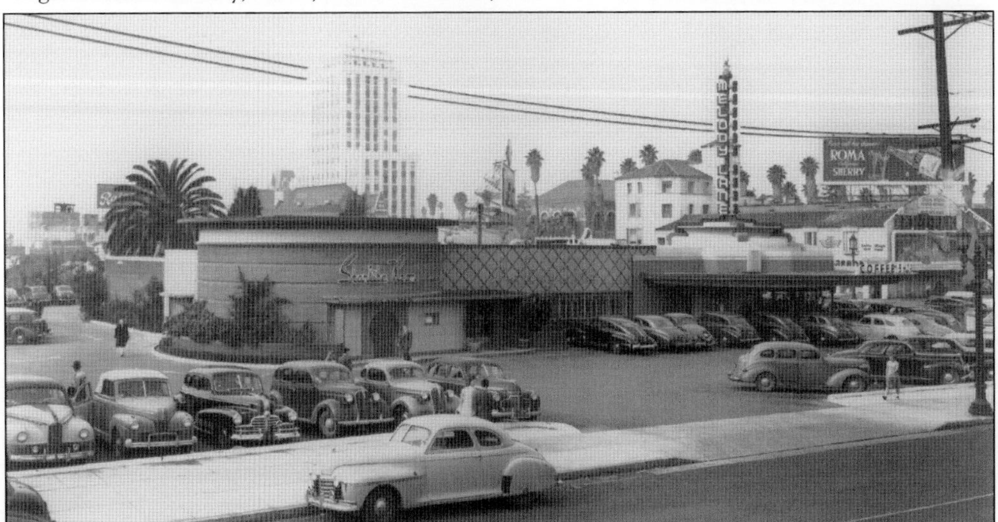

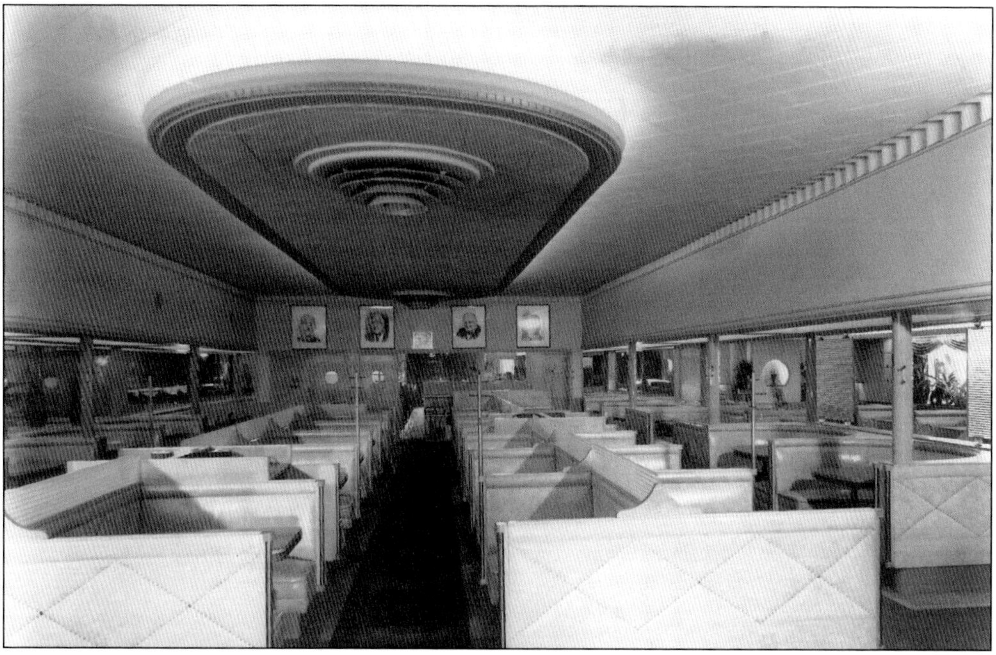

This interior shot of the Melody Lane on Wilshire Boulevard and Western Avenue, as seen in 1943, shows the dining room under a curved air-conditioning and lighting fixture. Prominently displayed on the back wall are photographs of the "Big Four," or the Allied Leaders of World War II—Generalissimo Chiang Kai-shek, Franklin Delano Roosevelt, Winston Churchill, and Joseph Stalin. (Courtesy Bison Archives.)

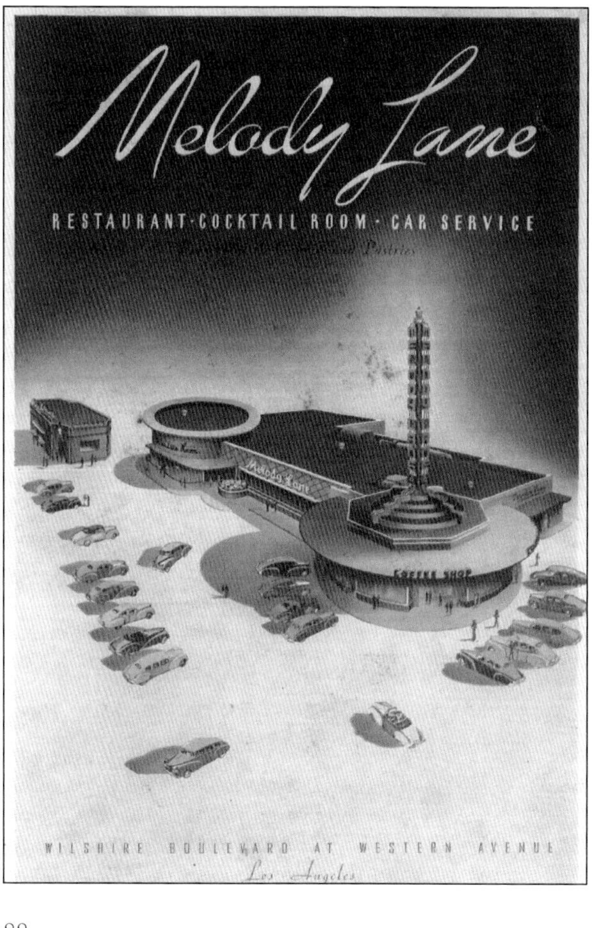

A Melody Lane menu from 1943 features the Wayne McAllister–designed drive-in restaurant, served by carhops. McAllister's famous designs include the Agua Caliente resort in Mexico; several prominent Las Vegas hotels, such as the Sands, Flamingo, and El Cortez; and dozens of restaurants and drive-ins that defined Los Angeles through the mid–20th century. Author and preservationist Chris Nichols has written *The Leisure Architecture of Wayne McAllister*, a reference book detailing McAllister's work.

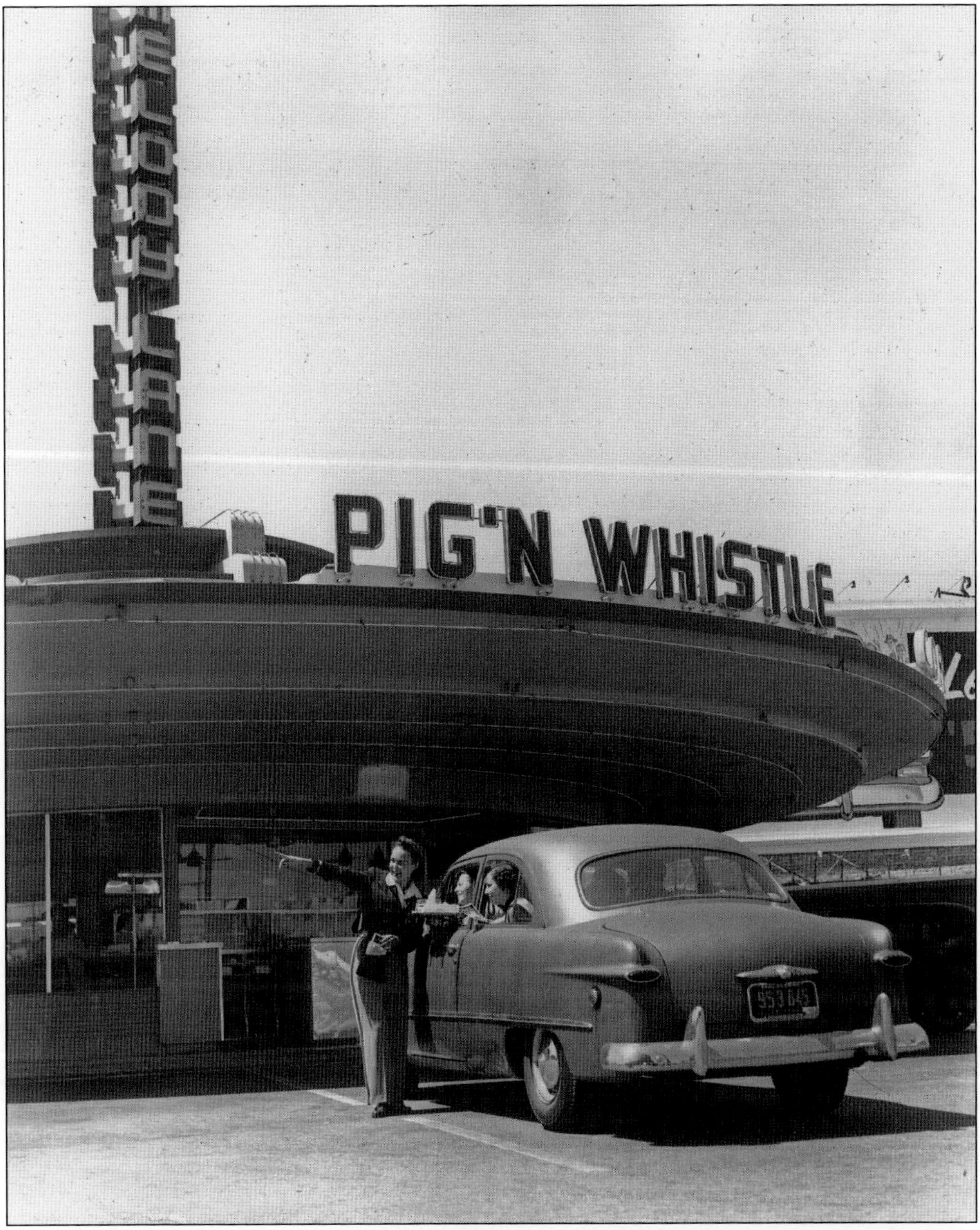

By the 1940s, every restaurant under the Pig 'N Whistle Corporation, with exception of candy shops, served liquor. Melody Lane was the first Los Angeles restaurant to add a cocktail lounge; by the mid-1940s, the chain surpassed dime-a-dozen drive-ins with the proverbial "hash-slingers" by adding elegant cocktail bars that appealed to people seeking a higher-class experience. In the 1945 film *Mildred Pierce*, Mildred (played by Joan Crawford) adds a cocktail bar to her restaurant (which is a dead-ringer for Melody Lane), explaining, "Why would I want them to eat here and drink somewhere else?" She subsequently becomes a big success with a whole chain of "Mildred's" restaurants stretching as far south as Laguna Beach (Melody Lane went as far as Long Beach). *Mildred Pierce* costar Eve Arden has one of her two stars on the Hollywood Walk of Fame in front of the Pig 'N Whistle at 6714 Hollywood Boulevard. (Courtesy the Watson family photograph archives.)

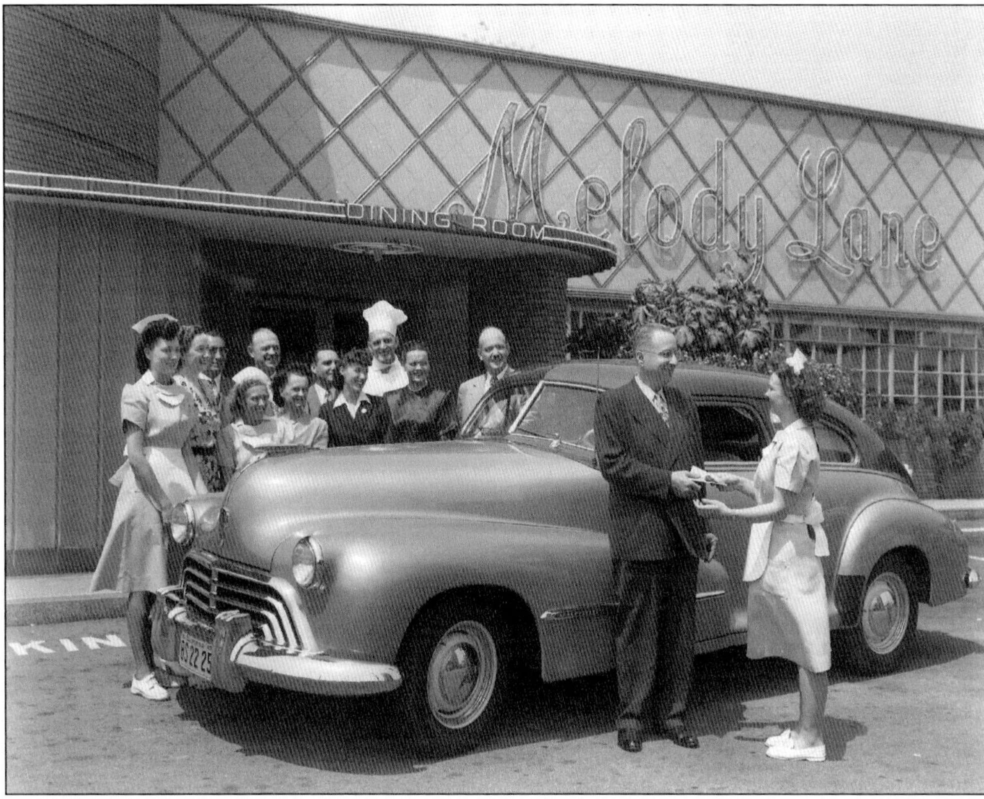

Pig 'N Whistle president Sidney Hoedemaker is seen here with the Melody Lane staff at the Wilshire Boulevard and Western Avenue location in 1947. He is handing an unidentified waitress papers and keys to a brand new Oldsmobile. Although it is unclear what the circumstances were surrounding this event, it is known that Hoedemaker was very generous to his employees. (Courtesy Bison Archives.)

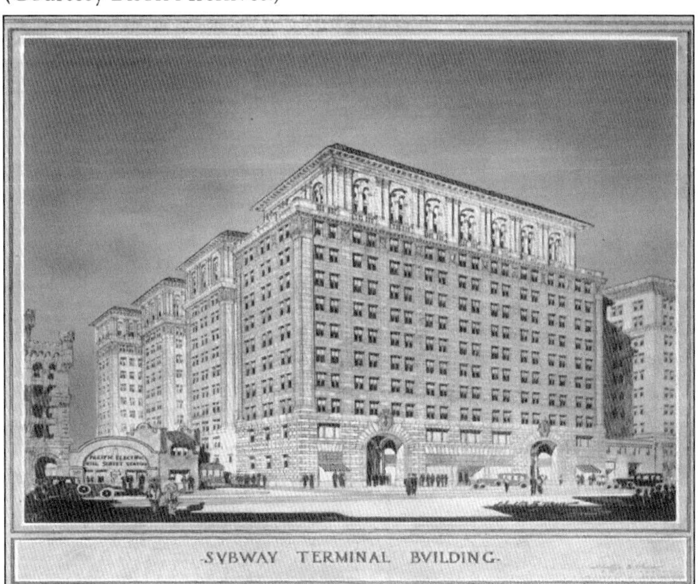

The Subway Terminal Building at 417 South Hill Street was designed in 1924 by architects Leonard Schultze and S. Fullerton Weaver of Schultze and Weaver and opened in 1925 to relieve traffic in downtown Los Angeles. Known as the "Hollywood Subway," it was close to Pershing Square, and Pig 'N Whistle opened a coffee shop across the street at 440 South Hill Street. During World War II, there were as many as 65,000 passengers traveling through this terminal daily.

The Standard Oil "Chevronettes" salute a photograph of Gen. Douglas MacArthur on March 30, 1942. General MacArthur was honored at Victory House in Pershing Square later that June by 1,000 members of the Rainbow Division who served under him in World War I. From left to right are Jean Kindley, Pat Hawkins, Lila Dean, and Mary Ellen Gleason. (Courtesy *Herald-Examiner* Collection, Los Angeles Public Library.)

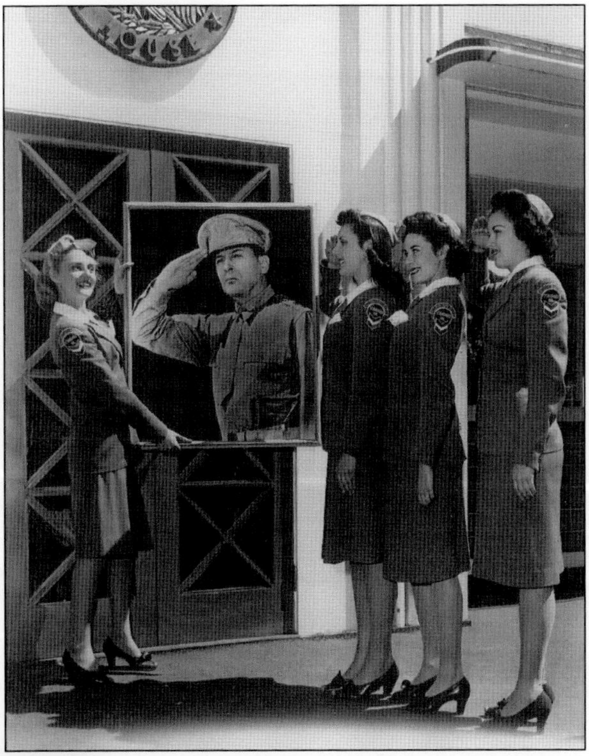

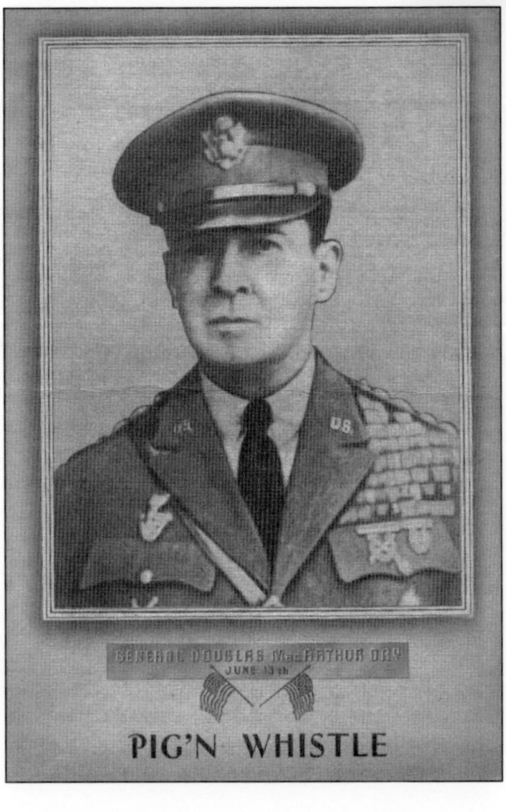

On June 13, 1942, Gen. Douglas MacArthur was celebrated, and the Pig 'N Whistle commemorated the event with a souvenir menu from the coffee shop on South Hill Street near Pershing Square. MacArthur tags (fund-raising buttons) were sold to raise money for the war effort, and leaflets were handed out with the following message: "Work! Fight! Give! Make Democracy live! Buy a MacArthur Tag and help put the Japanazis in the bag!"

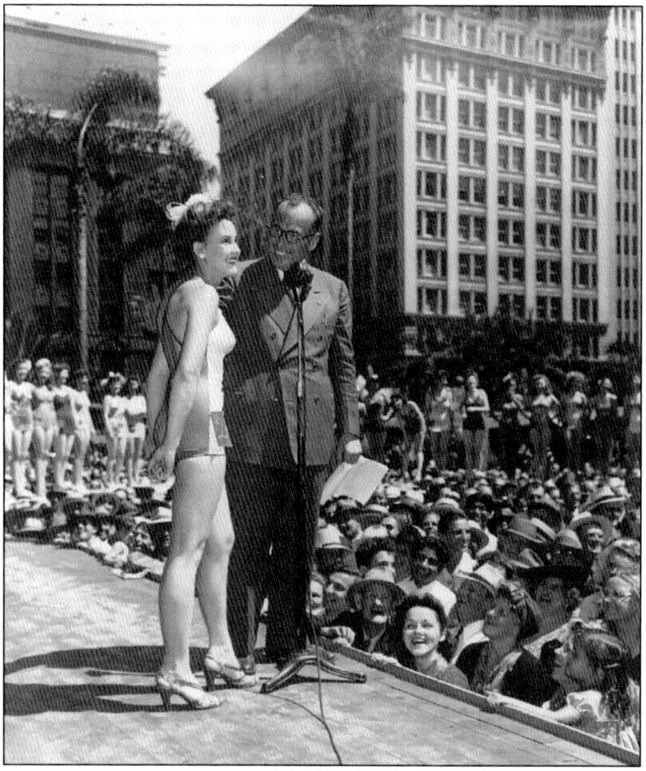

During World War II, Pershing Square hosted many events at Victory House to sell bonds and war tax stamps for the expensive war effort. On July 4, 1942, a beauty pageant to find "Miss Victory" was held. The Pig 'N Whistle coffee shop across the street was very popular during the war; it had an adjoining cocktail lounge called The Oasis and was frequented by soldiers and sailors passing through downtown Los Angeles. (Courtesy Ralph Morris/ Los Angeles Public Library.)

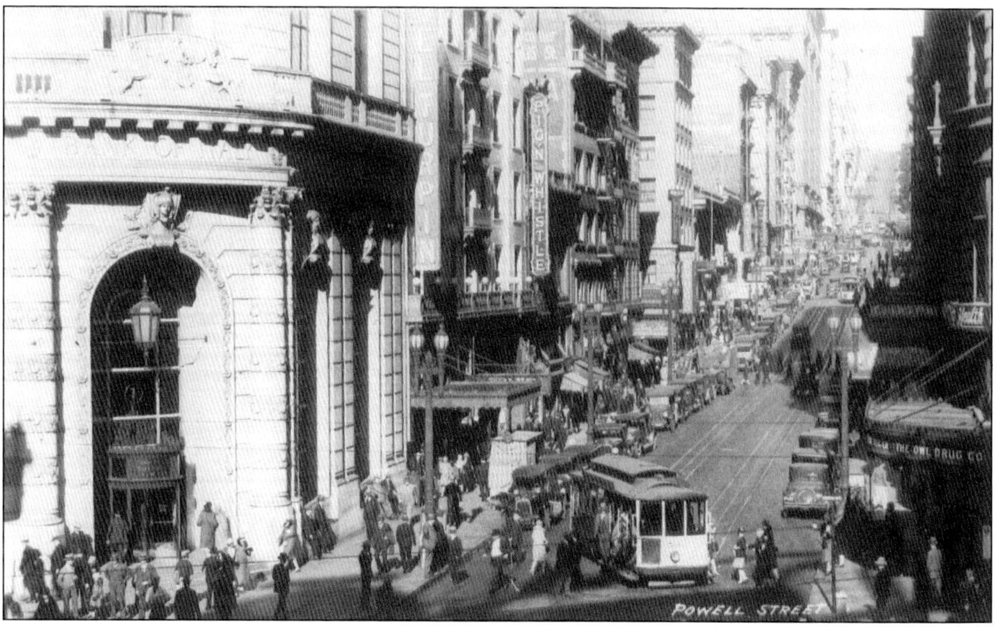

In the 1943 Edward Dmytryk film *Tender Comrade*, actress Kim Hunter is picked up by a soldier. When asked, "Where'd you meet him?" she replies, "On a street car about six months ago. We sat around the Pig 'N Whistle and he told me about his friends and about the army—and then he got kinda red and uncomfortable and he said let's go out and get some air . . . I don't have any appetite."

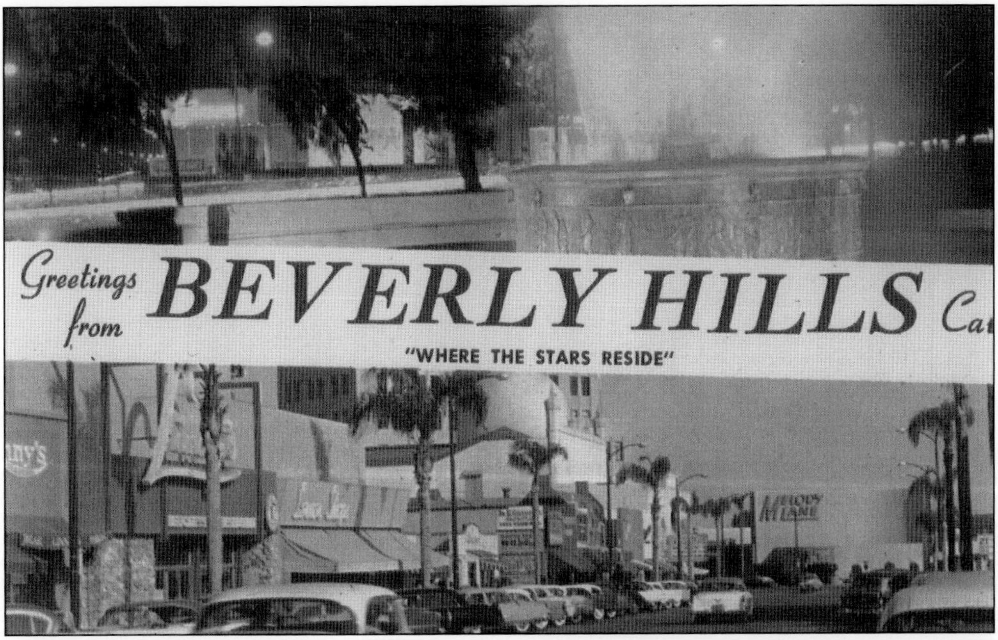

In 1946, ground was broken for another Wayne MacAllister–designed Melody Lane in Beverly Hills, the city "Where the Stars Reside." The property was owned by actor John Boles, and the *Hollywood Citizen-News* reported that the restaurant cost $400,000 to build. The restaurant was on the southeast corner of Wilshire Boulevard and Beverly Drive.

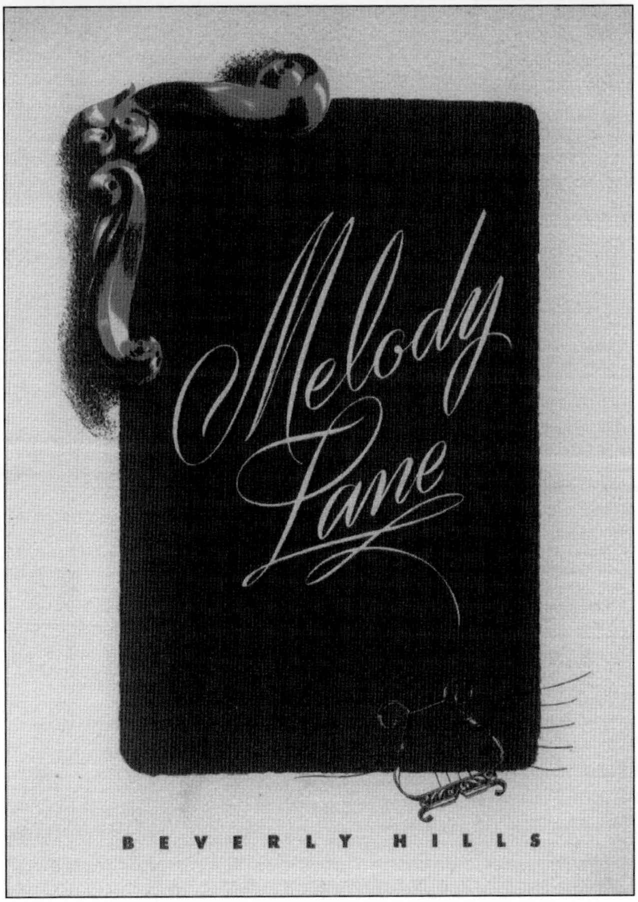

In 1952, the Melody Lane at 9454 Wilshire Boulevard in Beverly Hills was the newest and most popular of all the Melody Lane restaurants. Melody Lane Beverly Hills had a themed cocktail lounge named The Puppet Room, which was decorated with a number of marionettes hanging from the ceiling.

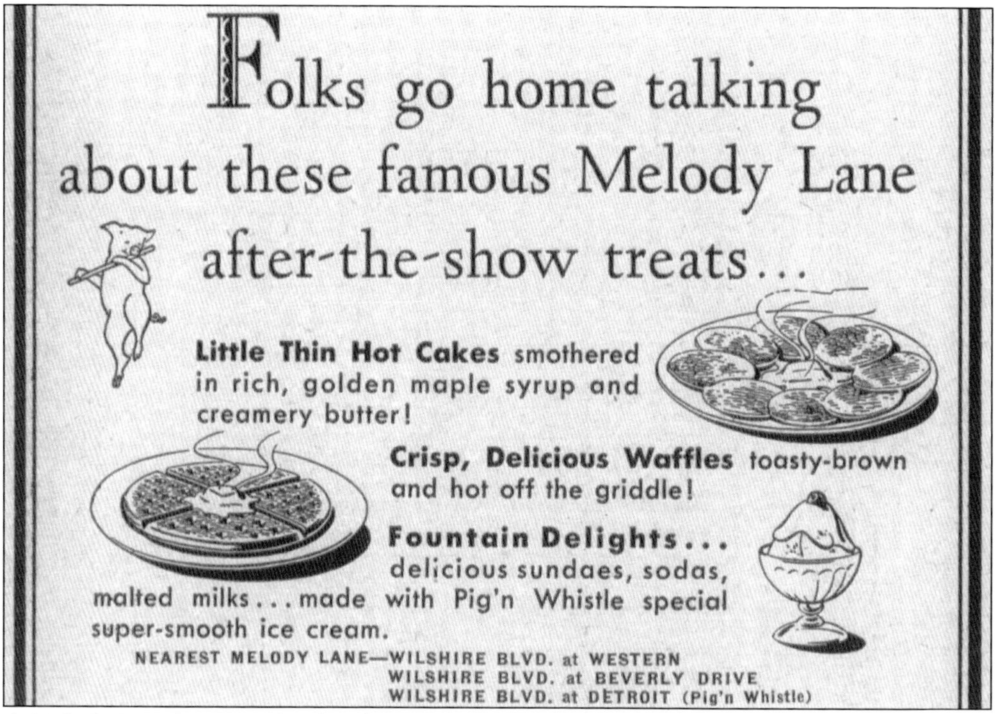

A Melody Lane/Pig 'N Whistle advertisement from 1948 advertises one of the most popular menu items: "Little thin hot cakes smothered in rich, golden maple syrup and creamery butter!" Breakfast items could be ordered all day by those seeing a late night show and wanting "crisp, delicious waffles toasty-brown and hot off the griddle!"

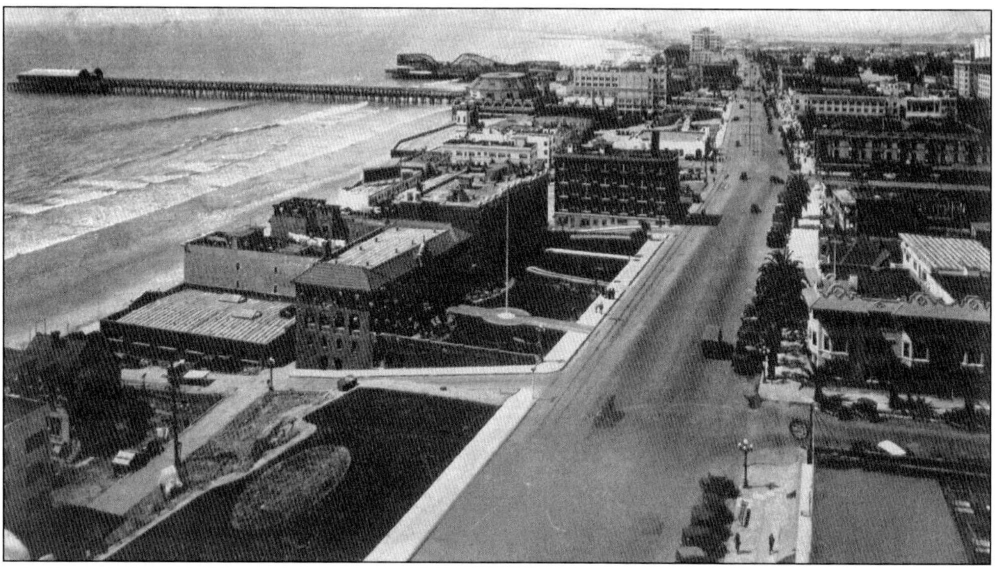

South of Los Angeles, the city of Long Beach became known as one of the biggest oil producers in the world. Sailors crowded the area during World War II, and it was the site of the Los Angeles air raid of 1942, when reports were made of shells being fired from the sea (it was later discovered that it was a false alarm). Melody Lane served the large naval population in the late 1940s and 1950s at its 252 East Ocean Boulevard location.

Six

Hollywood's Most Famous Corner

The intersection of Hollywood Boulevard and Vine Street became the epicenter for the entertainment industry during the 1930s and 1940s. In 1925, KFWB radio station was launched by Sam Warner and broadcast from Warner Bros. Studios on Sunset Boulevard. By 1928, the radio station moved to the roof of the Warner Theater at 6423 Hollywood Boulevard, and radio personalities mentioned that they were "live from Hollywood and Vine." Melody Lane and Pig 'N Whistle both advertised on KFWB, promoting, among other things, "Chef Pierre's Radio Specials."

The popular CBS Lux Radio Theater was located one block south on Vine Street, and the popular "Breakfast in Hollywood" radio show, which was broadcast live from Tom Breneman's restaurant, also emanated from Vine Street. This radio program was adapted into a Hollywood movie, *Breakfast in Hollywood*, in 1946 and starred Tom Breneman. There is a short scene that takes place right in front of the Melody Lane on Hollywood and Vine.

Hollywood and Vine was home to the second Brown Derby restaurant and the Hollywood Plaza Hotel, which had a Pig 'N Whistle restaurant. On the northwest corner, which was once the Richard Neutra–designed Laemmle Building (built as an office for Universal Pictures founder Carl Laemmle), architects S. Charles Lee and Wayne McAllister were called in to redesign the space for Melody Lane.

Sidney Hoedemaker left the Pig 'N Whistle Corporation in 1948 and soon after opened Hody's restaurant in the same space. The northwest corner of Hollywood and Vine had a huge billboard that advertisers had to reserve years in advance. It was one of the most expensive billboards in Hollywood and remained a fixture on Hollywood and Vine until 2008, when the building was destroyed by fire.

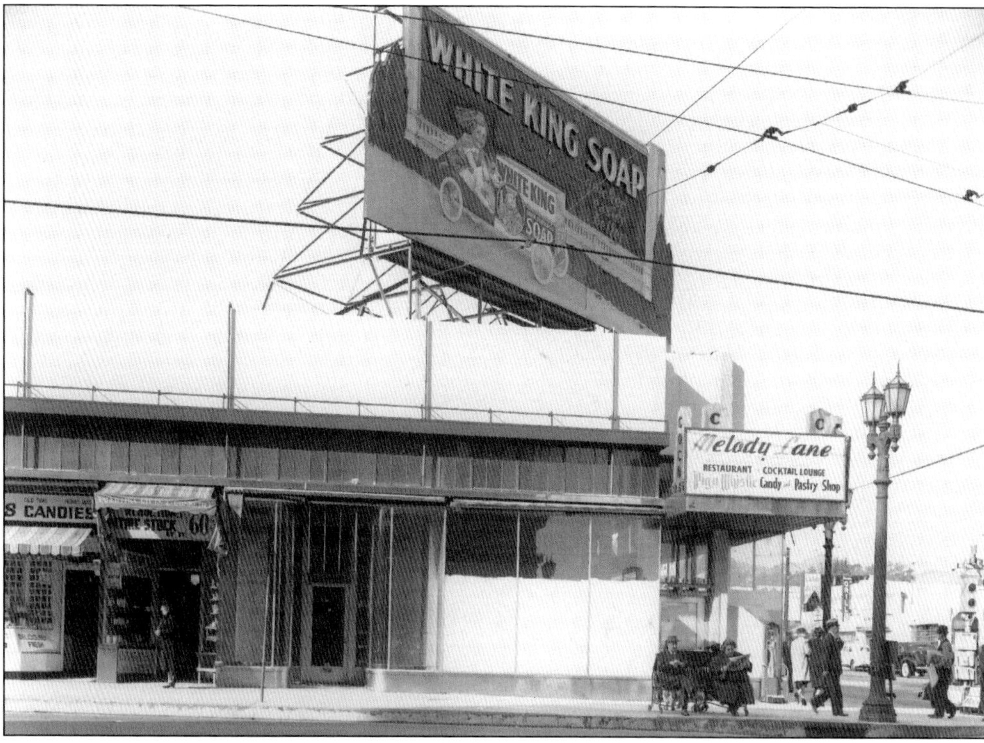

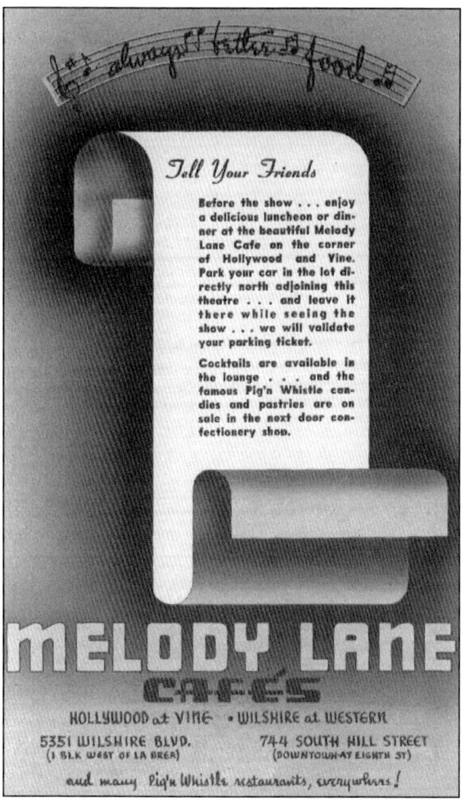

In 1939, the Coco Tree Café was on the northwest corner of Hollywood and Vine. The sign reads, "Melody Lane will occupy this corner soon with a beautiful restaurant and cocktail lounge." See's Candies and Valentina's Gifts and Cosmetics vacated the space for the remodel. (Courtesy Security Pacific National Bank Collection/Los Angeles Public Library.)

Melody Lane now had a restaurant on the two busiest intersections in Hollywood—Hollywood and Vine and Wilshire Boulevard and Western Avenue. The Hollywood and Vine location was completely remodeled in 1940. There were several theaters nearby: the Pantages, built in 1930, was down the street at Hollywood Boulevard and Argyle Street, and the Vine Street Theatre (later the CBS Radio Playhouse) was at 1615 Vine Street.

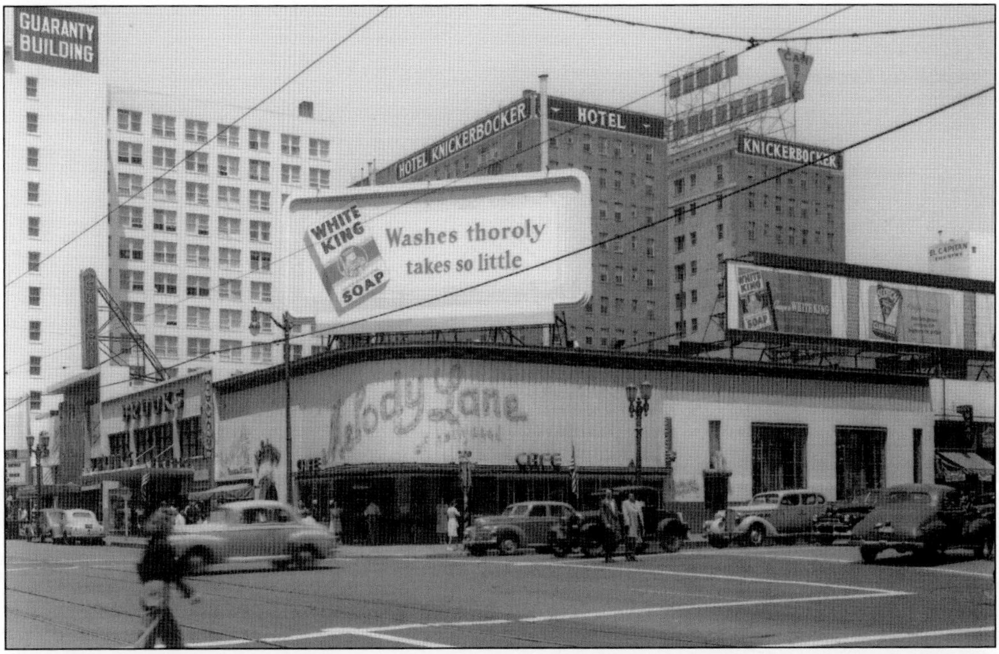

The Hotel Knickerbocker can be seen here behind Melody Lane in 1943; it was built in 1925 and enjoyed a colorful history with the film industry before being turned into a retirement home in 1970. The Pig 'N Whistle neon sign is on the left, and Chi-Chi, the newest addition to the chain, is seen next door. (Courtesy Bison Archives.)

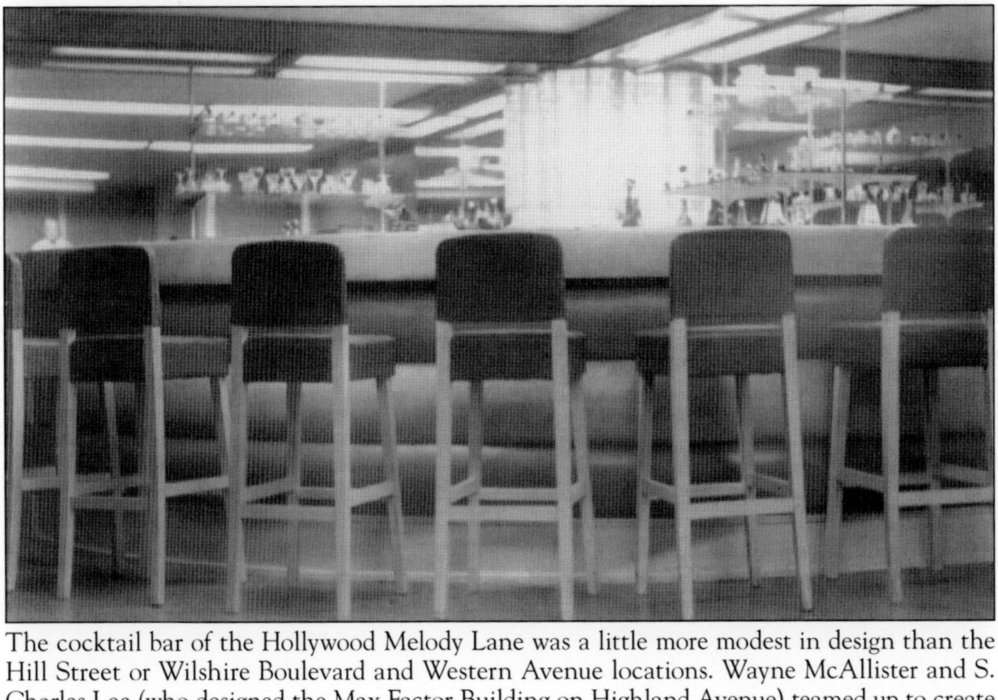

The cocktail bar of the Hollywood Melody Lane was a little more modest in design than the Hill Street or Wilshire Boulevard and Western Avenue locations. Wayne McAllister and S. Charles Lee (who designed the Max Factor Building on Highland Avenue) teamed up to create a rounded exterior, thoroughly erasing all traces of the original Richard Neutra design. (Courtesy Chris Nichols.)

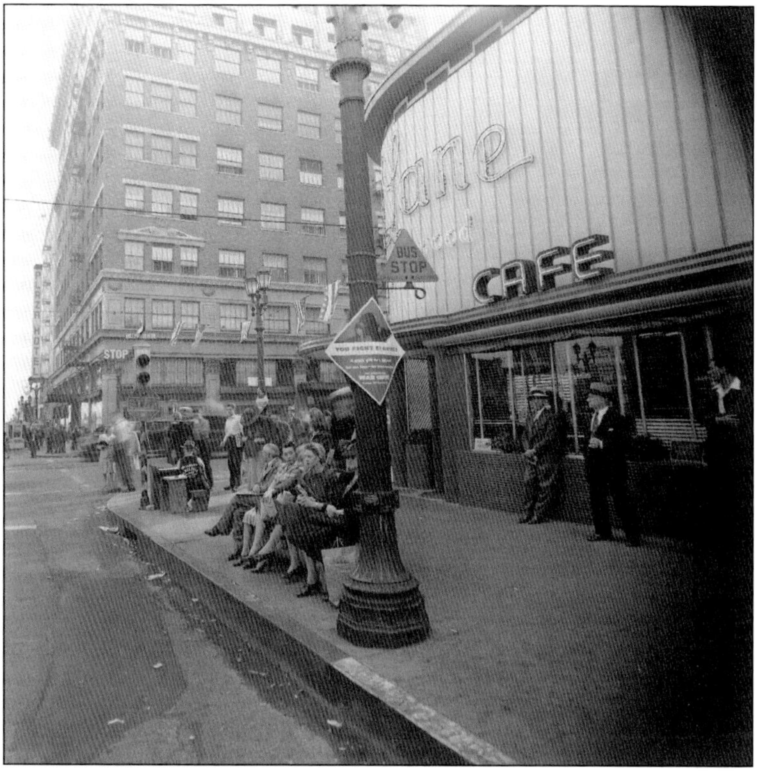

A shot of the exterior of Melody Lane on Hollywood and Vine shows a group of people waiting for a bus. The *Hotel Gazette* magazine from 1941 described Melody Lane as "one of the most handsome restaurants in the United States; the walls in the dining room are painted a rich blue, and the ceiling is rose tone. The draperies are in eggshell and rose and the carpeting is blue." (Courtesy Bison Archives.)

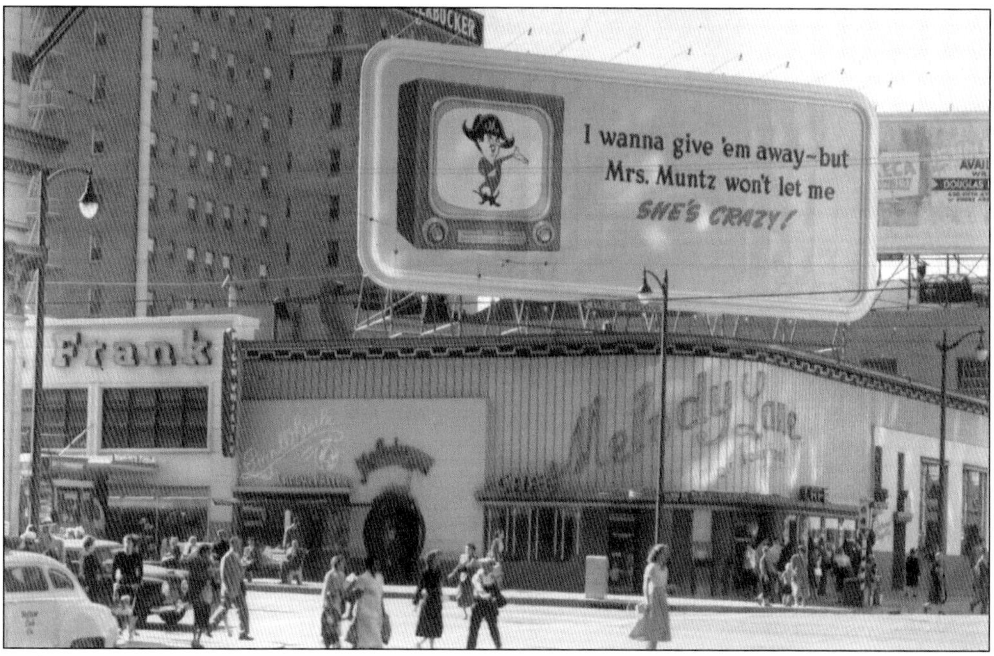

Earl William "Madman" Muntz was a salesman and inventor who starred in his own commercials and sold everything from cars to televisions. He employed stunts like mailing out television knobs with a card that read, "Call us and we'll show up with the rest of the set!" He was also known for his unusual costumes and sales pitches from the 1930s through the 1980s.

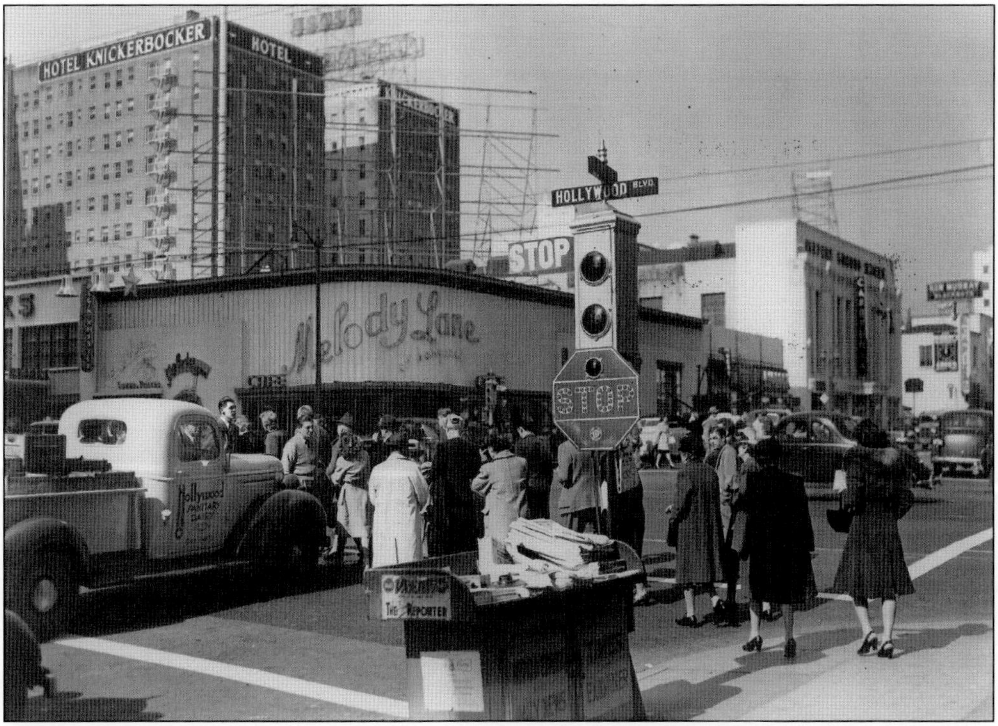

In this 1943 photograph, there is an unusual absence of a billboard over Melody Lane. The intersection is crowded with pedestrians and cars, as a Hollywood Sanitary Dairy truck is pulled up into the crosswalk. A newsstand in the foreground is selling all the major papers of the day. (Courtesy Bison Archives.)

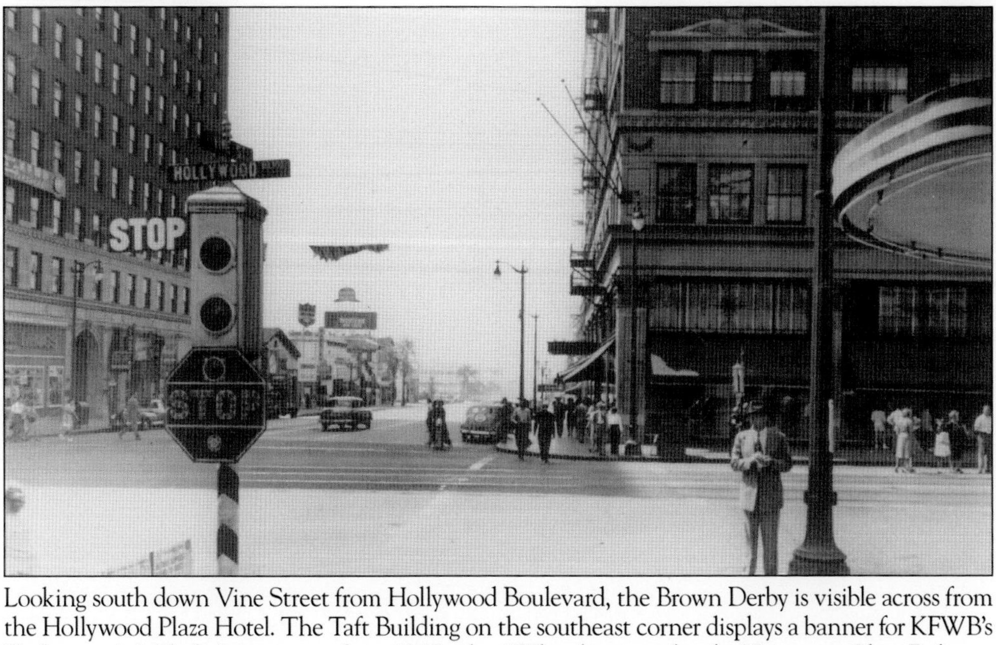

Looking south down Vine Street from Hollywood Boulevard, the Brown Derby is visible across from the Hollywood Plaza Hotel. The Taft Building on the southeast corner displays a banner for KFWB's Flashcast. A Melody Lane menu from 1948 asks, "What happened today? Listen to Clete Roberts, nationally famous news commentator, KFWB 6:00 P.M. nightly." (Courtesy Bison Archives.)

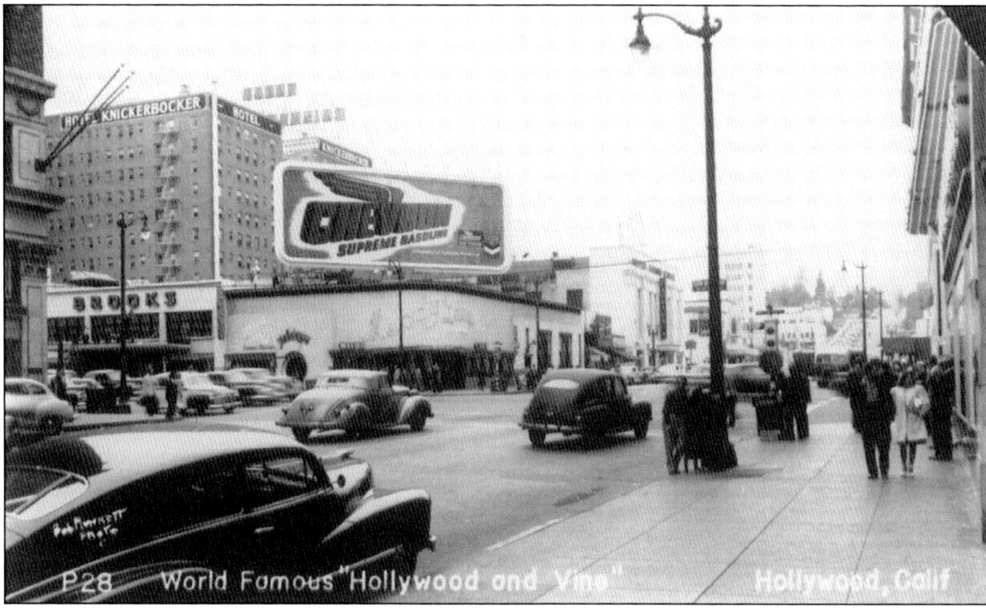

In yet another perspective, this view of Melody Lane is from the southeast corner of Hollywood and Vine. The Hotel Knickerbocker, Brooks clothing store, and the Dan-Dee shoe shop can be seen as well as an advertisement for Ken Murray's Blackouts playing at the El Capitan Theatre. Chevron gas is occupying the billboard; this famous landmark was destroyed by fire in 2008.

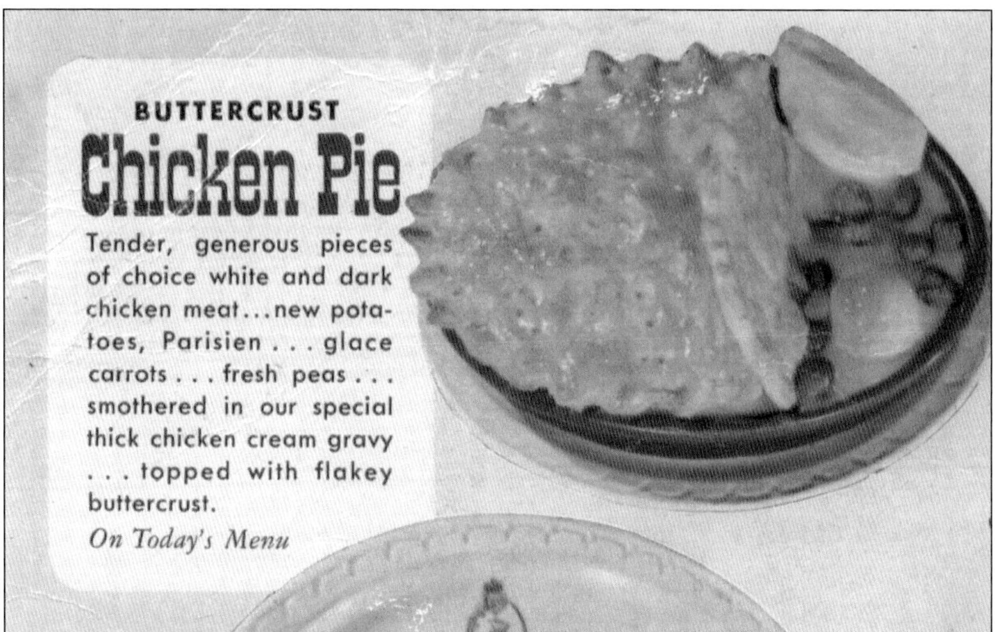

A staple on the Pig 'N Whistle menu since the restaurant's early days, the chicken pot pie is featured on a specials card from 1948. Today's Pig 'N Whistle menu has not forgotten this classic favorite; Alain Hajjar and Chris Breed have introduced a modern version of the chicken pot pie, with tender chicken breast and sautéed vegetables in a béchamel sauce topped with puff pastry.

This unidentified model was used in a variety of ads for Melody Lane and Pig 'N Whistle in the 1940s. Her uniform was worn by all Melody Lane/Pig 'N Whistle waitresses. In this ad, the reader is assured that "mothers like these dietetically correct nutritious meals—priced most moderately." From 1944, the advertisement also bears the "Buy Victory Bonds" stamp.

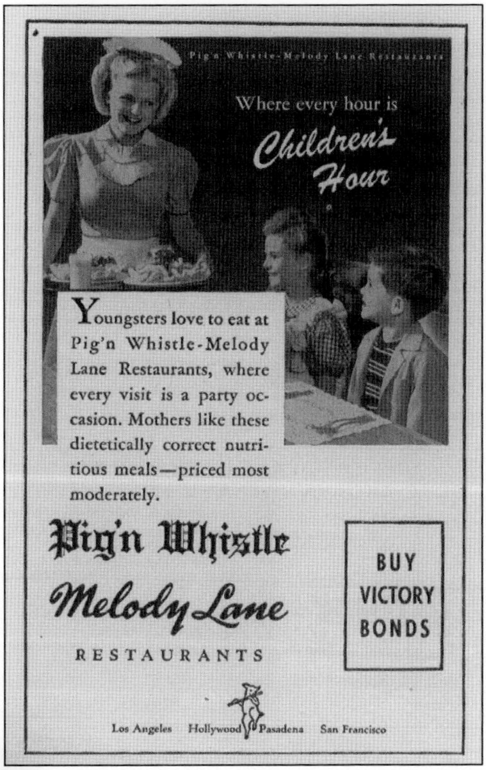

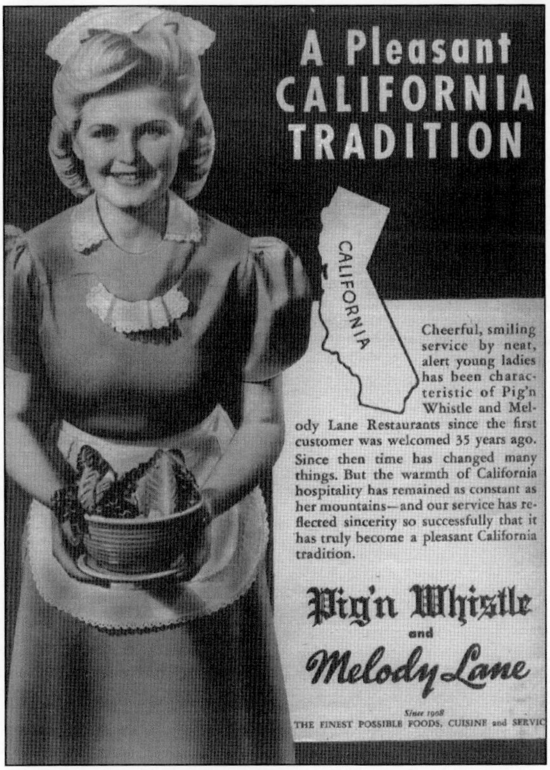

The same model is seen here in 1943; by this time the Seattle shop had been closed for five years, and Pig 'N Whistle was exclusively Californian. The advertisement promises "cheerful smiling service by neat, alert young ladies." Sidney Hoedemaker himself made sure that a "higher type of woman" was employed by his company.

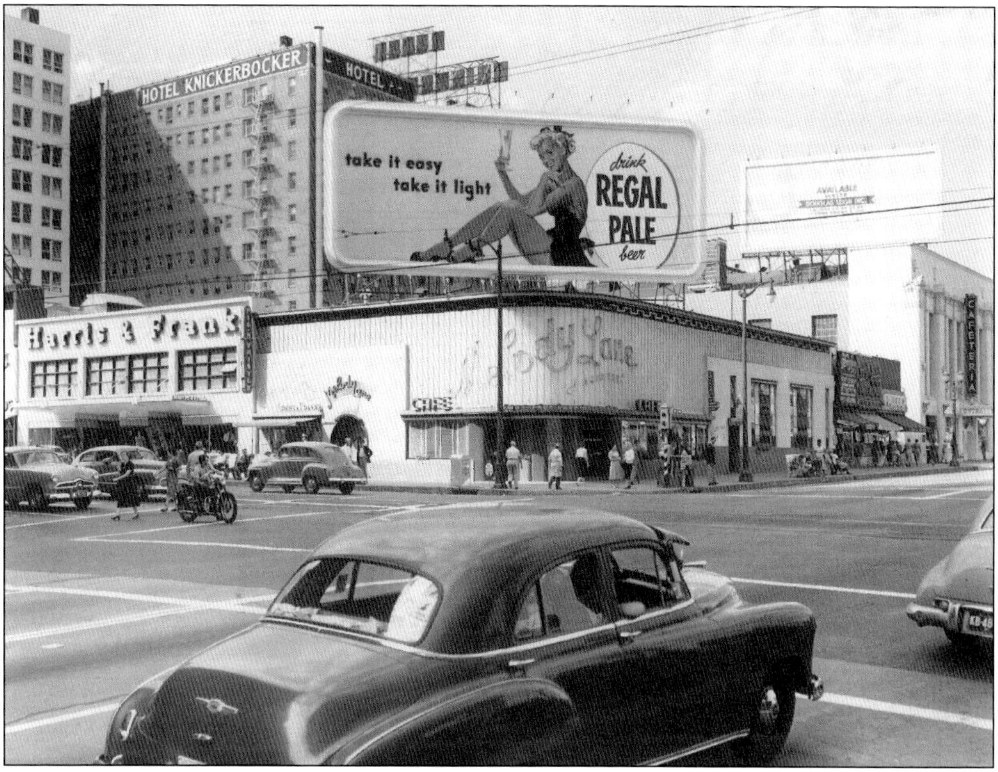

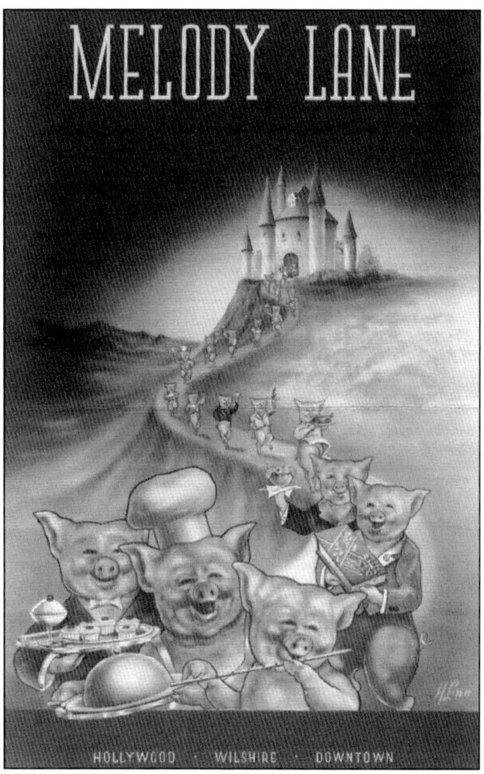

By 1951, Sidney Hoedemaker had moved on from the Pig 'N Whistle Corporation and started Hody's Family Restaurants. The Hollywood Melody Lane would remain open for a few more years before it closed and became a Hody's. The Brooks clothing store is gone and replaced by a speciality men's shop, Harris and Frank. The Regal Pale Ale girl is featured on the coveted billboard. (Courtesy Bison Archives.)

A wartime Melody Lane menu from 1943 advises, "Drastic rationing of ice creams, etc. compelled us to curtail our desert service." This was mailed and inscribed, "I was in the city. We had lunch at this place and picked this up to mail to you so you would not forget Melody Lane on Vine Street Hollywood. However ice cream is hard to get. A Burns' malted is only a dream."

With the addition of the Chi-Chi in 1947, all three restaurants were sharing the same H. Linn design. These menus were mailed free of charge to anyone handing it in to a hostess while dining, serving as an impromptu postcard. A 1945 message to Sgt. Weldon Lewis was inscribed, "My Darling. Just got the word. Your name was in the returns . . . Praise the Lord!" Another menu from 1940 read, "Dear Mother. Yesterday was election day in Los Angeles so Della went out with a group to celebrate. Instead of preparing dinner, I had it here. I had German fixed beef . . . it's called Sauerbraten. I'm not too wild about it tho. . . ." Another letter from Hollywood also mentioned the Brown Derby, which was a block away from Melody Lane: "Hi Sis! Having scads of fun. Had lunch here just before going down to CBS to hear Harry James. Of course you should know that Oggie and I could not pass up the Brown Derby, so that is where I'm dropping this line from!"

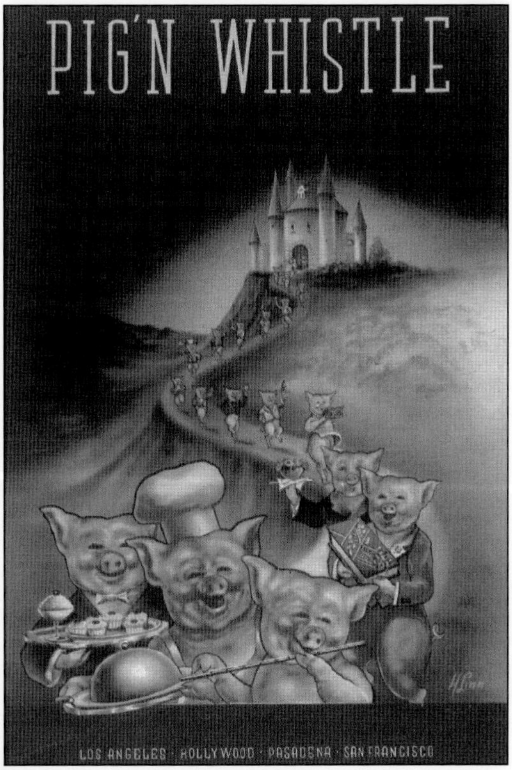

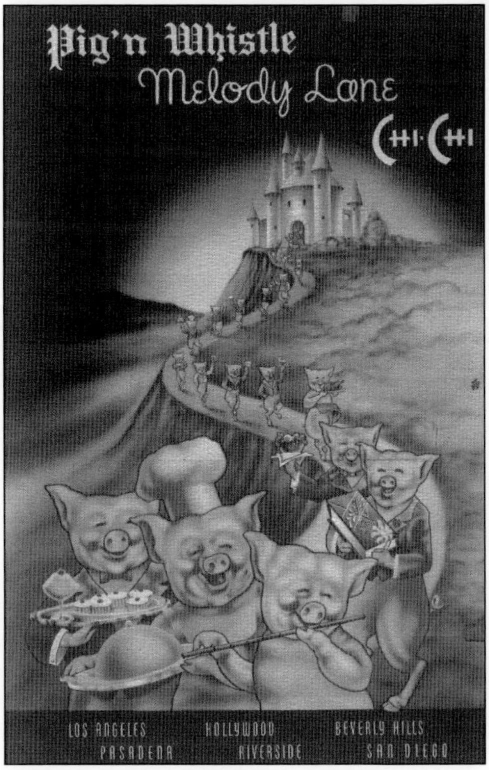

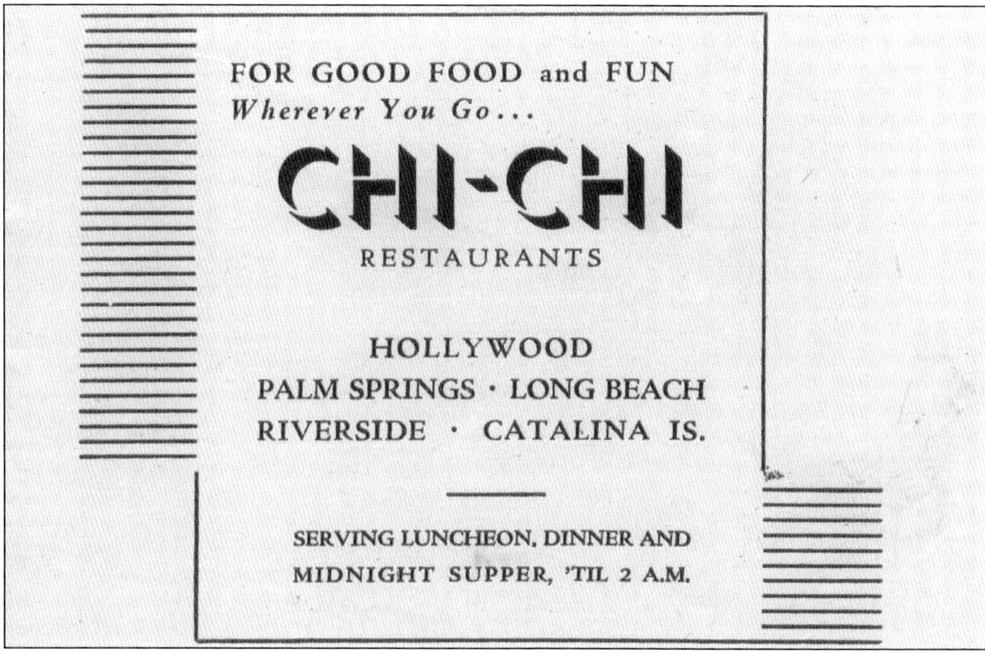

Chi-Chi was the third and final restaurant concept from the Pig 'N Whistle Corporation. A more exclusive dining experience, Chi-Chi did not cater to children like its counterparts. There were Chi-Chi restaurants from Catalina Island to Palm Springs. The Chi-Chi in Hollywood was at 6315 Hollywood Boulevard next door to Melody Lane on Vine Street.

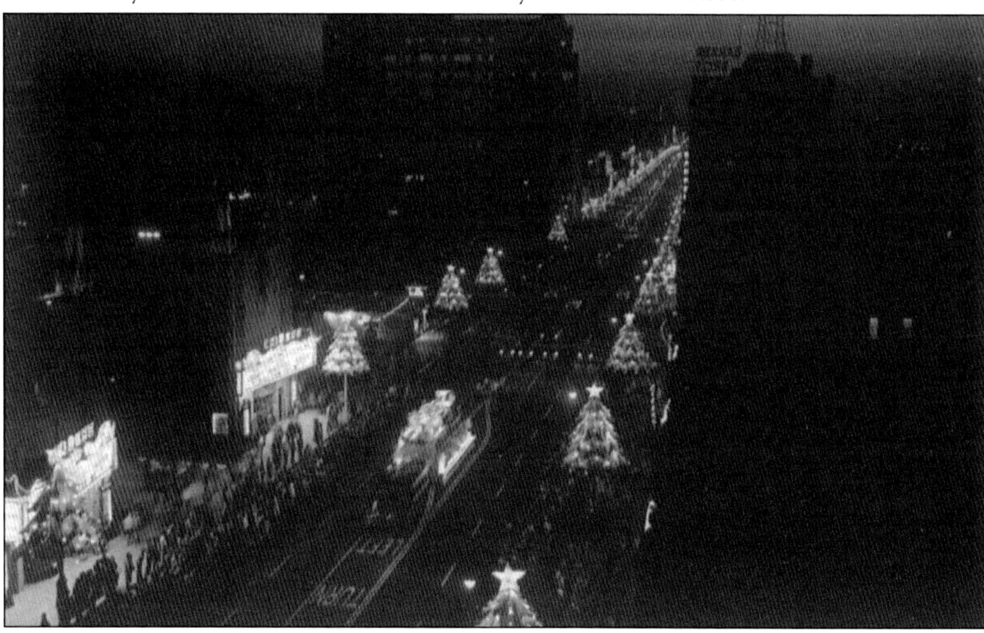

This postcard image shows the Santa Claus Lane Parade on Hollywood Boulevard in 1943. It began in 1928 as the smallest Christmas parade ever—one actress, Santa, and some live reindeer. By the 1930s and 1940s, it was considerably larger and had stars like Bette Davis, Gene Autry, and Mary Pickford lending their star power. The parade still runs today, though it is now known as the Hollywood Christmas Parade.

From Christmas 1946, this Pig 'N Whistle/Melody Lane newspaper advertisement features the same blonde model from previous Pig 'N Whistle advertising. It is interesting to see that there were 1,233 employees working for the chain at the time. (Courtesy Chris Nichols.)

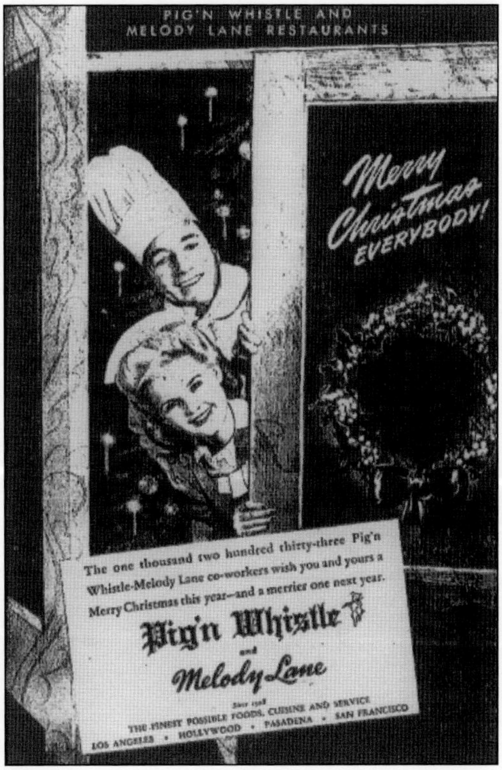

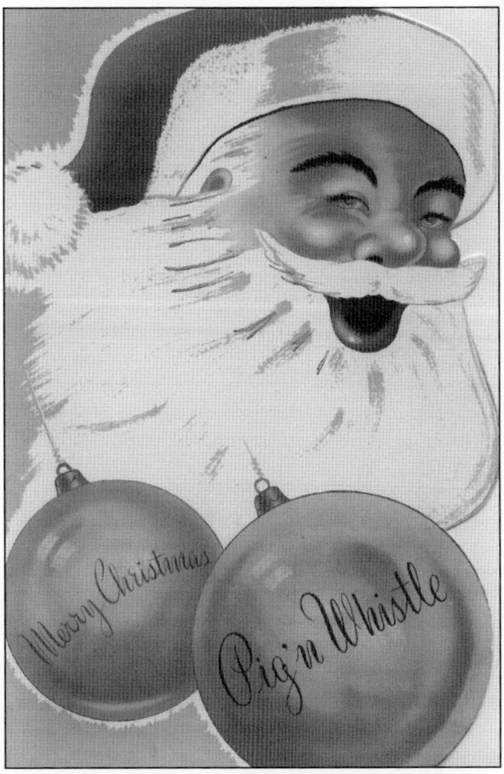

After watching the Santa Claus Lane Parade, a Christmas shopper could stop in and have dinner for a dollar. This Santa Claus menu from 1953 has a choice of roast young tom turkey, baked Virginia ham, or grilled top sirloin steak accompanied by candied sweet potatoes, a Bartlett pear, and hot mince pie.

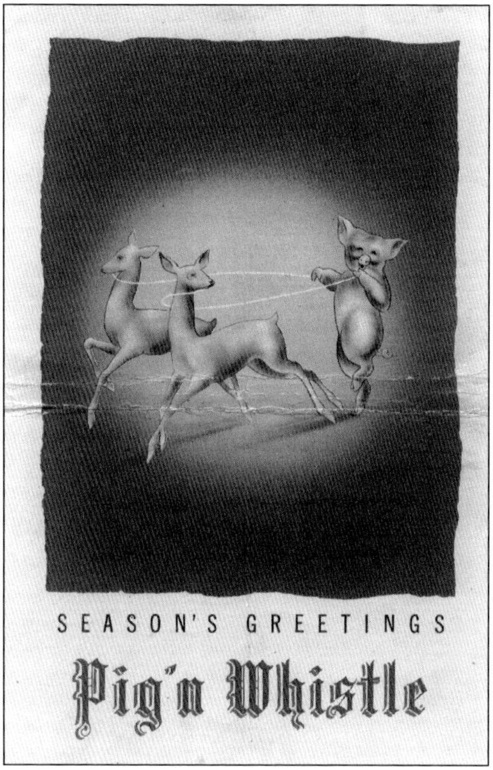

A pair of Christmas menus from 1941 and 1942 used a special silk-screened image of the pig and two reindeers. Christmas 1941 was especially hard for many Americans; soldiers and sailors were shipped out and did not get to celebrate the holiday at all. Those left at home were missing their loved ones and praying for their safe return. The Pig 'N Whistle menu is dated Sunday, December 28, 1941; the events at Pearl Harbor had occurred just three weeks before. This menu already bears the "Buy Victory Bonds for Defense" logo that was seen on all Pig 'N Whistle/Melody Lane menus through 1945. The menu selections are modest: flaked turkey a la king or lamb chops and minced chicken croquettes or buttered spaghetti.

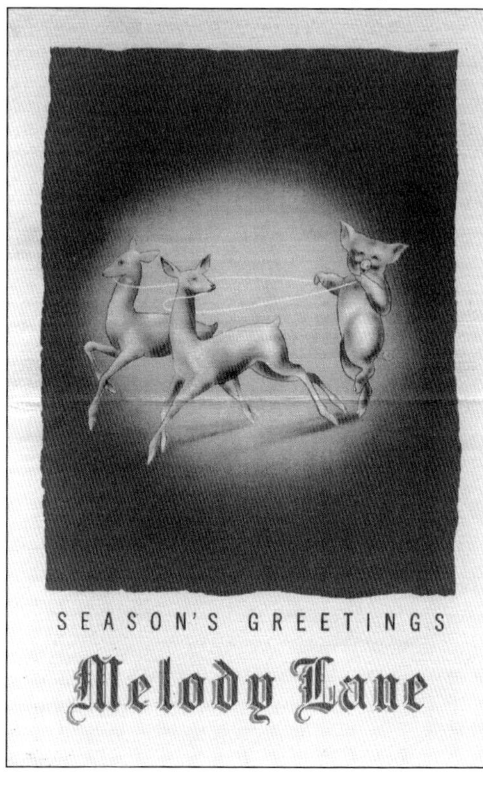

Another holiday that had a specially designed menu was Easter. The pig on this 1947 menu is dressed in shorts and wearing an Easter top hat while painting a brightly colored egg. The Pig 'N Whistle also made beautiful Easter candy boxes shaped like giant eggs made from California pottery. They were packaged in big yellow boxes adorned with dancing lambs and rabbits and nestled in Easter grass.

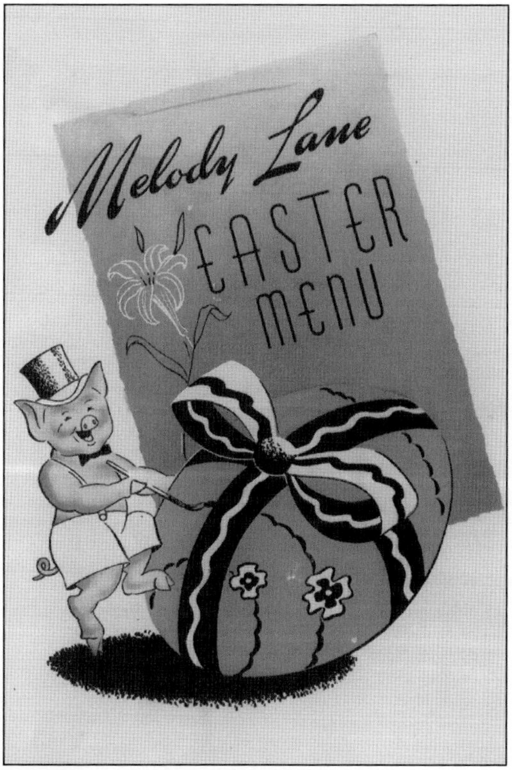

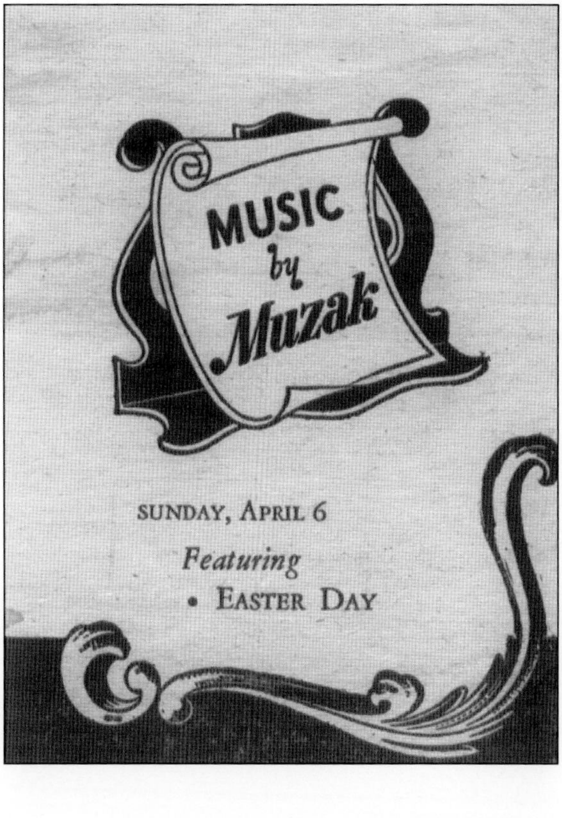

The Melody Lane menu for Easter Sunday, April 6, 1947, included this Muzak program. Again Sidney Hoedemaker had another first for Los Angeles by putting Muzak in his restaurants back in 1941. This program included the song's title and exact time that it would be played. "It Had To Be You," "California Sunbeam," "Bet Your Bottom Dollar," "Someone's Rocking My Dreamboat," "Easter Parade," and "For Sentimental Reasons" were among the selections.

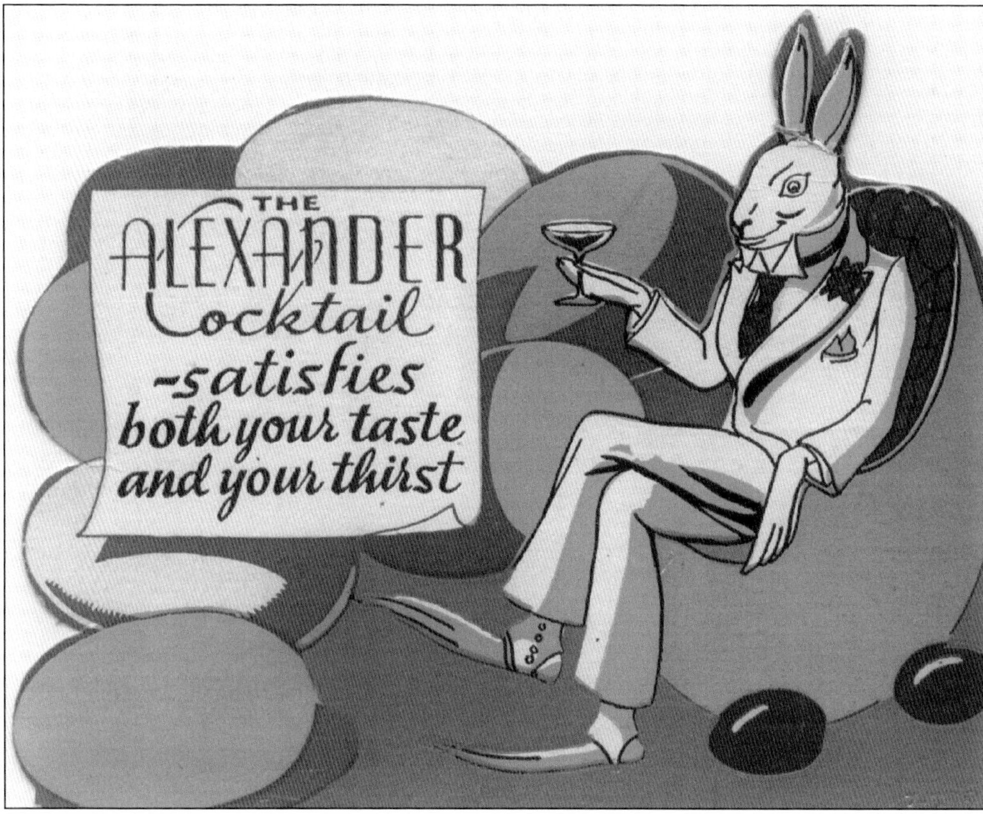

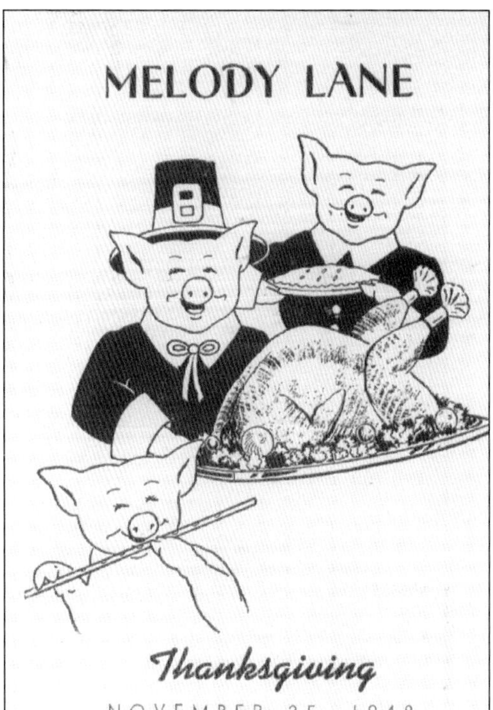

An Easter bunny enjoys an Alexander cocktail at Melody Lane. The Alexander had gin, crème de cacao, and cream. A beautiful metallic-painted tent card like this was found on all the cocktail tables in the lounge. The bunny is dressed in his Easter finery, down to his white spats. The jelly bean chair he is sitting in is influenced by the new modern design in furniture around 1947.

This Melody Lane Thanksgiving menu from November 25, 1948 has a deluxe dinner for $2, which included a glass of port or sherry. The 130 Post Street address for the San Francisco Pig 'N Whistle is listed on the back as the oldest continually running shop—it had been part of the chain for almost 40 years.

Seven

Hody's, the 1950s, and Beyond

After World War II ended, urban areas were abandoned by many American families for newly built suburbs with affordable housing and open space to raise families. The automobile was king in the 1950s. Cars were affordable, drive-in movies and large family restaurants became popular, and television also changed habits. There was no need to go to the crowded, smoggy city when families could enjoy entertainment from their living room.

The dawn of the fast-food era prodded Sidney Hoedemaker to leave the Pig 'N Whistle Corporation in 1948 and open a new restaurant that would fit the needs of the changing demographics. He started Hody's Family Restaurant in Baldwin Hills on La Brea Avenue and Rodeo Road in 1949. The location was near a planned community called the Village Green, which was built in 1942 and designed for families with automobiles. Another Hody's soon opened in the San Fernando Valley, and by the 1950s and 1960s, Hoedemaker had opened eight restaurants. Pig 'N Whistle and Melody Lane kept only a few stores open, and most were closed by the end of the 1940s. Melody Lane was gone by 1955, and by 1968, there were only two Pig 'N Whistles left. The ornate designs, the pipe organ music, and the old-fashioned sundaes all seemed like relics from the past.

In 2001, nightclub impresario Chris Breed and partner Alain Hajjar renovated and reopened the famous Hollywood Pig 'N Whistle that adjoins the Egyptian Theatre. The pair already enjoyed success with their exclusive supper club, Sunset Room, which opened in 1998 and enjoyed a five-year run. 2001 also saw the opening of the Kodak Theatre, the new home for the Academy Awards ceremony, nearby at Hollywood Boulevard and Highland Avenue. All eyes were on Hollywood again, and the celebrities that had been absent for so many years had now returned. The Pig 'N Whistle once again has become the focal point of a new Hollywood renaissance, and the glamour of Hollywood's Golden Age has returned.

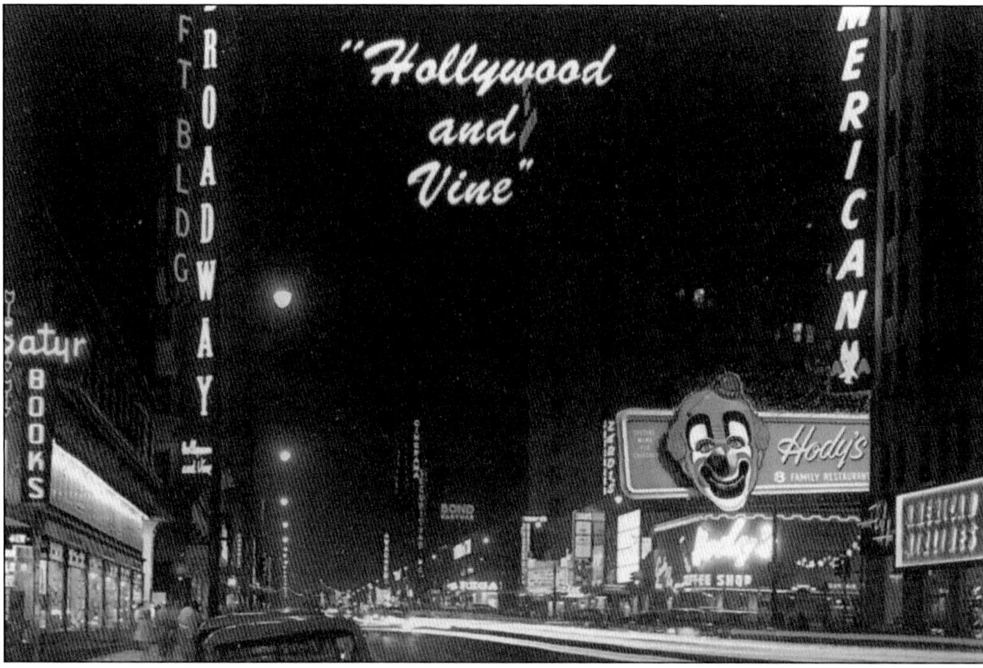

The Hollywood and Vine Melody Lane went out of business in 1955, and Sidney Hoedemaker quickly reclaimed the famous corner for Hody's. He had already opened several successful Hody's restaurants by this time, and the corner at Hollywood and Vine was still a hot property. (Courtesy Chris Nichols.)

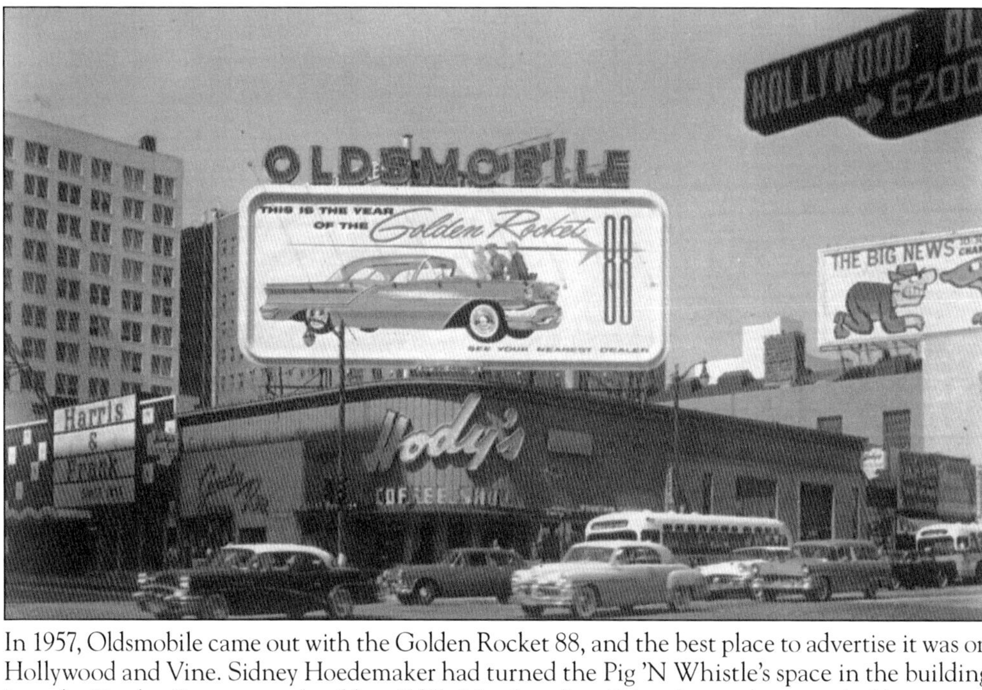

In 1957, Oldsmobile came out with the Golden Rocket 88, and the best place to advertise it was on Hollywood and Vine. Sidney Hoedemaker had turned the Pig 'N Whistle's space in the building into the Garden Room, a cocktail bar. Eddie Hoedemaker, Sidney's grandson, worked his way up to manager of this Hody's location by the time he was 18 years old. (Courtesy Chris Nichols.)

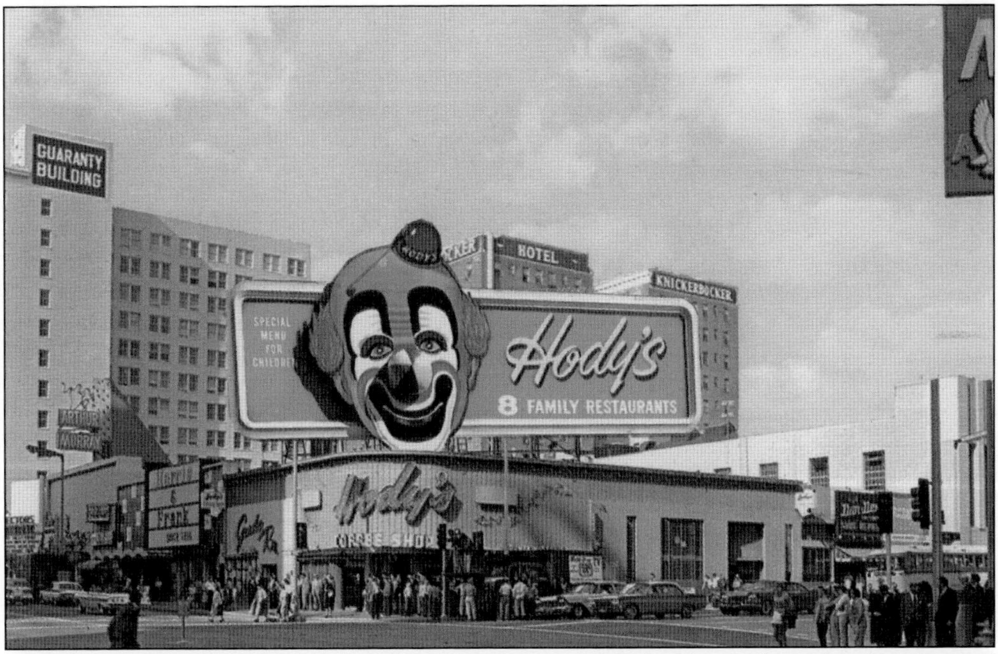

In this postcard view, Hody's has the billboard spot on top of the building, a feat Sidney Hoedemaker never accomplished with Melody Lane. The Hody's billboard clown had a giant inflated plastic nose. A crowd gathers in front for the filming of a television commercial. The Arthur Murray Dance School is in the spot Chi-Chi once held, and the Dan-Dee shoe store is still in business. (Courtesy Chris Nichols.)

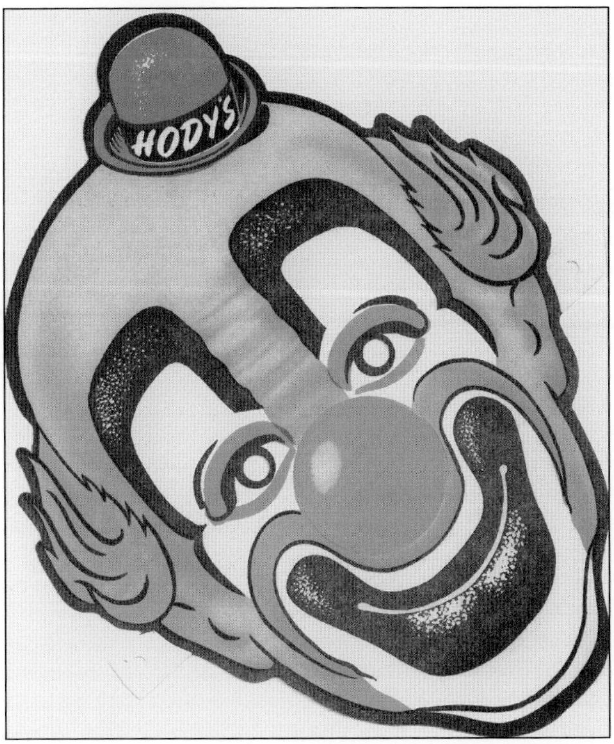

The Hody's clown mascot predated the McDonald's clown, but was most likely inspired by Bozo the Clown, who was a Capitol Records star just a few steps away on Vine Street. Capitol Records released a book and record set called *Bozo at the Circus* in 1946; he quickly became the Capitol Records mascot and was known as "Bozo the Capitol Records Clown." By 1949, Bozo had a program on KTTV-LA. This Hody's mask doubles as a kid's menu, like the Pig 'N Whistle had done years before. (Courtesy Chris Nichols.)

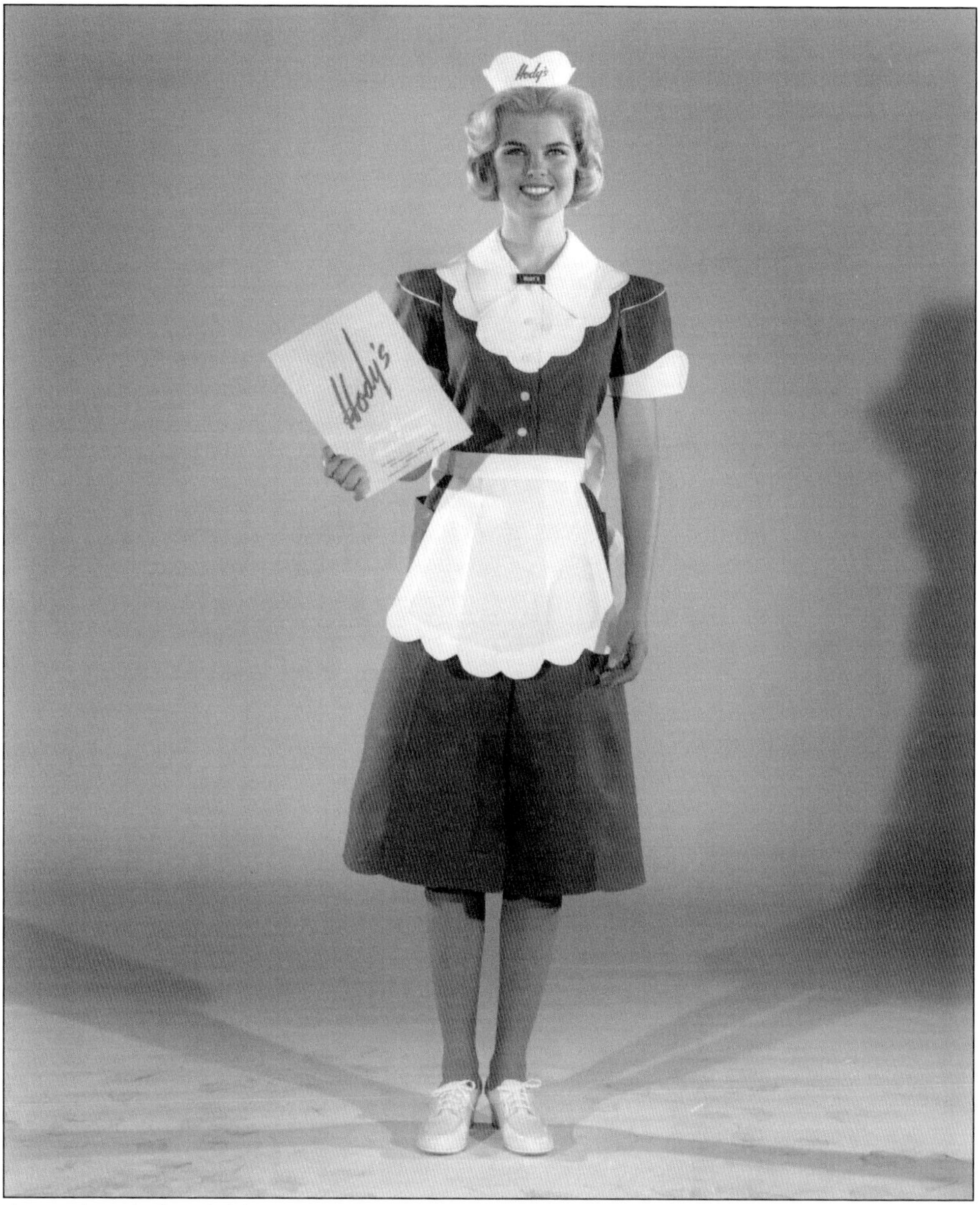

An unidentified model demonstrates what the Hody's uniform should look like: a crisply starched tiara, collar, cuffs, and tea apron; comfortable white nurse's shoes; a name tag symmetrically placed in the center of the collar; and a big smile. "In the old days," Sidney Hoedemaker said in a 1964 issue of *Cooking For Profit*, "a waitress was regarded as a hash-slinger—and this reputation was often justified. Today, we find that a better type, a more impressive woman is serving as waitress. This is because we have eliminated the extra steps, the heavy lifting, and other difficult aspects of restaurant work. We provide neat, comfortable uniforms the girls are proud to wear. Another consideration is that the day when a tyrannical chef ruled the kitchen is gone. Not uncommon 40 or 50 years ago was an obnoxious and dictatorial manner on the part of the chef. With the elimination of this situation, a higher type of girl has come to the restaurant industry to work." (Courtesy Security Pacific National Bank Collection/Los Angeles Public Library.)

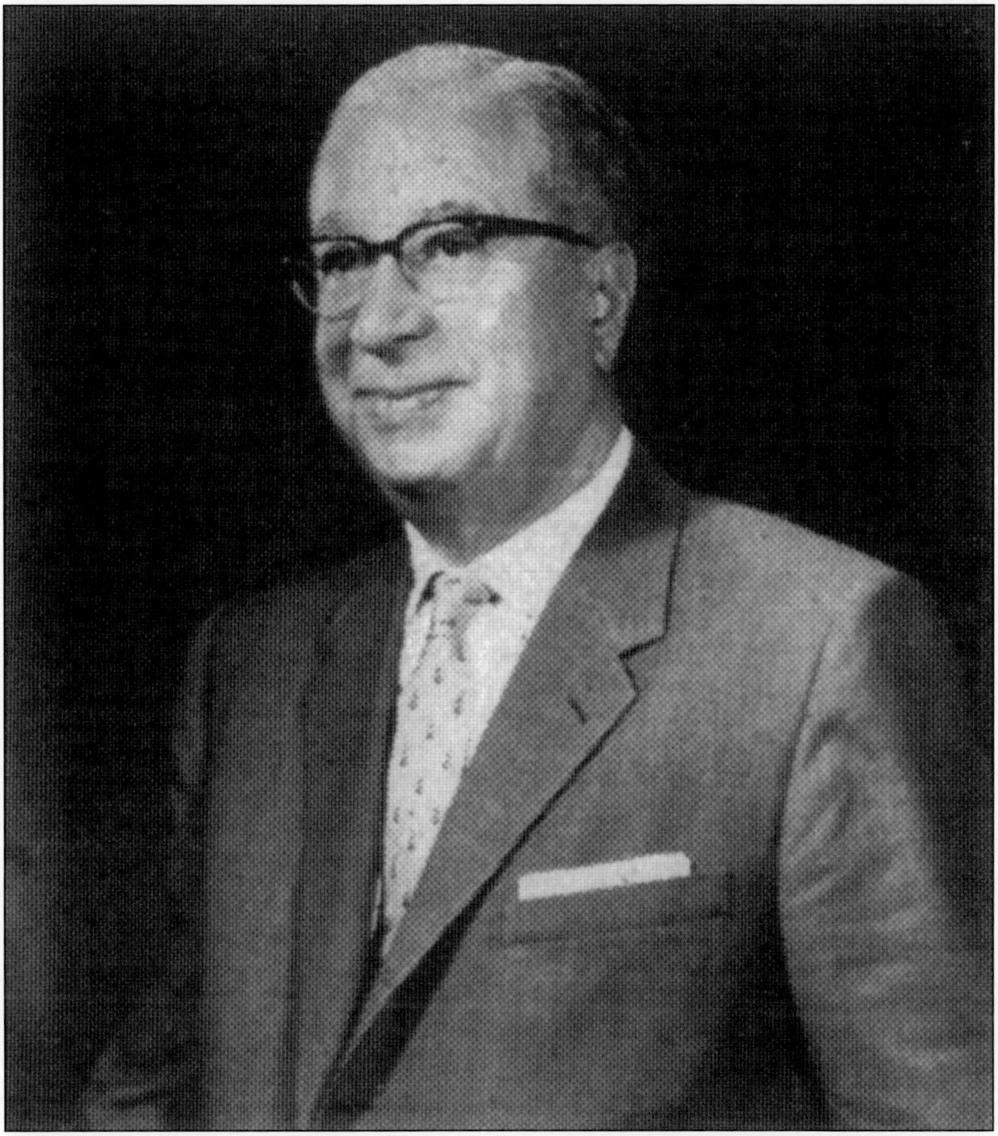

Sidney Hoedemaker contributed many ideas to the evolution of the restaurant industry. One of his concepts was the notion of atmosphere. He felt that atmosphere was more than decorations or furnishings, but the overall impression given by the restaurant: "Every new patron coming into a restaurant has a 'show me' attitude or even a chip on his shoulder regarding the restaurant," he said in *Cooking for Profit*. "The first impression the new patron gets upon entering the establishment is highly important. Is he greeted promptly, courteously, and with a smile? Is he treated as if his presence there is welcome and even as if he is someone special? A courteous, diplomatic, and smiling host or hostess can do a lot toward winning the confidence and respect of the new customer." (Courtesy Eddie Hoedemaker.)

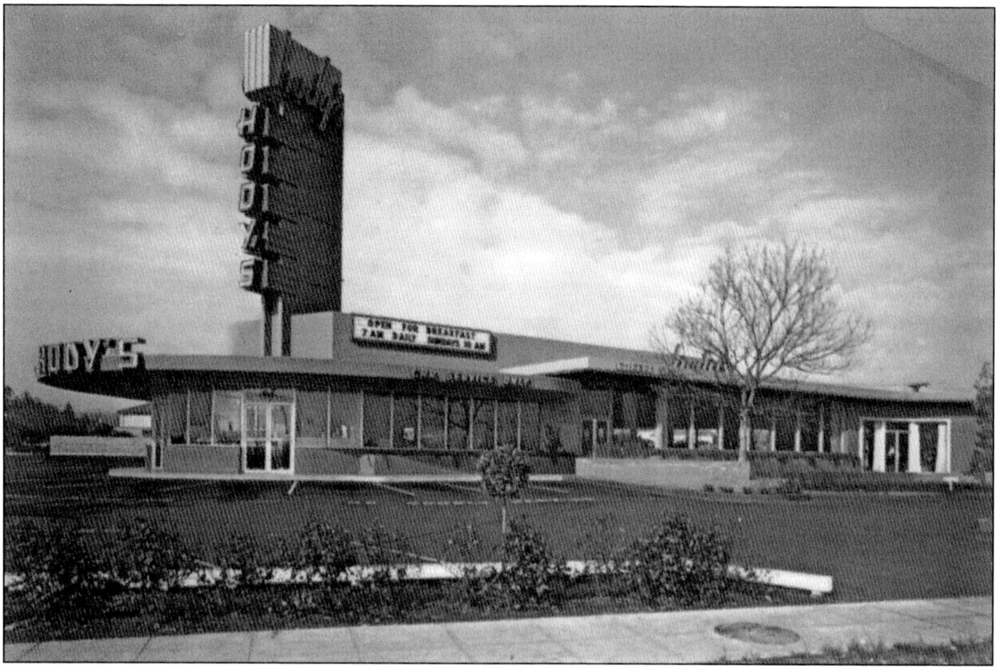

Wayne McAllister teamed up with Sidney Hoedemaker again in 1949 for Hody's first restaurant, built at 3553 South La Brea Avenue. It had a built-in cocktail lounge called the Garden Room and, like all of Hody's Family Restaurants, plenty of free parking. The South La Brea Avenue location was so popular that Hoedemaker opened a Hody's Cafeteria across the street at 3601 South La Brea Avenue, which was designed for take-out food only. (Courtesy Chris Nichols.)

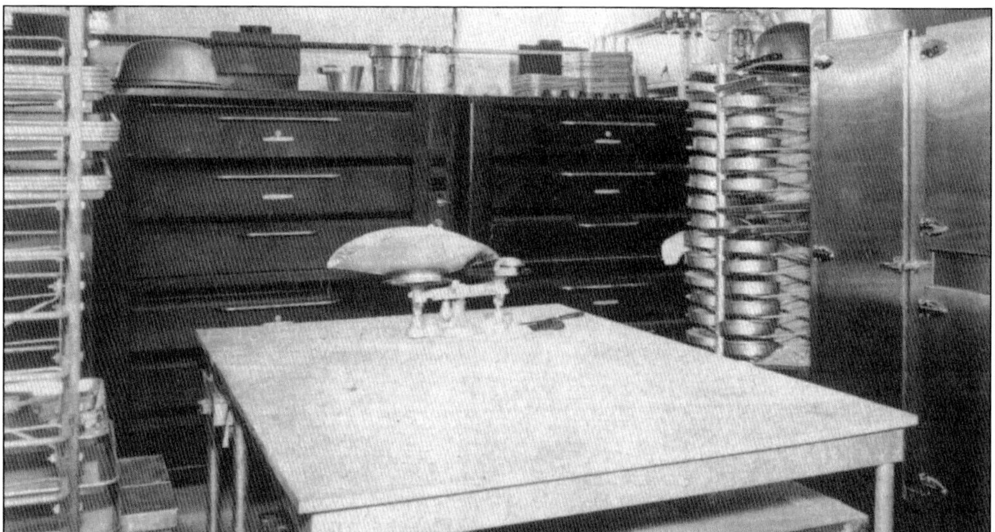

Like the Pig 'N Whistle operations, Hody's had its own bake shop to keep costs under control. The Hody's La Brea baking area is pictured above with its multi-deck, gas-fired ovens and plenty of table space for mixing and working with dough. Everything was measured in weight; Hoedemaker felt that restaurants lost a lot of money because "the only scales restaurant men know about are the ones that come on fish." (Courtesy Eddie Hoedemaker.)

Eddie Hoedemaker tells of getting his start in his grandfather's restaurant chain at Hody's La Brea. He worked as a busboy, fountain attendant, and host. There was a strict code of behavior expected by all Hody's employees, as detailed in the 1953 employee handbook titled *Courtesy*: "Never be grouchy, surly, or impatient—remember, the patron pays your salary; without him your salary stops, and you are out of a job." (Courtesy Chris Nichols.)

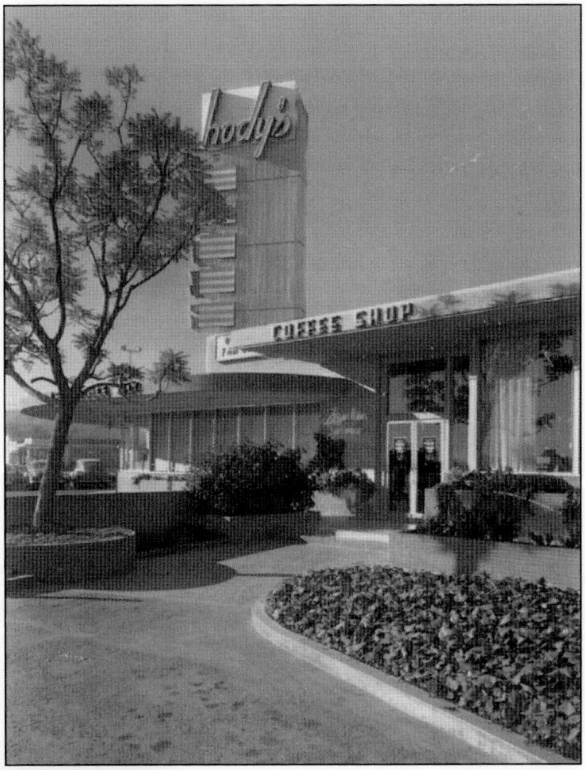

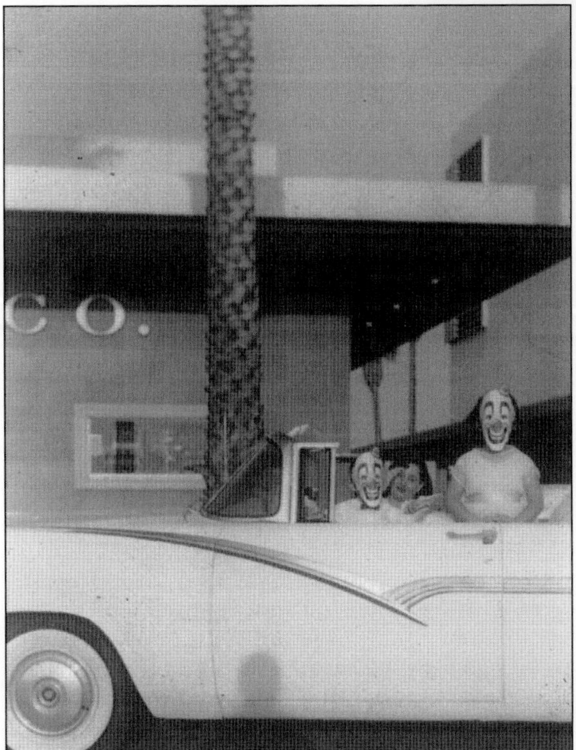

Here a typical family enjoys an outing together at Hody's Lakewood. From left to right are Vincent, Anita, and Cheryl Manocchi; Vincent and Cheryl are wearing their Hody's menu masks. Hoedemaker never let go of the concept of making his restaurants oriented toward children and families; it was part of his legacy. (Courtesy Chris Nichols.)

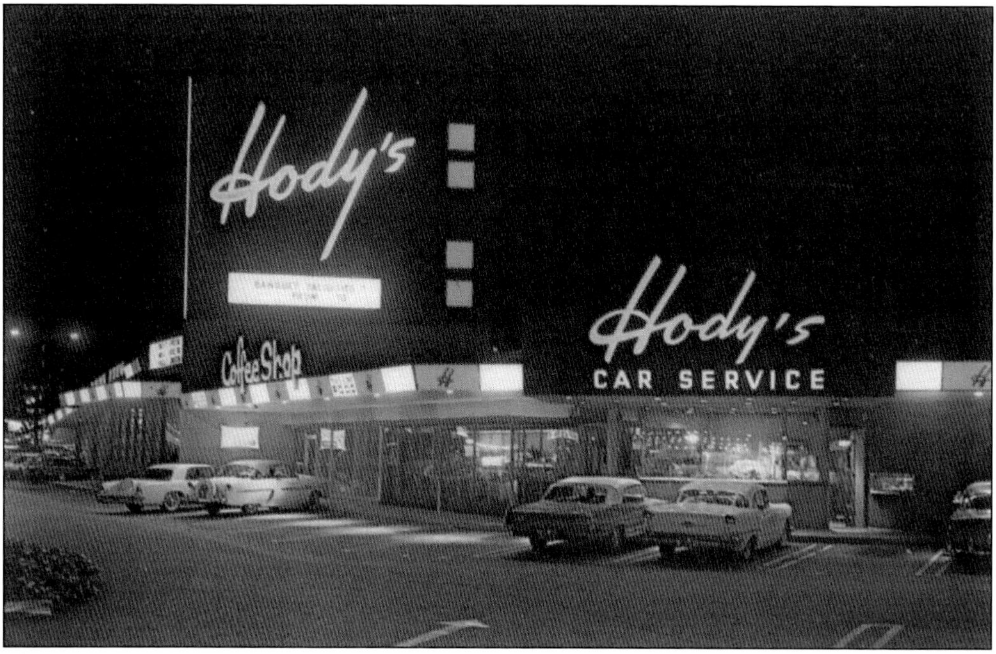

This attractive restaurant was located on Lankershim Boulevard and Oxnard Street in North Hollywood, in the heart of the San Fernando Valley. It had a coffee shop, cocktail lounge, car service, and a banquet room. One of the most popular Hody's locations, it stayed in business for almost 20 years until it closed in 1968. (Courtesy Chris Nichols.)

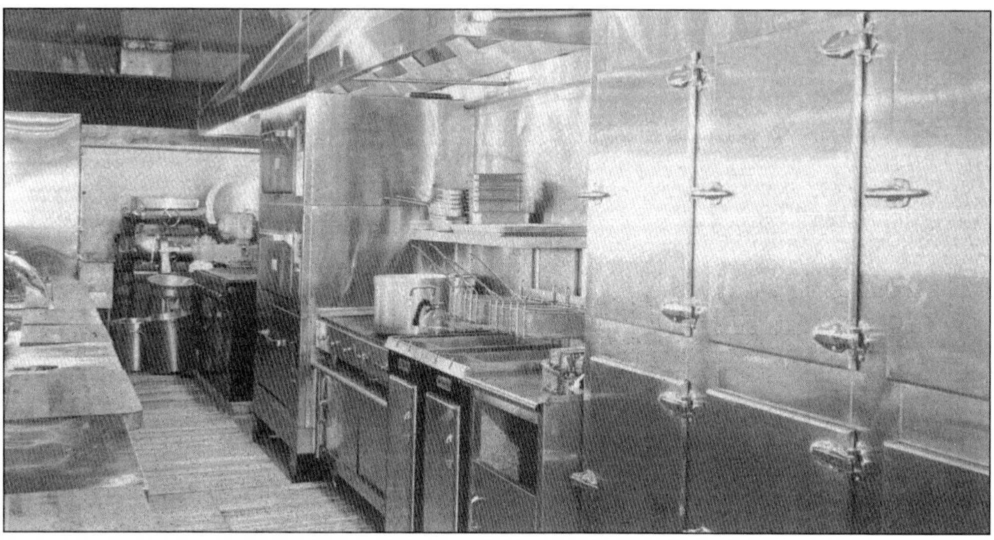

This 1964 photograph shows the sparkling clean stainless steel kitchen equipment that was used at the North Hollywood Hody's. The stove is gas-fired, and there are several deep fryers. The large stock-making pots can be seen in the back of the kitchen, which has wooden floorboards for the comfort of the cooks. (Courtesy Chris Nichols.)

There were eight Hody's Family Restaurants in all. With exception of the cafeteria, each had a cocktail room with names like the Garden Room, the Sequoia Room, the Hitching Post, and the Los Altos Room. Several had banquet facilities. The eight stores were Hody's La Brea, Hody's Lankershim, Hody's Lakewood, Hody's Los Altos, Hody's Sepulveda, Hody's Rodeo, Hody's Hollywood-Vine, and Hody's Panorama. (Courtesy Chris Nichols.)

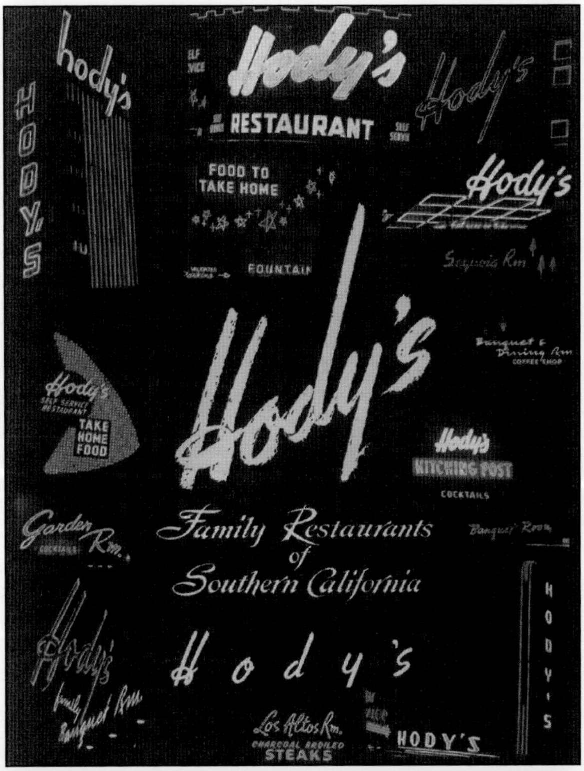

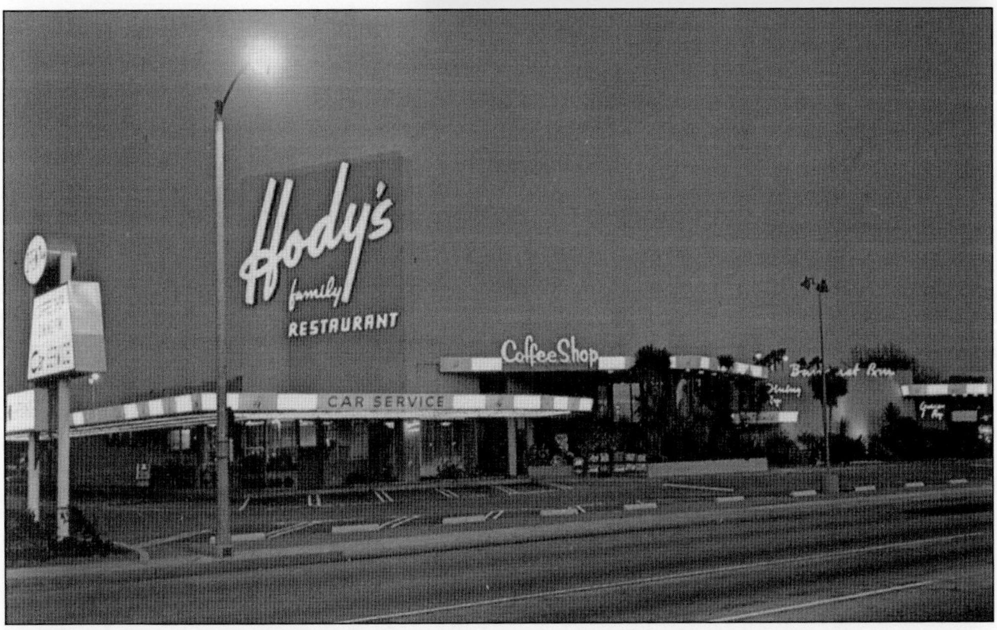

Hody's Lakewood was located on the corner of Lakewood Boulevard and Candlewood Street near the Lakewood shopping center. A 1956 advertisement for this location invites patrons to pick up a "wonderful, complete fried chicken boxed supper," to "picnic in the park" or "picnic before the show and avoid traffic." Each box contained a pair of "pliofilm mitts, for easier chicken pickin'." (Courtesy Chris Nichols.)

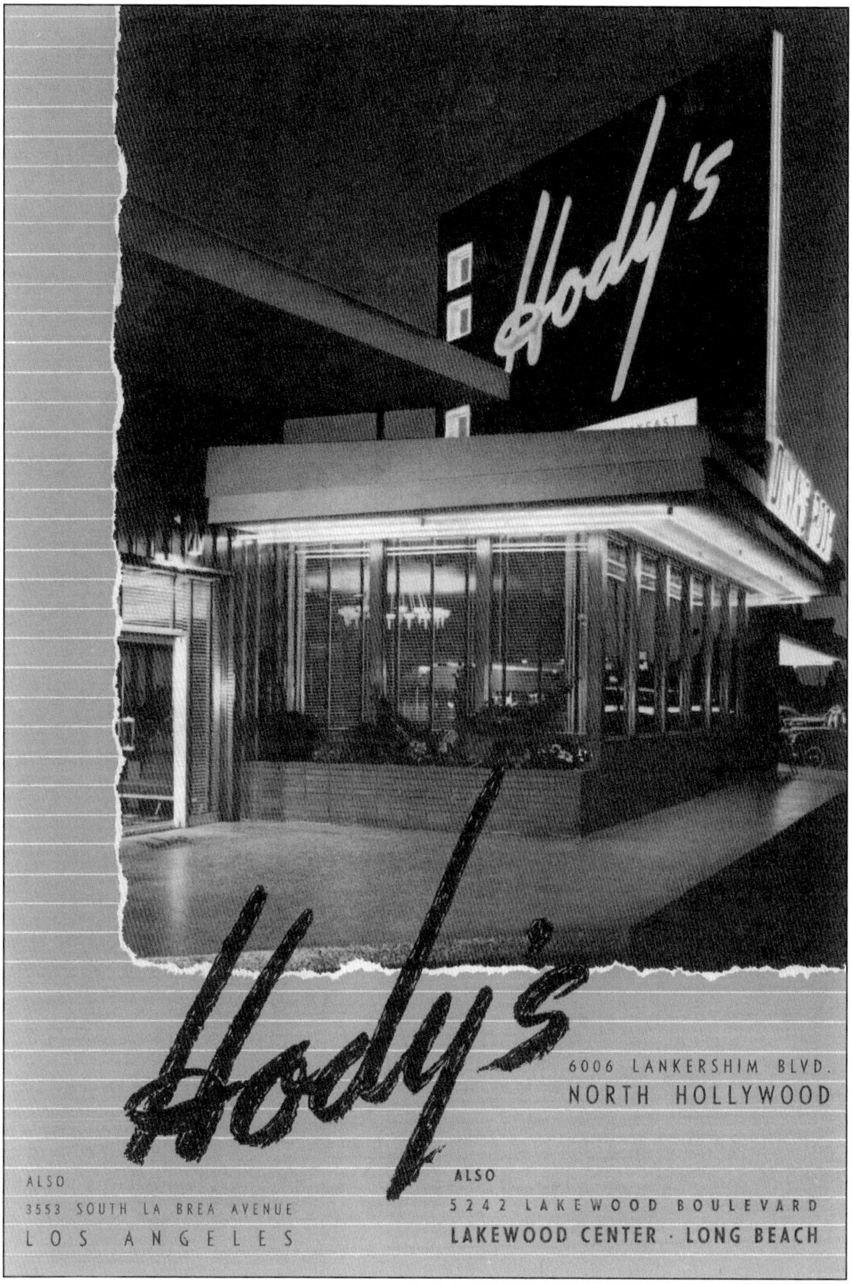

The San Fernando Valley Hody's closed on March 15, 1968, after a banquet by the Rotary Club of North Hollywood. Hoedemaker is quoted in the *San Fernando Valley News* as saying, "We have enjoyed the friendship and courtesy of San Fernando Valley patrons for almost two decades." Hoedemaker's only child, a son named Neil, was a World War II U.S. Coast Guard veteran who briefly ran a store in Okinawa. When he returned from service, he had no interest in following his father in the restaurant business, and the torch was instead passed to Hoedemaker's grandson, Eddie. Eddie started working at Hody's at the age of 14, but at age 18, he joined the service and served in Vietnam. While Eddie was overseas, the elder Hoedemaker passed away on July 18, 1969, and with his passing, so passed Hody's Family Restaurant. (Courtesy Chris Nichols.)

Noting the success of Hoedemaker's suburban chain of restaurants, the board at the Pig 'N Whistle Corporation decided to open a drive-in restaurant in the suburb of Gardena in 1953. It stayed open for only two years, and this surviving menu reflects a stripped-down version of the former menu. There is a "Melody Lane Hamburger De-Luxe on Toasted Bun" for 40¢ and "food is sold to take-out," mirroring Hody's style.

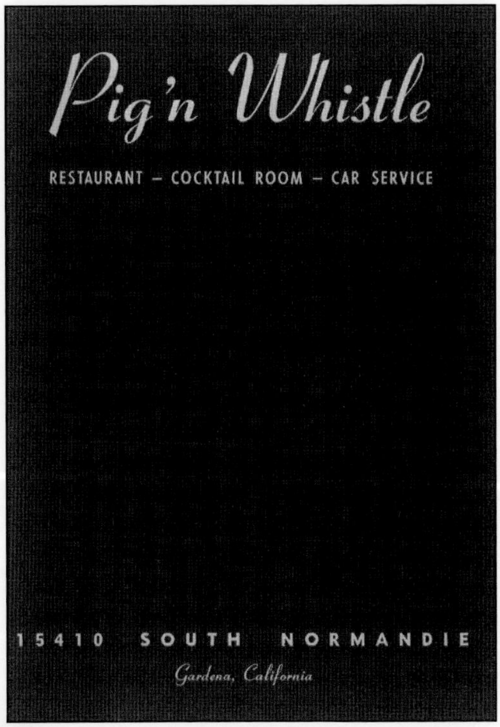

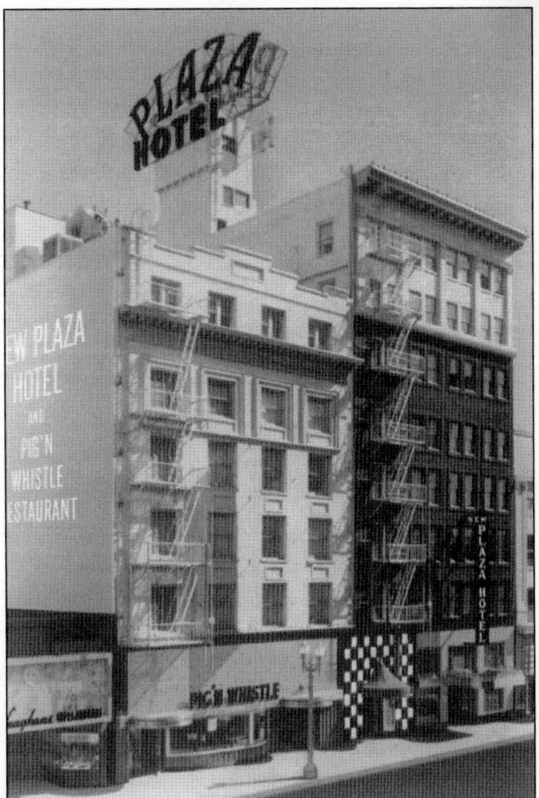

One other Pig 'N Whistle that remained open in the 1950s was a location in San Diego. It was located in the New Plaza Hotel on Fourth Street and Broadway and was complete with a cocktail lounge. This postcard was mailed in 1958.

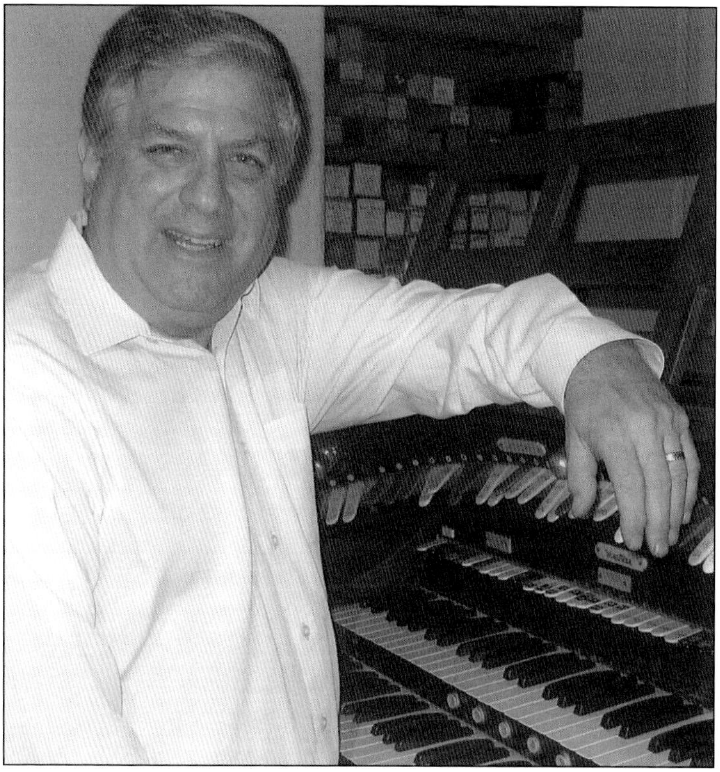

Ken Rosen is pictured here with the original Pig 'N Whistle organ that he and his wife, Jenice, purchased in 1972. While still students at California State University, Northridge, Ken and Jenice noticed that it was for sale at the First Christian Church of North Hollywood on Colfax Avenue, where it had been donated in 1952. Originally ordered in 1921 for the Garrick Theatre in Los Angeles, it was repossessed for nonpayment, shipped back to New York, and then later sold to the Pig 'N Whistle in 1927. (Courtesy Ken Rosen.)

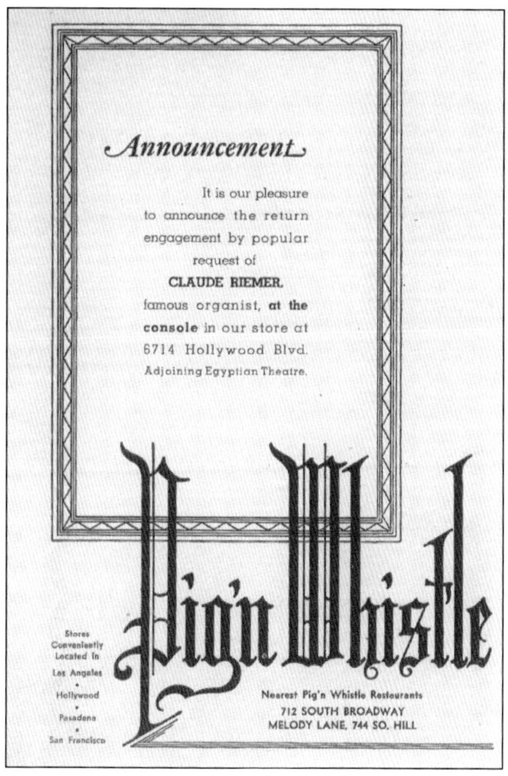

The Pig 'N Whistle's original organist was Claude Riemer, as this advertisement from 1938 states. The only shops that had Wurlitzer pipe organs were the 6714 Hollywood Boulevard location and the Melody Lane on Hill Street in downtown Los Angeles. Claude Riemer is remembered by a former Pig 'N Whistle patron who was interviewed for a *Visiting . . . with Huell Howser* episode on the Pig 'N Whistle.

Ken Rosen plays the Pig 'N Whistle's Mighty Wurlitzer, which he fully restored. Ken and Jenice Rosen built a 1,700-square-foot studio behind their home, "The Rosen Roxy," where Ken gives organ recitals to lucky guests. Ken also performs regularly for the American Theater Organ Society and to fans of silent cinema for Last Remaining Seats, the Los Angeles Conservancy's wildly popular annual silent film festival at the Orpheum Theatre.

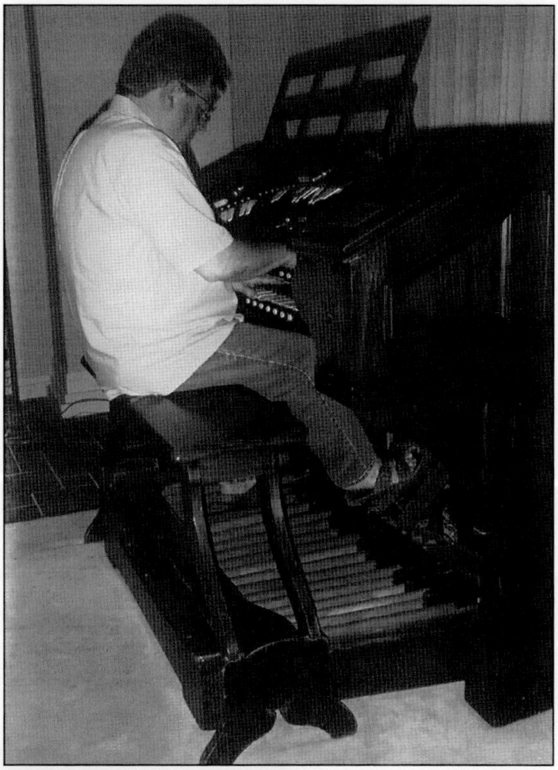

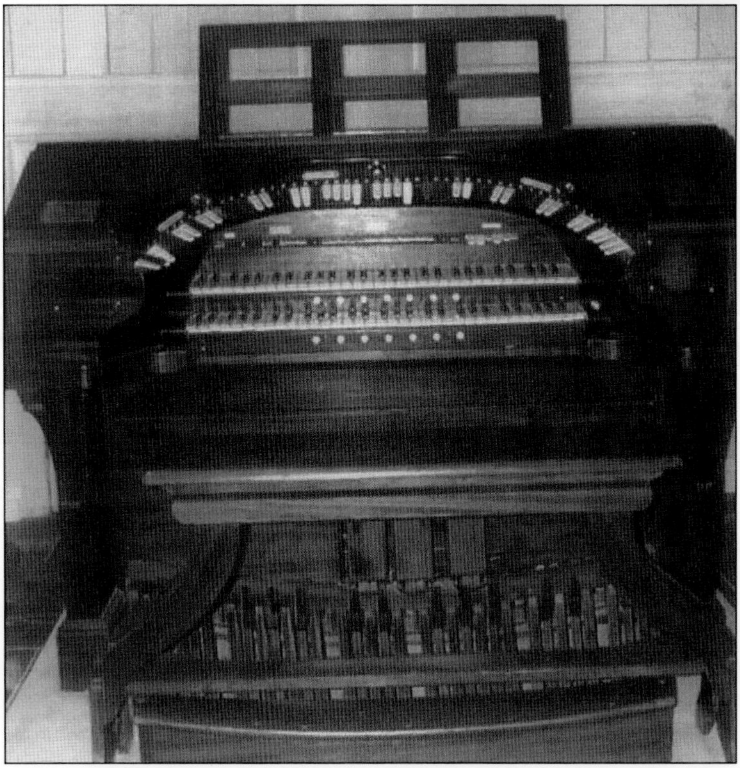

On February 18, 1927, the Eighth and Broadway Corporation delivered a new pipe organ for the grand opening of the Pig 'N Whistle in Hollywood. It remained at the 6714 Hollywood Boulevard location until 1952, but its spirit lives on there. Chris Breed tells of a night spent in the Pig 'N Whistle shortly after he reopened it in 2001 when he was abruptly awakened by loud sounds of ghostly pipe organ music echoing throughout the restaurant.

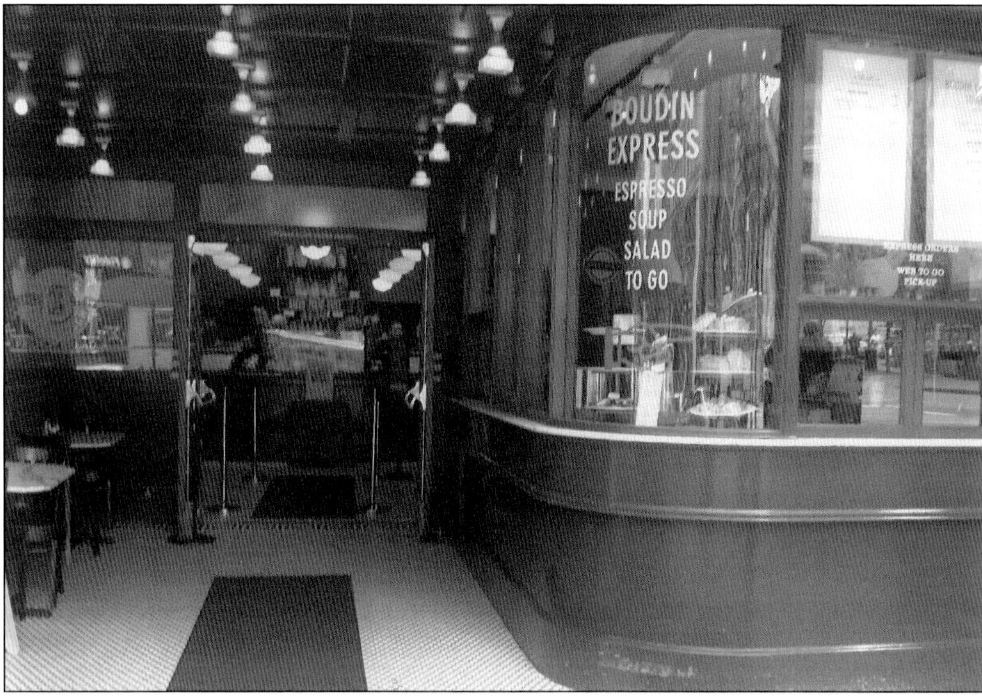

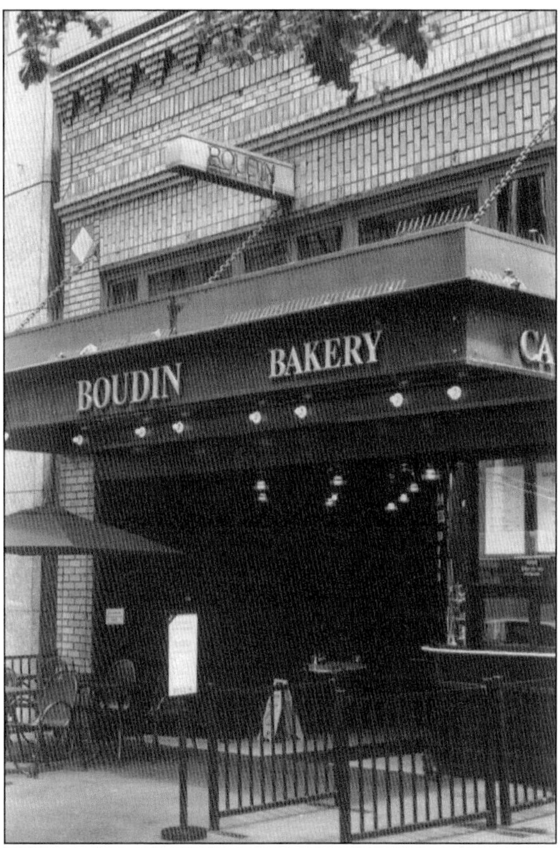

Of the four Pig 'N Whistles that were in San Francisco, the 621 Market Street location is the only one still standing. In 1941, it was listed on the back of a menu as "new and modern," although it had been in operation since 1926. The 1032 Market Street location closed in the early 1940s, and arson destroyed the building in 1965.

Boudin Bakery now occupies the space that was once a Pig 'N Whistle in the 1920s through the 1940s. Located at 619 Market Street, it once served the nearby Palace Hotel. It had a modest soda fountain, dining room, and a candy and pastry counter. Nothing remains of the soda fountain, and the inside appears to have been remodeled, but there are still beautiful tiles in the entranceway.

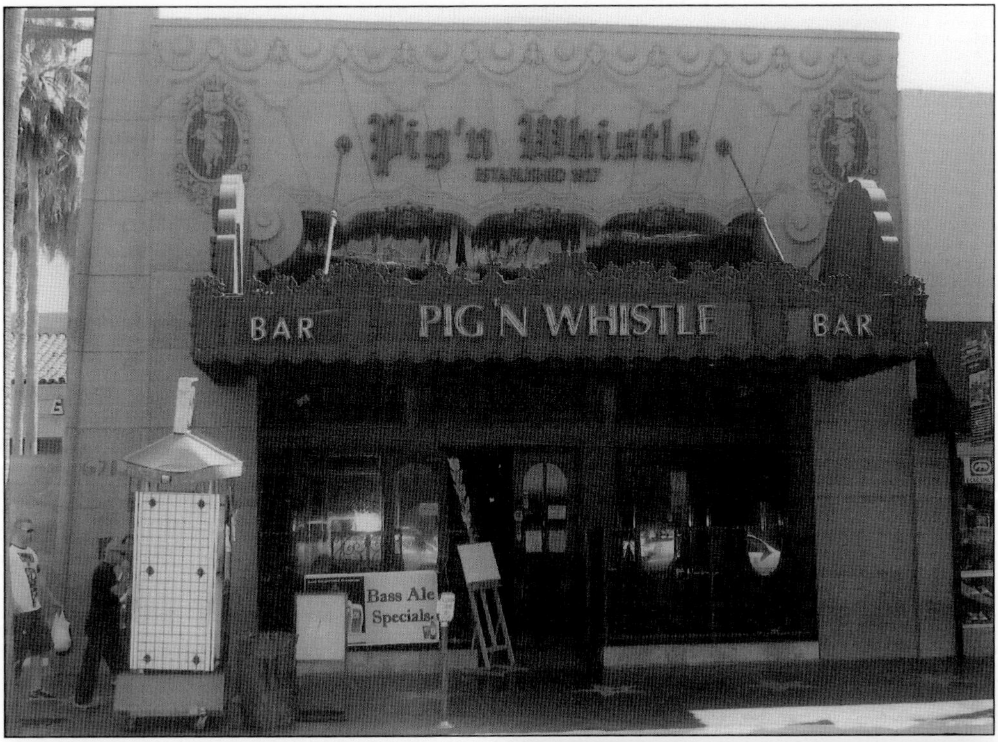

The Pig 'N Whistle at 6714 Hollywood Boulevard reopened for business after 50 years of other businesses occupying the space. It was once Vallera's Café Di Lusso, which was owned by Joe Vallera who was known as the "King of Italian Food" and was the originator of the Italian Kitchen on Eighth Street in downtown Los Angeles. This space was also a clothing store, and when Chris Breed and partner Alain Hajjar took it over in 1999, it was a Numero Uno Pizza. (Courtesy Bison Archives.)

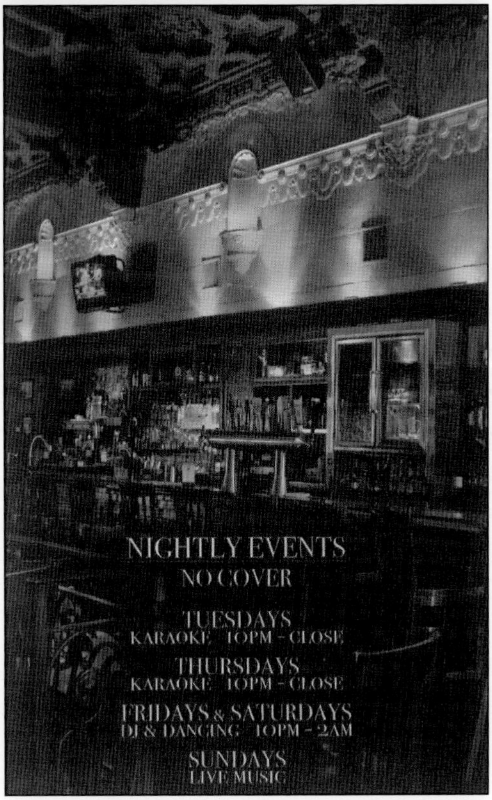

A detail from the current Pig 'N Whistle take-out menu shows the ceiling, which Chris Breed and his partner Alain Hajjar lovingly recreated from historical photographs. The ceiling had been covered up and was largely damaged and unusable. Molds of the old ceiling were made, and an exact replica of the original design was installed. Breed and Hajjar spent $1.5 million on the restaurant's design, which took one-and-a-half years to complete.

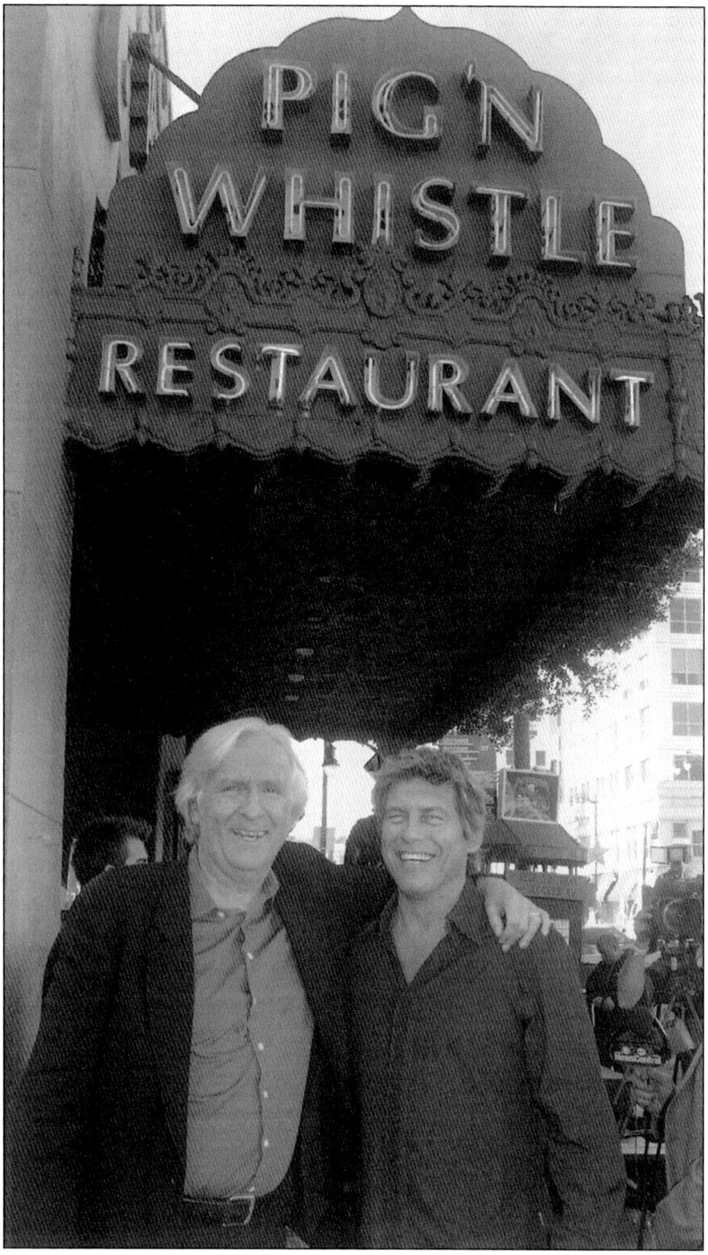

Pig 'N Whistle owner Chris Breed (right) poses with director James Cameron outside the restaurant. A longtime friend of Breed's, Cameron promised that if he ever received a star on the Hollywood Walk of Fame, he would place it outside the Pig 'N Whistle. Cameron received the star on December 18, 2009, which also coincided with the release of his film *Avatar*. California governor Arnold Schwarzenegger referred to Cameron, who directed him in the popular *Terminator* film series, as one of the greatest directors of all time. Breed is also a celebrity of sorts, having been the brainchild for the Roxbury nightclub that operated on Sunset Boulevard in West Hollywood from 1990 to 1997. The Roxbury was referenced in a popular *Saturday Night Live* skit called "The Roxbury Guys," which in turn was made into the 1998 film *A Night at the Roxbury*, starring Will Ferrell and Chris Kattan. (©2010 Bob Freeman.)

The grand reopening of the Pig 'N Whistle was a gala celebration that was held on March 19, 2001, and attended by such luminaries as Jack Nicholson, Dennis Quaid, Kevin Costner, and Rod Stewart. Alain Hajjar and partner Chris Breed revealed the new Pig 'N Whistle menu, which kept some of the classic American comfort food that the Pig 'N Whistle was known for, like its famous chicken pot pie, as well as the addition of some classic English pub fare. He has added karaoke on certain nights, which has also contributed to the restaurant's overwhelming success.

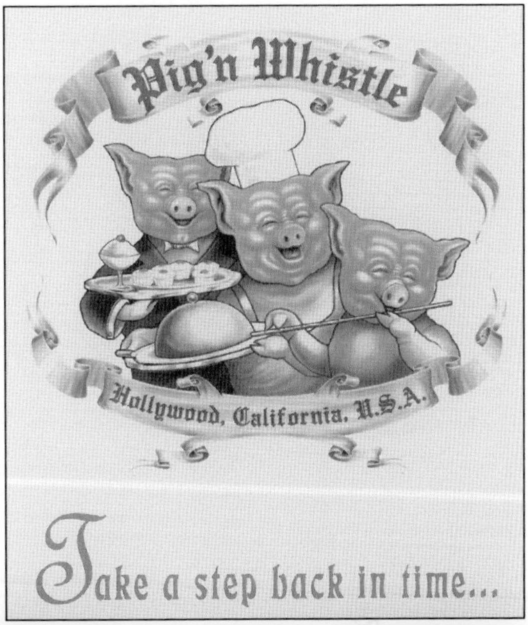

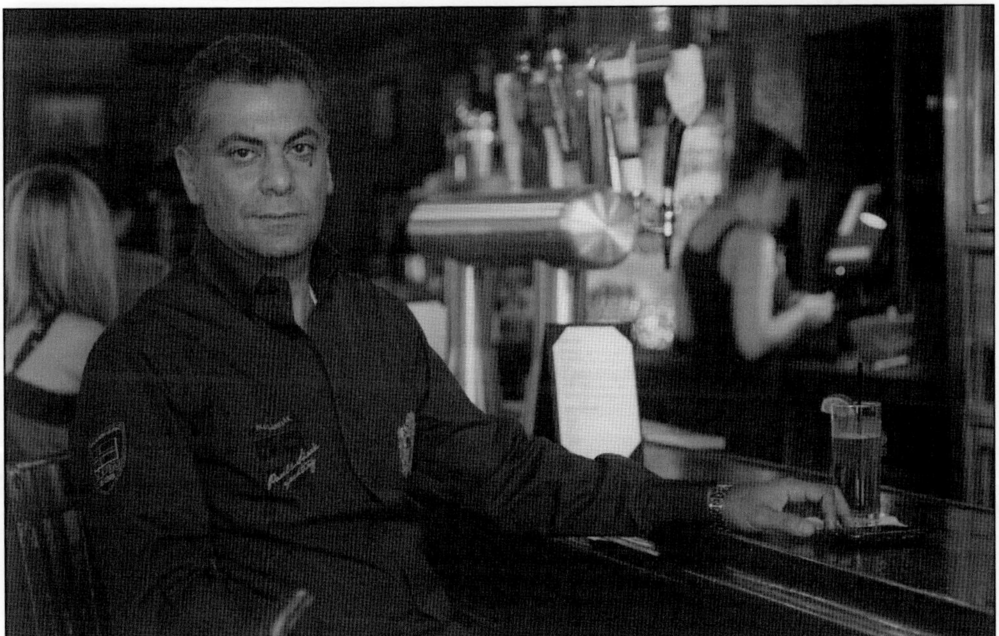

Alain Hajjar graduated from Beirut's St. Joseph University with a degree in civil engineering in 1986. Two years after graduation, he moved to Los Angeles, where he started his own firm, Edco Engineering and Construction, that merged in 2005 with ACS International. In 1992, he met Chris Breed at the Roxbury club where they had a great success. While on a project in Hollywood, Alain discovered the location of the Sunset Room, the first venture in Hollywood, which led to the opening of the Pig 'N Whistle, White Lotus, Cabana Club, Green Door, Kubar, and La Vida. Hajjar's vast experience in construction and his engineering background helped tremendously in the historical restoration of the Pig 'N Whistle. He is seen here seated at Pig 'N Whistle's bar, which he also built. (Courtesy Rony Peters.)

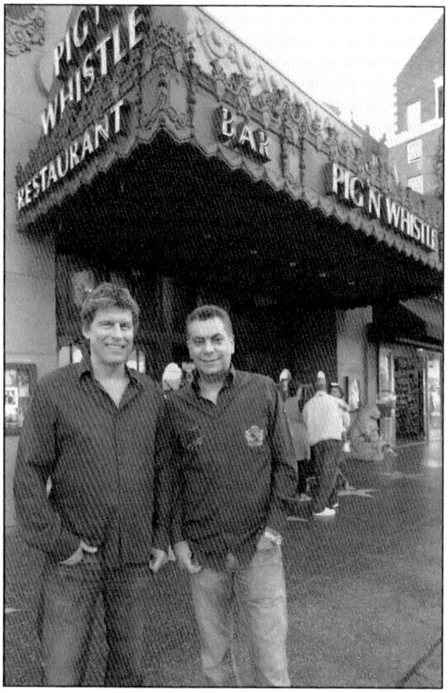

Hailing from Ramsey, Cambridgeshire, England, Chris Breed (pictured at left with partner Alain Hajjar) was first inspired by Hollywood through his father, Geoffrey James Breed. The senior Breed had a fascination for the Golden Age of Hollywood, and though a carpenter by trade, he was an independent filmmaker who showed his films in his own cinema club. By 1986, Breed was a professional rugby player and moved to New York; he moved to Los Angeles in 1988. (Courtesy Rony Peters.)

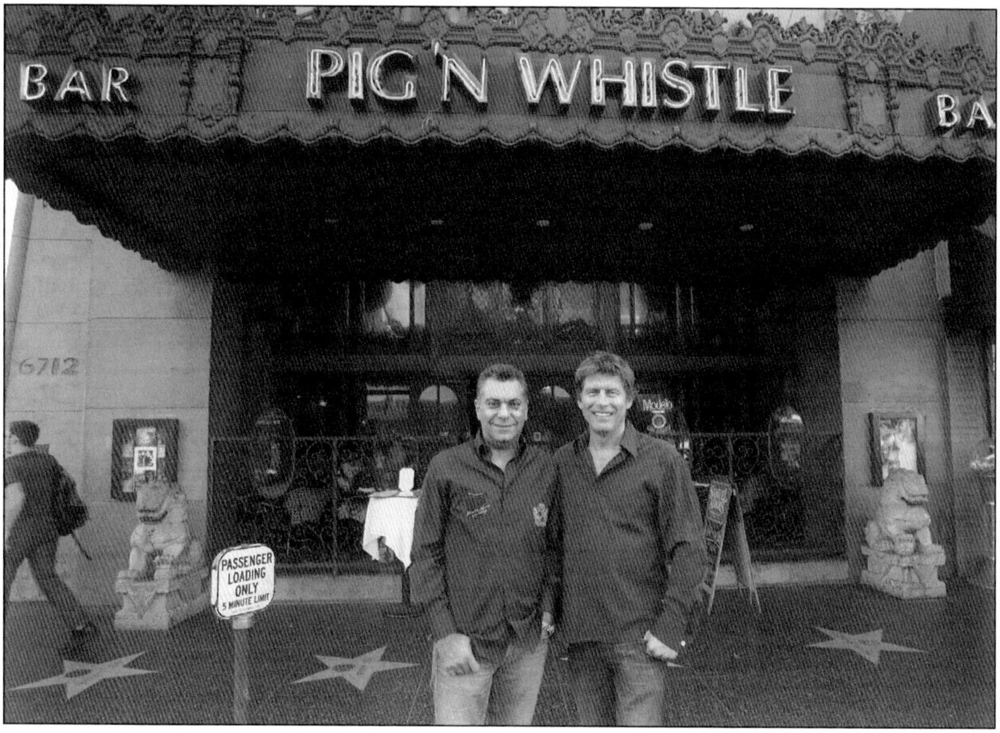

Alain Hajjar (left) and Chris Breed stand in front of the Pig 'N Whistle, which now functions as a bar and restaurant. Hajjar and Breed managed to keep the integrity of the Pig 'N Whistle, while also opening a string of other Hollywood hot spots—the Sunset Room, White Lotus, Cabana Club, the Green Door, Halo, and La Vida, all of which makes them what the *Los Angeles Times* has called "The Pioneers of Hollywood." (Courtesy Rony Peters.)

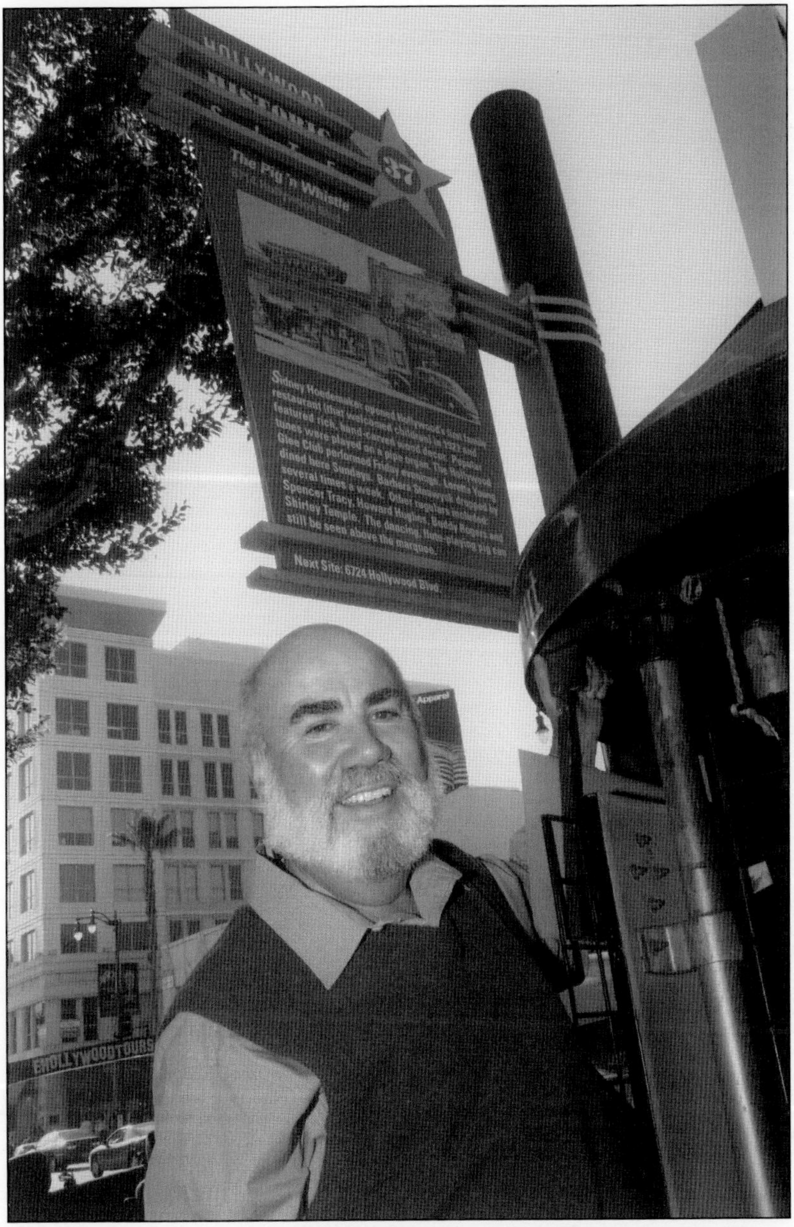

Eddie Hoedemaker poses near the Hollywood Historical Landmark No. 37 signage that has been placed outside the Pig 'N Whistle. Eddie got his restaurant start at an early age, working as a dishwasher, busboy, host, and fountain boy for Hody's on La Brea Avenue and Rodeo Road. He was carefully groomed by his grandfather, Sidney, to take over the Hody's restaurant chain and was taken out to dine at all the finest restaurants Los Angeles had to offer, like that in the Beverly Hills Hotel. By age 18, he was the manager of the Hollywood and Vine Hody's. Eddie joined the air force and went to Vietnam, where he served as a combat information monitor in 1969 and 1970. Unfortunately Sidney Hoedemaker passed away in 1969 while Eddie was away, and Hody's closed its doors for good. However, he was able to open his own bar and restaurant in 1973, Hody's Gold Post, which enjoyed success in Eagle Rock throughout the 1970s. (Courtesy Gary Leonard.)